D0486363

ILLUSTRATED LIFE OF
JESUS

POCKET REFERENCE EDITION

HERSCHEL H. HOBBS

HOLMAN
REFERENCE

NASHVILLE, TENNESSEE

Illustrated Life of Jesus, Pocket Reference Edition
© 2000, 2010 B & H Publishing Group
All rights reserved

ISBN: 978-0-8054-9541-6

A Holman Reference Book
published by
B & H Publishing Group
127 Ninth Avenue, North
Nashville, TN 37234
http://www.broadmanholman.com

Dewey Decimal Classification: 232
Subject Heading: JESUS CHRIST—BIBLICAL TEACHING\BIBLE. N.T.
GOSPELS AND ACTS

Cover Design: Greg Pope
Interior Design: Greg Pope
Composition: TF Designs

Scripture quotations, unless otherwise noted, have been taken from
The Holman Christian Standard Bible ®
Copyright © 1999, 2000, 2002, 2003, 2009

Scripture quotations marked ASV are from the
American Standard Version

Printed in China

1 2 3 4 5 6 7 15 14 13 12 11 10

DBS

TABLE OF CONTENTS

"*A* man who was merely a man and said the sort of things Jesus said would not be a great moral teacher. He would either be a lunatic – on a level with the man who says he is a poached egg – or else he would be the Devil of Hell. You must make your choice. Either this man was, and is, the Son of God; or else a madman or something worse. You can shut Him up for a fool, you can spit at Him and kill him as a demon; or you can fall at His feet and call Him Lord and God. But let us not come with any patronizing nonsense about His being a great human teacher. He has not left that open to us. He did not intend to."

— C.S. Lewis

INTRODUCTION

This study of the life of Jesus is approached with two assumptions: that the four Gospels were written by the men whose names they bear; and that these Gospels are trustworthy historical documents. It is not within the scope of this work to deal with technical points of literary or historical criticism, but to endeavor to employ the results of both in presenting "the greatest story ever told" about the greatest life ever lived. However, this presentation is made with the conviction that the above-mentioned assumptions are valid in the light of critical analysis.

The cover of the Book of Kells, an illuminated manuscript of the four Gospels created around AD 800. The four images on the cover represent characteristics of Christ most prominent in each of the four Gospels: man (Luke), lion (Matthew), ox (Mark), and eagle (John).

Each of the four Gospels possesses its own characteristics in keeping with the personality and purpose of the author. And yet when they are combined, they present a well-rounded, Holy Spirit-inspired story of the life of Jesus.

THE KINGDOMS OF
ISRAEL AND JUDAH
1 KGS. 12

- City
★ Capital city
○ City (uncertain location)
▲ Mountain peak
Israel
Judah
— International roads
--- Local roads

0 10 20 30 40 50 Miles
0 10 20 30 40 50 Kilometers

Beirut

PHOENICIA

Sidon

Ijon

Mt. Hermon

Damascus

Tyre

Litani River

Abel beth-maacah

Dan

Jeroboam built a sanctuary

Kedesh

ARAM

Achzib

Hazor

Lake Huleh

Acco

Chinnereth

Sea of Galilee

GESHUR

Mt. Carmel

Gath-hepher

Aphek

Ashtaroth

Megiddo

Mt. Tabor

Edrei

Dor

Taanach

Jezreel

Beth-shan

Ramoth-gilead

Dothan

Ibleam

Pehel

Jabesh-gilead

MEDITERRANEAN
SEA

Socoh

Tirzah

Samaria

Mt. Ebal

Political capital of Israel
from Omri onward

ISRAEL

Shechem

Mt. Gerizim

Mahanaim

Penuel

Succoth

Jabbok River

Joppa

Aphek

Shiloh

Adam

Jeroboam built
a sanctuary

Upper
Beth-horon

Bethel

Jericho

Rabbah
(Amman)

AMMON

Lower Beth-horon

Mizpah

Gezer

Ramah

Geba

Heshbon

Aijalon

Ekron

Gibeah

Ashdod

Gath

Jerusalem

Mt. Nebo

Medeba

Ashkelon

Azekah

Bethlehem

Mareshah

Beth-zur

Tekoa

Gaza

Lachish

Hebron

Dibon

PHILISTIA

Adoraim

Zaph

Arnon River

Gerar

Carmel

DEAD
SEA

N. Besor

JUDAH

Maon

Arad

Beersheba

King's Highway

Kir-hareseth

Negeb

MOAB

Int

W. el-Arish

Zered River

Tamar

Bozrah

Eastern
Desert

Kadesh-
barnea

EDOM

Wilderness

THE HISTORICAL ENVIRONMENT OF THE GOSPELS

In the light of the above it is well to take a brief look at the historical environment of Palestine in the time of Jesus, for His life was not lived in a vacuum. Jesus Christ was a real Person who lived in a given period of history, and it is impossible fully to understand the Gospel record without taking this fact into account.

Following the death of Solomon, his kingdom was divided into the northern kingdom of Israel and the southern kingdom of Judah. In 721 BC Israel was taken into captivity by the Assyrians, who left behind only a small remnant. In turn the Assyrians sent in people of foreign lands who later intermarried with these Israelites to produce the Samaritan people. In 586 BC the kingdom of Judah fell to the Babylonians who took large numbers of its people into captivity. When the Babylonian empire gave way to the Persian empire, the latter, under Cyrus, permitted the Jews (so-called after "Judah") to return to their land. A remnant did so and rebuilt Jerusalem. In their efforts they were opposed by the Samaritans. This, plus the fact that the Samaritans were a mixed race, led to a hostility between the Jews and Samaritans extending into the time of Jesus.

If one turns the page from Malachi 4 to Matthew 1, he does more than turn a page. He takes a step four hundred years into the future, and he finds himself in an environment far different from the one he knew. For during this period violent changes had taken place in Palestine.

Under Persian rule Judea was a part of the satrapy of Coele Syria. Its affairs were administered by the high priest under the control of the Syrian governor. With the fall of the Persian empire to Alexander the Great in 330 BC, Palestine was under his rule until his death in 323 BC. As a result of Alexander's campaigns, the Greek language and Greek culture were introduced into Palestine. By the first century the Greek language had become a universal language throughout the Roman Empire.

Following the death of Alexander, his empire was divided into five parts. Two of these, Egypt and Syria, continued to figure in the history of Palestine. From 320–198 BC the Ptolemaic kingdom in Egypt ruled in Palestine, to be succeeded by the Seleucid kingdom of Syria (198–167 BC). In 175 BC Antiochus Epiphanes came to the throne in Syria. His reign was

THE DIVISION OF
ALEXANDER'S EMPIRE
ABOUT 275 B.C.

● Modern city
● City
▲ Mountain peak
⚔ Battle
 Seleucid kingdom
 Antigonid kingdom
 Ptolemaic kingdom
 Hellenistic province

Ptolemy and Seleucus were victorious at the battle of Ipsus, resulting in the death of Antigonus (301 B.C.)

Seleucus allied with Ptolemy against Antigonus' fighting many battles in the eastern Mediterranean

Antigonus initiates conflicts by attacking Ptolemy

Antigonus forces Seleucus to abandon Babylon

characterized by savage persecution of the Jews. He was set on imposing Greek customs and religion on them. Some readily accepted them, but for the most part they were refused. The violent persecution brought on the Maccabean revolt in 167 BC. Judea won her independence, and for approximately one hundred years she existed as an independent nation. But it was a period marked by wars without and internal struggles for power within. Weakened by this internal strife, Judea fell an easy prey to the Romans

under Pompey in 63 BC. At this time Roman rule was extended over all of Palestine. So Judea, a part of a Persian satrapy in Malachi 4, had become a portion of a Roman province in Matthew 1.

At the time of Jesus' birth, Herod the Great ruled in Palestine as a puppet king under the Romans. His reign was characterized by political intrigue and unrest. Jealous for his throne Herod tolerated no threat to it. As a result he put to death many members of his own family, including his favorite wife, Mariam, and her two sons, Alexander and Aristobulus. Herod died in 4 BC. His kingdom was divided among three of his sons. Archelaus reigned for a short period as the ethnarch of Judea but was replaced by a Roman procurator or governor. Herod Antipas was made the tetrarch of Galilee and Perea, and Herod Philip ruled in the same capacity in Iturea and Trachonitis. Under Roman rule the Jewish Sanhedrin, the ruling body among the Jews, was shorn of most of its power. Its jurisdiction was confined to religious and civil matters. High priests were appointed and deposed repeatedly by the Romans.

Thus the proud and politically ambitious Jews were reduced to political and military servility. Roman soldiers and tax-gatherers were seen everywhere throughout the land as a constant reminder and source of discontent and hatred among the populace.

During all of this time, there had been significant developments in the religious life of the Jews. The Babylonian captivity had thoroughly purged them of idolatry. Upon their return to Judea, they rebuilt the temple and reinstituted the temple services and the annual feasts. At this time a new institution appeared—the synagogue. Nothing is known as to its origin. It may have been during the Babylonian captivity when the Jews had no temple. At any rate, following their return from captivity, synagogues began to spring up everywhere. On each Sabbath day they were filled with people assembled for worship and for the teaching of their Scriptures. This institution later was to play a major role in the early spread of Christianity.

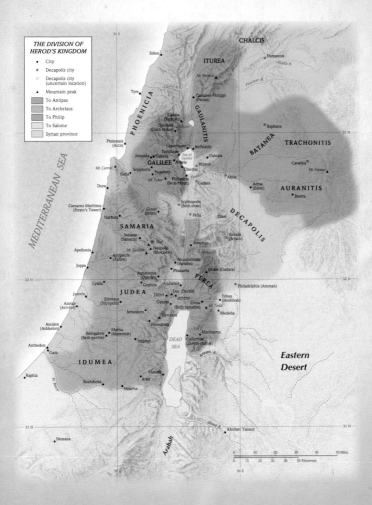

THE DIVISION OF HEROD'S KINGDOM

- City
- Decapolis city
- Decapolis city (uncertain location)
- ▲ Mountain peak
- To Antipas
- To Archelaus
- To Philip
- To Salome
- Syrian province

By the time Jesus came on the scene, there were two major parties among the Jews, namely, the Pharisees and Sadducees. They were both religious and political in nature. As with the synagogue, it is also true that the origin of these parties is shrouded in mystery. In all probability they arose gradually. Following the return from captivity there may well have developed two schools of thought among the Jews. One group followed both the Law and the Prophets and placed great value on the interpretations of them by leading teachers. The other group chose to follow only the Law or the five books of Moses. The former were extremely zealous for their religion and were even willing to die for it. The latter became more broadminded and sought to adjust to changing conditions. The one developed a bitter hatred for foreigners, but the other was more friendly toward them.

Whether or not this may be a correct surmise, Josephus, the Jewish historian, tells us that by 145 BC the Pharisees and Sadducees were distinct parties holding to the above-mentioned views respectively. The name *Pharisee* means a "separatist." During the Maccabean revolt they represented the patriots of the time, opposing bitterly every effort to impose Greek customs and religion on the Jews. Thus they became very popular with the people, and, therefore, were the larger party. At the time of Jesus they were fanatically opposed to the Romans who ruled over the Jews. Not only did they adhere to the Law and the Prophets, but they developed an almost endless number of traditions in interpreting the Scriptures. Their system included the most meticulous rules of outward conduct, which they identified with religious righteousness. A sad result of these rules is that they served to stifle the spiritual aspects of religion.

The name *Sadducee* probably came from the Hebrew word for "righteous." Thus they were content merely to be righteous according to Jewish standards but cared nothing for the meticulous rules of conduct set forth by the Pharisees. They were a small group numerically but included men of influence and wealth. As the ruling party they worked closely with the Roman rulers and were opposed to anything threatening to upset the status quo and to endanger their privileged position of wealth and power.

The attitude of these two parties toward the Scriptures was reflected in their theological beliefs. The Pharisees believed in miracles, angels, and the resurrection of the dead; the Sadducees rejected all of these beliefs. And while both were primarily religious parties, they had lost all sense of a true spiritual experience. The Pharisees had gone to seed on tradition, outward conduct, ritualism, and formalism. The Sadducees, on the other hand, were more concerned with economic prosperity and political power. It is in these dual positions that one can comprehend their hostile attitudes toward Jesus and His opposition to them.

THE WORLD INTO WHICH JESUS CAME

Against this historical environment it is possible to visualize the world into which Jesus was born. Within the changing tides of history God had been producing His history within history. Through Alexander the Great the world received a universal language—Greek—whereby the gospel might be preached and written in the most perfect and expressive lan-

A fragment of the Septuagint, the Greek translation of the Hebrew Scriptures. This fragment dates between 50 BC and AD 50.

guage ever known to man. The Romans brought law and order, built roads, and opened sea lanes. This wherewithal produced the environment and means of travel whereby the evangels of grace would move and work.

In the meantime the pagan religions had largely run their course and had led mankind into a blind alley of spiritual frustration. Even the Hebrew religion had deteriorated into a Judaism bereft of the spiritual power to satisfy the longings of the human heart. A spiritual darkness had settled over the world. The only twin rays of light came from the Jews themselves: the worship of the one true God and the abiding hope of the Messiah. But wherever the Jews were scattered throughout the empire, they carried with them their Scriptures and their Messianic hope. That this expectancy had fanned the flickering flames of hope in hearts everywhere may be seen in the references found even in pagan writings of the time that there was an almost universal expectancy among the Jews that a world deliverer would arise in Palestine.

It was of such a time that Paul wrote, *"When the time came to completion, God sent His Son, born of a woman, born under the law, to redeem those under the law, so that we might receive adoption as sons."* (Gl 4:4–5).

CHAPTER I
THE PERIOD OF PREPARATION
THE PREEXISTENCE OF CHRIST

The story of the life of Jesus Christ did not begin in Nazareth or Bethlehem but in eternity. It is true that Jesus of Nazareth was God; it is even more correct to say that God became Jesus of Nazareth. *"In the beginning was the Word, and the Word was with God, and the Word was God"* Himself (Jn 1:1).

The "Word" or *Logos* was commonly used for reason or speech. Ancient writers employed it in various ways. To Heraclitus it was the principle controlling the universe. The Stoic philosophers used it to express the soul of the world, and Marcus Aurelius by it connoted the generative principle in nature. Philo, the Jewish-Alexandrian philosopher-theologian, employed it as a substitute for the Hebrew word *Memra* (Word) and used it almost in a personal sense. But the Apostle John personalized it and used it as a name for the Messiah, along with the Son of God, Son of Man, and other personal names for deity.

This eternal Christ was the creator of the universe from subatomic particles to suns. Apart from Him not even one thing came into being which did come into being. Furthermore, He was and is the source of all life, a life which is the light of men. Through the centuries the darkness of evil had sought to snuff out this light but without success. And in God's own

"All things were created through Him, and apart from Him not one thing was created that has been created. Jn 1:3; See also Col 1:16; Heb 1:2

time this Light, this Logos, entered into the arena of history that He might destroy the works of darkness.

No greater words were ever penned than:

"The Word became flesh and took up residence among us. We observed His glory, the glory as the One and Only Son from the Father, full of grace and truth" (Jn 1:14)

Yes, the eternal Christ who is God Himself became a flesh and blood man. He pitched His tent of flesh and dwelt for a little while among men. He was God as though He were not man. Yet He became man in every sense of the word, apart from sin, that He might both identify Himself with man and fully reveal the Father to men. When God revealed His law, He did so through Moses; but when He revealed His grace and truth, He did so through Jesus Christ.

"Long ago God spoke to the fathers by the prophets at different times and in different ways. In these last days, He has spoken to us by His Son,

whom He has appointed heir of all things and through whom He made the universe. He is the radiance of His glory, the exact expression of His nature, and He sustains all things by His powerful word. After making purification for sins, He sat down at the right hand of the Majesty on high" (Heb 1:1–3).

THE GENEALOGY OF JESUS CHRIST

When Christ entered bodily into the arena of history, He did so as a Jew. This was in keeping with the eternal purpose of God. For in a world filled with paganism, it was the Jews who had clung to the idea of the one true God, Yahweh.

The Jews placed great value upon lineage. The Old Testament testifies to this fact. Josephus introduced his own autobiography by giving his genealogy, which he says he found in the public records. These records were kept by the Sanhedrin. Herod the Great was of mixed ancestry, and for that reason, along with many others, was despised by the Jews of unmixed ancestry. Out of spite he destroyed all the genealogical records so that he could say that no one could prove a better pedigree than he could.

Therefore, to the Jewish mind, the record of the life of Jesus would be incomplete without His genealogy, and the gospel accounts include two such records. Luke is said to have listed Jesus' genealogy according to the line of Mary His mother. He began *"was thought to be the son of Joseph,"* and ends with *"son of Adam, son of God"* (Lk 3:23–38). Matthew, on the other hand, traces His lineage through Joseph, the foster-father, as was required by Jewish law. In a genealogy it was not required that every name be listed, but only that the line be established.

Matthew began his record with the simple yet profound statement *"The historical record of Jesus Christ, the Son of David, the Son of Abraham"* (1:1). He divided the genealogy into three sections of fourteen generations

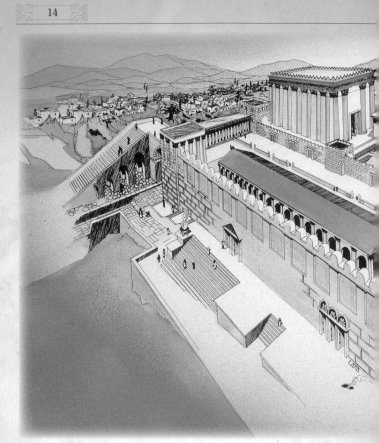

Herod the Great initiated a large number of expensive building projects including the enlargement of the temple in Jerusalem. This project began in 19 BC and was not finished until AD 63, just seven years before the temple was destroyed by the Romans.

each: Abraham to David; David to the Babylonian captivity; the captivity to the birth of Jesus. It was through Abraham that God's covenant of grace was given. The Hebrew nation reached its greatest glory under David whose throne became a symbol of the everlasting kingdom of the Son of David.

It was during and following the Babylonian captivity that the Messianic hopes of the Jews burned the brightest. So "Jesus Christ, the Son of David, the son of Abraham" was the Messiah, the Desire of all nations.

Certain other matters of interest emerge from an analysis of Jesus' genealogy. For instance, certain notorious sinners are included in His line. Judah and David were adulterers. Solomon, Manasseh, and Amon were worshipers of pagan gods. Furthermore, contrary to Jewish custom, the genealogy included the names of women. Tamar had sinned with Judah. Rahab is called a harlot of Jericho. The Hebrew word translated *harlot* means "public woman." She may not have been a harlot, but simply a public woman or innkeeper. She was a Canaanite. Ruth was a Moabitess. Neither of these last two women were Hebrews. Of interest also is the fact that the lineage of Jesus includes some who had lived in political bondage.

Therefore the genealogy of Jesus is more than a mere recitation of names. It shows that He was the son of Abraham, the Son of David, and the fulfillment of prophecy. Also it becomes the gospel in miniature. Jesus came not to call the righteous but sinners to repentance. In His lineage He is identified with sinners, and in Christ *"There is no Jew or Greek, slave or free, male or female; for you are all one in Christ Jesus. And if you are Christ's, then you are Abraham's seed, heirs according to the promise"* (Gl 3:28–29).

THE BIRTH OF JOHN THE BAPTIST

It was probably the year 7 BC just three years before the death of Herod, king of Judea. With a strong hand and a suspicious, vengeful nature the king in his luxurious palace watched over the affairs of state, while totally unknown to him an event of the ages was transpiring in the temple just a few blocks away.

Zechariah, a priest, was taking his turn ministering in the temple. He and his wife Elizabeth lived in a small village in the hill country of Judea. Zechariah was a son of Aaron married to a daughter of Aaron, something like a preacher married to a preacher's daughter. He was of the priestly course of Abijah, one of twenty-four such courses. According to custom each course served in the temple for eight days twice during a year. Zechariah was fulfilling such a duty at the time.

Once in his lifetime each priest was permitted to minister in the holy place. It was on this particular day that Zechariah was enjoying his once-in-a-lifetime privilege.

Suddenly the angel Gabriel appeared to him. He quieted the priest's fears by telling him that his prayers had been answered. He and Elizabeth were childless, and even though they were of an age beyond the normal age of becoming parents, nevertheless Elizabeth was to bear Zechariah a son whose name would be John. This son was to undertake a special mission in God's redemptive plan. He was to be the forerunner of the Messiah, calling on the people to prepare for His coming.

Quite naturally, because of the biological problem involved, Zechariah doubted. Perhaps both as punishment for his unbelief and as a sign as to the truth of the angel's words, he was stricken dumb until the child was born. The waiting congregation wondered at the priest's tarrying in the holy place, and even more so when he emerged unable to speak. But they perceived that he had seen a vision.

It was as the angel had said. For Elizabeth soon was found with child, and in due course she delivered a son to her husband. Amid great rejoicing their neighbors wanted to name him Zechariah, but to their surprise the mother said that he would be called John. Zechariah asked for a writing tablet, and thereby confirmed his wife's words. At that moment his tongue was loosed as the father praised God and prophesied concerning what manner of child and man his son should be.

News of this marvelous event spread throughout the hill country of Judea, but Herod in his palace was too preoccupied with the mundane affairs of state either to hear or to heed the wonderful works of God which transpired in his domain. For unknown to him the stage had been set for the mightiest event of the ages—the birth of Christ—who was to be born King of the Jews!

CHAPTER II
THE BIRTH AND CHILDHOOD OF JESUS
THE ANNUNCIATION TO THE VIRGIN MARY

It was three months before the birth of John the Baptist. If strange things were happening to Elizabeth, an even stranger experience awaited her cousin, Mary, who lived many miles to the north in Nazareth of Galilee. Mary was a virgin maiden betrothed to a village carpenter, Joseph by name, and probably many years her elder. In Jewish life the betrothal was more than an engagement and less than marriage in the present-day sense. It usu-

Nazareth. Basilica of the Annunciation

ally lasted for one year, during which time unfaithfulness on the part of the woman was punishable by death.

There is every evidence from both her words and deeds that Mary was a chaste and pious young woman. Nevertheless she was naturally startled when one day the angel Gabriel suddenly appeared to her. He was on another mission of glad tidings from heaven to earth, for he told Mary that she was highly favored of God in that she was to become the mother of the virgin-born Son of God. Quite naturally this raised a biological problem, and Mary herself became the first person to utter a question as to the possibility of the virgin birth: *"How can this be, since I have not been intimate with a man?"* (Lk 1:34).

But Gabriel brushed aside biological problems by telling Mary that this was to be a divine birth. Like begets like. Men and women beget sons and daughters, and God in the Virgin Mary would beget the Son of God. As proof of God's power to perform His word, Gabriel cited the conception of the aged Elizabeth, which to say the least was a supernatural act on the part of God.

Mary gave consent of her will to the will of God. It was not as simple as the saying of it, for hers was a secret she could share with no one in Nazareth, not even with Joseph. Most certainly it would bring down upon her the scorn of her neighbors. It might mean the loss of her betrothed, and it could mean death itself by stoning. But God had spoken, and she obeyed.

Shortly thereafter Mary hastened to Judea to visit her cousin. Maybe it was to verify the angel's words. More likely it was to seek comfort and courage from the one person who would understand; and when Mary had greeted Elizabeth, John the Baptist, whose voice one day as the forerunner of the Messiah would echo throughout the wilderness of Judea, leaped in his mother's womb at the presence of his Lord who now reposed in the virgin womb of His mother. In response to the twofold blessing of Elizabeth on Mary and her unborn child, the virgin mother uttered words of poetic beauty. They were words fraught with the knowledge of the Hebrew Scriptures. By them one is reminded of the song of Hannah when God answered her prayers in the birth of Samuel (1 Sm 1:9–18).

The curtain of silence is reverently drawn about the three following months, but they must have been days of prayer and rejoicing by two kindred spirits in whom the Lord had wrought wondrously. Just before the Baptist was born, Mary returned to Nazareth.

Mary's secret could be hidden no longer; and when Joseph knew her condition, he was greatly troubled. As far as he knew she had been unfaithful to him, and in that state of mind two courses were open to him. Either he could expose her as a public example, which probably would mean her death, or else he could put her away privately. His love for her triumphed over his injured sense of justice, and he chose to follow the latter course. But before he could do so, God, in a dream, let him in on His and Mary's secret, and never does Joseph appear greater than in his choice to protect Mary and the Babe with his name. He shared her shame before men and her glory before God.

THE BIRTH OF JESUS

In faraway Rome Augustus Caesar ruled his vast empire with an iron hand. True to Roman fashion he was primarily concerned that his subjects should keep the peace and pay their taxes. In 8 BC he had inaugurated a periodical census every fourteen years in order to enroll his people for taxation. According to Tacitus even the *regna*, the dependent kingdoms, were included in this census.

It was probably two years later that this census was carried out in Palestine. Herod, the vassal king, would not think of disobeying Augustus. Yet, knowing the Jew's aversion to paying taxes to Rome, he delayed it as long as he dared. Even then he sought to placate the Jews by adhering to their customs in dealing with them along tribal lines. So when the order for enrollment was finally given, it called for every Jew to be enrolled at the place where the tribal register was kept.

Thus it was that Joseph and Mary journeyed from Nazareth to Bethlehem, for they were descendents of David and members of the tribe of Judah. Though they were peasants, royal blood flowed in their veins. By this time Mary was great with child, and this journey of approximately one hundred miles worked a great hardship on her. Nevertheless the decree of Caesar must be obeyed.

However, she and Joseph moved under a greater word than that of the Roman emperor, for God had said that His Son, the Messiah, should be

Joseph and Mary's journey from Nazareth to Bethlehem may have taken close to a week.

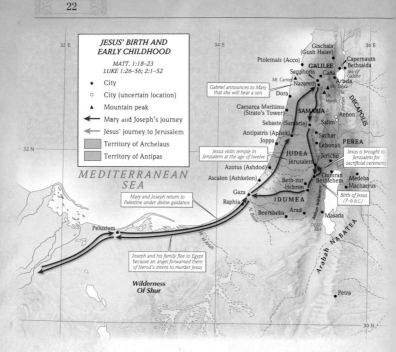

JESUS' BIRTH AND EARLY CHILDHOOD

MATT. 1:18–23
LUKE 1:26–56; 2:1–52

• City
○ City (uncertain location)
▲ Mountain peak
← Mary and Joseph's journey
← Jesus' journey to Jerusalem
▨ Territory of Archelaus
▨ Territory of Antipas

Gabriel announces to Mary that she will bear a son

Jesus visits temple in Jerusalem at the age of twelve

Mary and Joseph return to Palestine under divine guidance

Jesus is brought to Jerusalem for sacrificial ceremony

Birth of Jesus (7–6 B.C.)

Joseph and his family flee to Egypt because an angel forewarned them of Herod's intent to murder Jesus

MEDITERRANEAN SEA

Wilderness Of Shur

born in Bethlehem. Augustus knew nothing of this prophecy, and cared less. But unknowingly he was an instrument in the hands of God, as his decree, like an invisible cord, drew the virgin mother toward her destiny.

After several days of travel, late in the afternoon these weary travelers climbed the last rocky, steep ascent leading into Bethlehem. The streets were crowded with hundreds of other men and women bent upon the same mission. Clouds of dust boiled up from the stirring of the hundreds of feet of men and animals. A bedlam of noise characteristic of such a scene filled the ears of the weary couple from Nazareth as they laboriously made their way to the village inn. But it was already filled to overflowing.

So because there was no lodging to be had, Joseph bedded his wife down in the area provided for the animals. It was here that Mary *"gave birth to her firstborn Son, and she wrapped Him snugly in cloth and laid Him in a feeding trough"* (Lk 2:7).

Thus was the Son of God born. Not in a king's palace nor in the home of the wealthy or mighty, but to a peasant mother whose delivery room was a stable. No physician stood by to assist. Only the gnarled hands of a village carpenter came to her aid, but they were hands made tender by a conquering love and a devotion to God. As the newborn Babe slept through the night, He was under the watchful eyes of His mother and foster father, but most of all He was secure under the never-failing gaze of His Heavenly Father.

The next morning Bethlehem roused from her sleep. It was business as usual as the bazaars rang with the noise of commerce. The enrollment was finished, and the crowds moved out to return to their homes. Caesar's bidding had been done, and the village of David returned to normal. Only a few simple folks knew that on that night in this little village there had transpired the greatest event in the history of the world.

In infinite proportion it was much like the little community near Hodgenville, Kentucky. Early one morning a man was returning from a trip to Elizabethtown some miles away. He met a neighbor who was eager to learn what was happening in the outside world. After telling him of wars in Europe and events in Washington, the man asked, "What has happened here while I was away?" The neighbor replied, "Nothing. Oh, I believe that Mrs. Lincoln did give birth to a baby boy last night. I hear that they named him Abraham. But nothing important ever happens around here." Nothing important. If he had only known!

The magi made the long journey to worship the young King and present Him gifts of gold, frankincense, and myrrh.

"And you, Bethlehem, in the land of Judah, are by no means least among the leaders of Judah: because out of you will come a leader who will shepherd My people Israel" (Mt 2:6).

THE HOMAGE TO THE INFANT

The birth of Jesus was largely unnoticed by the world. Outside of the Bible no ancient historian took note of the event. They were so bent on recording the affairs of men and nations that they failed to recognize God's *history within history*, whereby in the person of His Son He had entered into the arena of time to answer the universal cry of men's hearts. But it did not occur without recognition by those whose hearts were prepared to receive it.

Heaven itself rejoiced over the glorious event. For the angelic hosts burst asunder the barrier of invisibility to proclaim the Savior's birth and to sing the first Christian anthem dedicated to His praise.

For their audience they had a handful of lowly shepherds, the simple folk who counted for little in the tides of history ever beating upon the shores of time. But their hearts were firmly fixed in the promises of God upon which they meditated in the quiet hours of the night. In Bethlehem's fields where Ruth had gleaned in the fields of Boaz, later to become his bride and the Moabite ancestress of the Savior; where David had tended his sheep, all the while contemplating upon the glory of God and upon Him who was to be born; there the shepherds first heard the glad tidings that unto them had been born a Savior, Christ the Lord.

The shepherds hastened to Bethlehem to find it as the angels had said. They found Mary, and Joseph, and the Babe lying in a manger. God in a cradle! Upon hearing from the shepherds about the heavenly declaration, Mary placed this event alongside the message of Gabriel, pondering them in her heart. And she knew that God had fulfilled His promise. The shepherds returned to their work, carrying back into their mundane sphere the memory of an experience that would forever cast an aura of glory about them and about all others who in humble trust come to Him who fills the universe with His presence, yet who for a little while was contained in a baby's crib.

When Jesus was eight days old, He was circumcised according to Hebrew law. It was at this time also that He was formally given the name *Jesus*. This is the Greek form of the Hebrew word *Joshua* or *Yeshua*, meaning *Jehovah is salvation*. Thus was obeyed the word of God through Gabriel who said, *"You are to name Him Jesus, because He will save His people from their sins."* (Mt 1:21).

The second group to pay homage to the Christ-child were two aged saints in the temple in Jerusalem. Again in keeping with Hebrew law forty days after Jesus' birth, Mary and Joseph took Him to the temple to make the prescribed sacrifice for the purification of the mother and the dedication of the child. These peasant people received scant notice as they offered the sacrifices of the poor: two doves and two young pigeons. The priests were too busy with their sacrifices and teaching the Scriptures to notice Him who was Lord of the temple. But two saints in Israel did take note of Him.

One was the aged Simeon. He had been promised by the Holy Spirit, probably in answer to his prayers, that he should not die until he had seen the Lord's Christ. When he looked upon the infant Jesus, the Holy Spirit told him that this was He. So taking Him into his arms he blessed God, and in words of poetic beauty declared Jesus to be *"a light for revelation to the Gentiles and glory to Your people Israel"* (Lk 2:32). Then he added words of an ominous note as to Mary he spoke of the sword that should pierce through her soul. Mary would realize the full import of these words when one day she would see her Son hanging on a cross. Truly her soul must have been a study of mingled lights and shadows as she heard Simeon's prophetic utterance.

The words of Simeon aroused the soul of Anna, an aged prophetess who dwelt in the temple day and night as she was absorbed in prayer and worship. She also approached the infant, praising God and speaking of the Christ to all who were looking for the redemption of Jerusalem and Israel.

And the One bringing salvation was made evident to those whose hearts dwelt in the Lord and feasted upon the promises of His Word. So it was then; so it is now and always.

Mary and Joseph marveled at these things as they returned to Bethlehem. Apparently they decided not to return to Nazareth, for the next time that they are mentioned in the Gospel narrative (Matthew) they are dwelling in a house in Bethlehem.

Probably some days or even months later a strange caravan arrived before the palace of Herod the king in Jerusalem. Wise men or Magi from the east came inquiring, *"Where is He who has been born King of the Jews? For we saw His star in the east and have come to worship Him."* (Mt 2:2).

Who were these Magi? Tradition numbers them as three, stemming from the gifts they presented before the Babe. Furthermore, it identifies them as coming from Europe, Asia, and Africa respectively. But these are traditions unsupported by the Gospel record.

In all likelihood they came from a land east of Palestine, probably from the Mesopotamian valley. Herodotus tells of such a people as being a former Median tribe. They had attempted an unsuccessful rebellion against the Persians. Therefore, they became a priestly tribe very much like the Levites among the Israelites. They were skilled in philosophy, medicine, and natural science. Especially were they students of astrology, the forerunner of modern astronomy. According to the ancients a man was believed to be affected by the star under which he was born. Any unusual phenomenon in the heavens was said to herald some special intervention of God into the natural order.

It is of interest to recall that at this particular time an air of expectancy hovered over the ancient world. Wherever the Jews went, they carried their Scriptures telling of the promised Messiah. It is not surprising, therefore, to read from Tacitus, in the first century BC, "that at this very time the East was to grow powerful, and rulers coming from Judaea were to acquire universal empire" (*The Histories*, Book V). Later both Suetonius and Josephus echoed the same thought. There was an almost universal expectancy regarding a Savior. Ancient inscriptions reveal this title as being ascribed to many rulers, including Augustus Caesar himself.

One can hardly question but that the Magi were aware of this expectancy. Probably they had received it from the Jews themselves who were in their land in abundance. They may even have been students of the Hebrew Scriptures. So when in the East they discovered an unusual star in the heavens, they interpreted it as signifying a great divine event, as the birth of some unusual person. Therefore, they journeyed to Judea, the land in which this expectancy centered.

Many attempts have been made to identify this star with known astronomical phenomena, but no such explanation meets the requirements of the biblical language describing it. The gospel record calls it "His star," pointing to a special star for a special event. If one accepts the position that God created the universe, there is no reason why He could not have created this star for the purpose of heralding the greatest event in history, namely, the incarnation of God in human form.

Nevertheless, when the Magi inquired of Herod as to the whereabouts of the one *"born King of the Jews,"* he summoned the chief priests and scribes. From them Herod learned that the Scriptures taught that He should be born in Bethlehem. Learning this, the Magi departed. They rejoiced when once again the "star" appeared in the night sky. Following it they were led to the house where the young child was, and falling down before Him they worshiped Him, presenting unto Him gifts: gold, frankincense, and myrrh.

These gifts are not without significance. Gold, the gift for a king; frankincense, suggestive of worship and sacrifice, the gift for a priest; myrrh, used to embalm the dead, the gift for one who is to die. Thus there was prophecy in these gifts. Jesus was born to rule in the hearts of men. As

Harbor at Alexandria, Egypt. Joseph, Mary, and Jesus may have lived in Alexandria among a Jewish community until Herod the Great died in 4 BC.

their High Priest He opened the way of man to God, and He did so in His atoning death.

Their mission accomplished, the Magi prepared to return to their home. But being warned of God that evil stalked the land, they gave Jerusalem and Herod a wide berth in so doing. In their coming to Bethlehem, they had blazed the path over which many who are wise would come to kneel before Him who is Truth.

The words of the Magi, *"He who has been born King of the Jews,"* struck a note of terror in the heart of Herod. Though he was in the twilight of his years, still he held tenaciously to his throne. To hold on to it, he had killed too often to let any impending threat go without notice. He had even killed members of his family as we have already noticed. So feigning a desire to pay homage to this Child, he asked the Magi to bring him tidings as to the Child's whereabouts. Homage indeed! At the hand of a sword!

Therefore, when he learned that the Magi had avoided him, he sent troops to dispatch the infant King. To insure that they did so they were to slay every child up to two years of age in the area about Bethlehem. But his satanic plot was thwarted. Having been warned of God, Joseph already had taken Mary and the Babe to Egypt. However, the "innocents" died in Herod's futile effort. How many? No one knows. One may wonder why no record of this murderous deed is found outside the Bible, but such a foul deed by this despot whose hands dripped with the blood of royalty hardly merited notice in the chronicles of time. Augustus Caesar himself characterized the man when he said that it was better to be Herod's sow (*hus*) than his son (*huios*), for the sow had a better chance to live.

Herod died in 4 BC. As the crowning act of his infamy, he sought to insure mourning throughout the land at his death. Knowing that the people would rejoice at such news, he gave orders that the most distinguished

Nazareth, Israel. A dramatically lit carpenter shop, with rustic wooden table and wooden hammers, mallets, and other tools of the trade, an authentic representation of carpentry tools used in ancient times.

citizens of Jerusalem should be arrested. At the moment of his death, they too should be killed. Thus at the simultaneous announcements joy would be muffled and tears would flow throughout the land. Happily at Herod's death the order for this mass murder was never given. Such was the man who sought to kill the Savior at His birth.

These groups gathered about the Christ Child in His birth hour are not without a broader significance than the event of the moment. For while they were real people in actual experiences, they are suggestive of others of their kind through the succeeding ages. The humble, simple folk find in Jesus the answer to their deepest needs. The devout ever gather about Him in worship and praise. Wise men find in Him the answer to the intimate questions of life as they lay the fruits of their labors at His feet, and worldly systems ever oppose Him as they see in Him one who ultimately will bring to naught all of their schemes. But to all who come to Him in faith, He is ever God's Son born to be King.

THE SILENT YEARS

How long the little family remained in Egypt is a matter of speculation. It could have been for only one year. But at the death of Herod, God told Joseph that they should return to Palestine. Upon learning that Archelaus, Herod's son, reigned in Judea, Joseph followed God's guidance to return to their former home in Nazareth, and with this the curtain of silence falls upon the life of Jesus for more than twenty-five years. Only once is the curtain parted to give one brief glimpse of the young lad Jesus.

Human curiosity is such that it yearns for more detail as to these early years. It is not surprising, then, that in the years following the life of Jesus there arose many apocryphal gospels purporting to reveal His child-hood. They tell many ridiculous stories about Him. According to them He made birds of clay, pitched them in the air, and they flew away. When

His playmates angered Him, in a fit of anger He turned them into little goats. Instead of Jesus being subject to His parents, He is pictured as being a problem to them and to the neighbors. One has but to compare these stories with the dignified, beautiful account of Luke to understand that man's fanciful imagination can become a dangerous thing. The one clear statement in the canonical Gospels covering approximately eleven years of Jesus' childhood is that *"the boy grew up and became strong, filled with wisdom, and God's grace was on Him"* (Lk 2:40).

But even though the Scriptures are largely silent, there are many things to be learned about this period. His home was that of a peasant carpenter, but Joseph was tender, wise, and a godly man. Every Jewish lad was required to learn a trade. Under Joseph's wise guidance Jesus learned the trade of carpentry. However, in all likelihood it was His mother who exerted the greater influence upon Him. From the Gospels it is clear that she was a woman pure and sensitive of soul. She possessed a great knowledge of the Hebrew Scriptures. God makes no mistakes. And He entrusted His Son to a mother full of grace and a foster father who nobly stood beside her in the stewardship God had placed upon them.

Jesus grew up in a normal home. After His birth there were other children born to Joseph and Mary. His half-brothers were named James, Judas (Jude), Joseph, and Simon. There were at least two half-sisters whose names are not given. In later life they did not accept Jesus as the Christ until after His Resurrection. Thereafter James and Jude became leaders in the Early Church; each wrote an epistle bearing his name.

There is strong evidence that Jesus' brothers and sisters did not understand Him. From this it may be inferred that they were never close to Him. Therefore, Jesus must have spent much of His time in the company of His mother or else alone.

An overview of modern Nazareth from the southwest

As a normal Jewish lad Jesus received His education first in the home and later in the synagogue under the tutelage of a scribe. Quite naturally this centered largely in the Scriptures, but His eager mind thirsted after knowledge, and He was "filled with wisdom" gained in the school of God.

It is quite evident that Jesus spoke at least three languages. He quoted the Scriptures from the original Hebrew and not from the Greek transla- tions. On more than one occasion He spoke in Aramaic, the current tongue among the Jews. And it is most likely that He was conversant in the Greek language, since it was commonly spoken in Palestine at that time.

The teachings of Jesus reveal His tremendous understanding of both nature and human nature, and Nazareth and its environs was an ideal place in which to learn both. Nazareth is located in a beautiful valley surrounded by the hills of Zebulon and joined on the west by the Plain of Esdraelon. In the springtime beautiful flowers abounded. As Jesus wandered these hills

He learned about nature. He knew the habits of birds and animals. Farmers sowing and reaping were a common sight to Him.

In the closely knitted life of a village He had a perfect laboratory in which to observe human nature at its best and worst. Nazareth was a notoriously wicked town, and by observing it the boy Jesus saw the sordid nature of sin and its degrading effect upon men. But He saw the better side of life also. His mother busy at the ordinary chores of the home: kneading dough, baking bread, patching worn garments, sweeping the floor or searching for a lost coin. And then there was contact with the neighbors. Even today one may see the well, which until recent years was the only source of water for the village. How often Jesus must have gone with His mother to draw water and to listen as the women exchanged morsels of news! All of these things bore fruit in His later life as He drew upon the ordinary things of daily life to impart eternal truth.

Then there was the larger scope of learning. For One who never set foot out of Palestine, except as an infant, Jesus possessed great knowledge of the world in which He lived. How as a lad He must have dreamed as from a nearby hill He gazed upon the blue waters of the Mediterranean whose waves lapped the shores of the ancient world! The caravan route brought a constant stream of travelers through Nazareth. With wide-eyed wonder Jesus must have listened

As a Jewish boy, Jesus grew "in wisdom and stature and in favor with God and with people" (Lk 2:42).

as He drank in the many stories of distant lands. All of these things plus the liberal Greek atmosphere of Galilee, served to develop in Jesus a cosmopolitan view enabling Him to overcome any temptation toward a narrow Jewish nationalism. His heart went out to all nations and to all men, and the very simplicity of His surroundings made Jesus unusually sensitive against the stale and sophisticated emptiness of the teachings of the religious leaders of His day.

During all of these years Joseph and Mary made annual visits to Jerusalem for the Passover. Whether or not they took Jesus with them is not known, but when He reached the age of twelve He became a "son of the Law," and began to observe the ordinances of Jewish worship. So at twelve years of age He did accompany His parents to this great feast. While there He spent much time in the temple. The parents evidently traveled in a caravan, so that when they left Jerusalem to return to Nazareth they went a full day's journey before discovering that Jesus was not with them. Returning to Jerusalem they finally found Him in the temple among the teachers both listening and asking questions. His hungry mind was feasting upon this intellectual and spiritual experience, and the learning of His years is evidenced in the astonishment of all as to His comprehension of the things of God.

The natural relation Jesus bore to His mother and Joseph is seen in her mild rebuke that He had caused them such anxiety. But He replied, *"Why were you searching for Me? . . . Didn't you know that I had to be in My Father's house?"* (Lk 2:49).

This statement definitely reveals Jesus' consciousness of His unique relation with His Heavenly Father. Was it just now dawning upon Him? Or had He known it all along? To say dogmatically either way is mere speculation, but in all likelihood there had never been a moment in His conscious life when this awareness was not present with Him.

However He was still subject to His parents. With them He returned to Nazareth. There He continued to advance or to cut His way forward *"in wisdom and stature, and in favor with God and with people"* (Lk 2:52). Yes, Jesus learned. It was in keeping with His complete identity with man, apart from sin, that He learned as must any other child. But He learned His lesson well.

From this point on Joseph is not mentioned as being alive. Tradition says that he died when Jesus was a youth, maybe sixteen years old. Thereafter, Jesus assumed the duties of a man. He became the carpenter of Nazareth and the breadwinner in the family. Doubtless Mary more and more turned to Him for strength and help. This within itself may not have improved the attitude of the brothers and sisters toward Him.

Nevertheless, the Savior of men was a hard-working artisan among His neighbors, until one day God whispered in His heart that the time of His public ministry had arrived.

CHAPTER III
THE TIME OF THE BEGINNING
THE MINISTRY OF JOHN THE BAPTIST

It had been four hundred years since a prophet of God had appeared among His people. Since the days of Malachi there had been a famine of prophetic preaching in Israel. During this interval the temple ritual had continued, but even this had largely lost itself in the dry desert sands of a meaningless rote. Still there remained hungry hearts that waited and prayed for the coming of the Messianic age. And then came John the Baptist. It was probably late in AD 25 or the early spring of AD 26. John was of the priestly line. A priest began his ministry at the age of thirty, so John was probably that age when he appeared in the mission for which he had been prepared.

With the sense of a true historian, and following the custom of the ancients, Luke dates this event according to the rulers of the day. *"In the fifteenth year of the reign of Tiberius Caesar, while Pontius Pilate was governor of Judea, Herod was tetrarch of Galilee, his brother Philip tetrarch of the region of Iturea and Trachonitis, and Lysanias tetrarch of Abilene, during the high priesthood of Annas and Caiaphas, God's word came to John the son of Zechariah in the wilderness"* (3:1–2).

Of him Alexander Maclaren said, "John leapt, as it were, into the arena full-grown and full-armed." His message was not his own but that of God, as in the wilderness of Judea he declared, *"Repent, because the kingdom of heaven has come near!"* (Mt 3:2). Like some new Elijah dressed in rugged

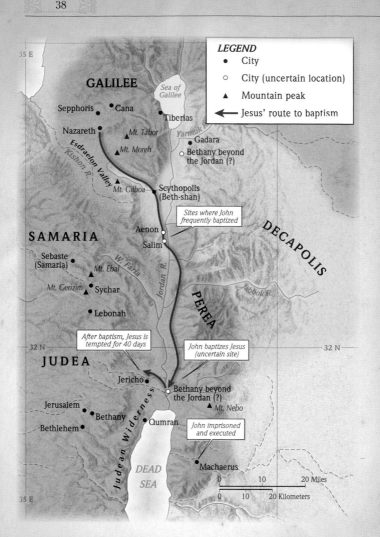

LEGEND

- City
○ City (uncertain location)
▲ Mountain peak
← Jesus' route to baptism

GALILEE

Sea of Galilee

Sepphoris • Cana
• Tiberias
Nazareth ▲ Mt. Tabor
Yarmuk R.
• Gadara
○ Bethany beyond the Jordan (?)
▲ Mt. Moreh

Esdraelon Valley

Kishon R.

▲ Mt. Gilboa
Scythopolis (Beth-shan)

Sites where John frequently baptized

Aenon
DECAPOLIS
Salim

SAMARIA

Sebaste (Samaria) •
▲ Mt. Ebal
W. Faria
Jabbok R.
Mt. Gerizim ▲ • Sychar
PEREA
• Lebonah

After baptism, Jesus is tempted for 40 days

John baptizes Jesus (uncertain site)

32 N
32 N

JUDEA

• Jericho
○ Bethany beyond the Jordan (?)
Jerusalem • ▲ Mt. Nebo
• Bethany
• Qumran
Bethlehem •

John imprisoned and executed

Judean Wilderness

• Machaerus

DEAD SEA

0   10   20 Miles
0   10   20 Kilometers

35 E
35 E

John the Baptizer in Aenon and Salim

clothes made of camel's hair and bound with a leather girdle, he strode suddenly into the arena of history to herald the approaching King. His body fed upon the frugal fare of locusts and wild honey, but the soul of this son of the desert was nourished by a revelation from God falling upon him as manna from heaven.

It is no wonder that the multitudes left their homes, cities, and villages to hear him, for his preaching echoed the voice of God. Both his message and his mission bristled with the words of the Old Testament prophets. A steady stream of repentant sinners was being baptized in the Jordan River as evidence of their readiness to participate in the coming kingdom.

But not all who came did so with such willingness, for when word reached Jerusalem about this revival meeting, some Pharisees and Sadducees came to investigate it. Seeing this delegation the Baptist boldly charged them: *"Brood of vipers! Who warned you to flee from the coming wrath?"* (Mt 3:7). He saw them as a brood of snakes fleeing for safety before a desert fire. It was a shocking figure but one readily understood by them. Challenging them to repent, he reminded them that they could no longer smugly claim that as descendents of Abraham they were already in God's kingdom. Looking about at the multitude of desert stones, he said that God could of them raise up such children to Abraham. But the relationship He demanded was a spiritual one. If they expected to participate in His kingdom they must not only repent but show evidence of it in their works, for the ax of God's judgment was already laid at the roots of the trees. Any tree failing to yield such fruit would be cut down and cast into the fire.

Hearing these scorching words the crowds asked, *"What then should we do?"* (Lk 3:10). And fitting his words to the need in each case John told them, not how to be saved, but how to prove the genuineness of their repentance (Lk 3:11–14).

Separating the chaff from the grain (Ps 1:4)

However, John's message was not solely one of judgment, for it sounded the note of hope also. The people were in a state of eager expectation. In reply to their question if he were the Christ, John said that there came One after him who was infinitely greater than he was. He was not even worthy to unloose the shoes of the One whom he heralded. Instead of baptizing them with water, as he had done, this One would baptize them in the Holy Spirit and the power of fire. He would come for both salvation and judgment. Drawing upon a common scene in Palestine, then as now, he pictured this One as one winnowing grain. As both wheat and chaff were thrown upward, they were separated by the wind. The grain was gathered and stored; the chaff was used for fuel. So would the One coming after John separate the true from the false. Salvation for the one; condemnation for the other! Such was the gospel John preached in the wilderness of Judea.

THE BAPTISM OF JESUS

John the Baptist was six months older than Jesus, so evidently his ministry had covered that period of time when it took a most unique turn. Luke notes that at this time Jesus was about thirty years of age (3:23). Even though He was not of a priestly line, still He was to serve as the Priest. Thus He began His public ministry when He reached His thirtieth birthday.

The news of John's ministry spread like wildfire throughout Palestine. Finally it reached the village of Nazareth, and hearing it Jesus knew that His time had come. So closing His carpenter's shop He went forth to meet His destiny.

Suddenly the Forerunner stood face-to-face with his Christ. Whether or not they had met before is not certain. Since they were related it is possible that they had done so as children, but the probability seems to have been otherwise. In all likelihood John's parents had died when he was very young. Thereafter, he became a child of the desert; it could be that he was reared by some desert group such as the Essenes. At any rate it would appear that he and Jesus for the first time stood face-to-face on the banks of the Jordan.

And yet John seems instinctively to have recognized Jesus as the Christ. A divinely given sign by which he would know the Christ had not yet been fulfilled (Jn 1:33–34). Without question John had baptized those who expressed their repentance; but when Jesus stood before him, he hesitated, stating that he should be baptized by Jesus rather than Jesus be baptized by him. Jesus brushed aside his hesitation, saying, *"'Allow it for now, because this is the way for us to fulfill all righteousness.' Then he allowed Him to be baptized"* (Mt 3:15).

So John and Jesus went down into the waters of the Jordan. Following Jesus' baptism a most remarkable thing happened. The heavens were

The Jordan River in Israel

opened, and John saw the Spirit of God descending as a dove upon Jesus. Then he heard a voice out of heaven saying, *"This is My beloved Son. I take delight in Him!"* (Mt 3:17). John had his sign. He knew that Jesus was the Christ, and this fact had been authenticated by the presence of the triune God. In all probability only John and Jesus saw the "dove" and heard the "voice." It was a dual sign given only to them and not to the multitude. *The revelation of God is given only to those who are prepared to receive it.*

What is the significance of this divine manifestation? The dove is symbolic of gentleness, innocence, and meekness. Furthermore, the Levitical law prescribed one dove, along with a lamb, or two doves only for the poor, as a sacrificial offering. So the anointing of Jesus by the Spirit in the form of a dove foretold His ministry as a sacrifice for sin, and the Father's approval of the Son further attested His sinless purity as a fit offering for sin. Jesus had lived as a man for thirty years. So completely was He one in the will of God that He was well-pleasing to God. Elsewhere throughout His ministry the Father would repeat this approval, but it came first as Jesus stood in the flowing waters of the Jordan.

Why was Jesus baptized? The baptism of John symbolized repentance from sin and a willingness to participate in the coming kingdom. But that Jesus' baptism involved more than these is evidenced by John's hesitancy to baptize Him, for Jesus had committed no sin from which He should repent. (And He was Himself the King of the kingdom.) It is quite true that in His baptism Jesus authenticated the mission of John, but His own words express an even greater purpose—*to fulfill all righteousness*" (Mt 3:15). It was to perfect the righteousness that Jesus came to establish, the righteousness of God in Christ Jesus.

And how was this made possible? Through the death, burial, and resurrection of Jesus. He identified Himself with the sins of men and gave them victory over them. Therefore He submitted to baptism at the hands of John, but in so doing He portrayed what He would do in order to redeem man from sin. He died for man's sin; He was buried; He rose from the grave in triumph over sin and death. So His baptism at once looked both backward and forward. Backward to the fact of man's sin and Jesus' identity with sinful man. Forward to His redeeming act as the sacrifice for the sins of the world. Thus at the outset of His ministry Jesus symbolized what all believers through the subsequent centuries have portrayed when they act in obedience and follow Him in baptism.

THE TEMPTATIONS OF JESUS

Immediately following His baptism Jesus retired into the wilderness of Judea. This He did under the leading or driving (Mk 1:12) of the Holy Spirit. The purpose of this retirement was that He might be tempted by Satan.

The traditional Mount of Temptation is a wild, barren mountain just west and north of Jericho. From the time of the Crusades it has been called *Quarantania*, a name derived from the forty days of fasting. One can still stand on the mound of ancient Jericho and view it as it rises sharply and forebodingly out of the desert. Here for forty days Jesus was alone with no companions but the wild beasts of the desert. These days He spent in fasting, not as a ritual but in preoccupation with the will of God. He had embarked upon His ministry. What kind of ministry would it be? He was the King of the kingdom. What would be the nature of His kingship? These were the questions so occupying His mind that He lost all sense of hunger. Finally He became aware of His physical needs and it was then that Satan made his attack upon the Son of God.

Why should Jesus be tempted of Satan at this time? It has been noted that Jesus came into the wilderness *"to be tempted by the Devil"* (Mt 4:1). "To be tempted" is an infinitive of purpose meaning to test, to prove, either in the good or evil sense. God would permit Jesus to be tested to prove the good; Satan would test Jesus in an effort to prove Him imperfect. It is in this latter sense that the experience may be called temptation.

At this point the question naturally arises as to whether or not Jesus could yield to temptation. Of course He did not possess a sinful nature. Nor was He guilty of antecedent sins that made Him liable to yielding to the overtures of Satan. But it must be admitted that He had the power to yield or else the temptations were not real; and if they were not real, then He merely pretended to be tempted. Such would make Him guilty of hypocrisy, the sin which Jesus assailed more than any other. It must be remembered that Jesus had completely identified Himself with man, apart from sin, and He was tempted in His humanity, not in His deity. As such He had the power to sin, but a more glorious truth is that He also had the

Quarantania, the Mount of Temptation as seen from the top of Old Testament Jericho

power not to sin. And so He is *"One who has been tested in every way as we are, yet without sin"* (Heb 4:15).

Another question presents itself. Were these temptations merely psychological experiences, or did they involve a bodily confrontation between Jesus and Satan? Some hold to the former position, but there is no reason why the latter could not be true. As God was manifested in bodily form, in like fashion Satan, the adversary, appeared to Jesus in bodily form. The struggle that raged on Quarantania and in Jerusalem was but a visible phase of the conflict going on in the spiritual realm. *Devil* means "slanderer," and Satan ever slanders God to man (Gn 3:4) and man to God (Jb 1:9–11). Such was the struggle that raged in the temptations of Jesus.

Before examining the three temptations themselves, it is well to note that in resisting them Jesus did so in the realm of His humanity, not His deity. For his purpose Satan assumed that Jesus was the Son of God, but Jesus did not call upon His divine power to resist the evil one. Indeed, the first two temptations were designed to lead Him to do so, yet He did not separate Himself from man in this struggle. Apart from His sinless nature and life Jesus called upon no power that is not available to any man as he faces temptation. His only weapon was the Scripture, the sword of the Spirit, and He wielded it within the center of the will of God.

In order to understand the temptations of Jesus in the wilderness, two things must be kept in mind. They must be cast against the backdrop of current Jewish expectations concerning the Messiah. The Jews thought of Him as the ruler of an earthly kingdom, doing great wonders, and providing them with an abundance of material prosperity, and Jesus was aware of these things being so evident in the three proposals of Satan. Furthermore, these temptations were aimed at the three areas of man's being in which he may be tempted: physical appetites, aesthetic nature, and spiritual ambition. These areas are evident in Satan's temptation of Eve: *"Then the woman saw that the tree was good for food* [physical appetite] *and delightful to look at* [aesthetic nature], *and that it was desirable for obtaining wisdom* [spiritual ambition]" (Gn 3:5–6).

The first temptation was directed at physical appetite: *"command that these stones be made bread"* (Mt 4:3). This involved Jesus' use of His divine power for selfish purposes. It expressed distrust in God's benevolence and power to care for His own. But more, it suggested that He should be a *bread Messiah*, ministering only to the physical needs of men. Every age has produced such, as power-mad rulers have enslaved their subjects under the guise of giving them prosperity in material things.

In reply Jesus quoted from Deuteronomy: (Note also the other two temptations.) *"Man must not live on bread alone but on every word that comes from the mouth of God."* (Mt 4:4; Dt 8:3). Man must have bread, but he needs far more than bread. Jesus refused to call upon His divine power to provide for His own human needs. He had identified Himself with man and would trust in His Father to provide His every need. He came to give men more than bread for their bodies, it was the living Bread for their souls.

The second temptation was aimed at Jesus' aesthetic nature. Transporting Jesus into the temple area in Jerusalem, Satan caused Him to look from its highest point into the valley far below. He preyed upon the natural tendency of dizziness: "throw Yourself down." Put God to the test. And then Satan also quoted from Scripture: *"For it is written: He will give His angels orders concerning you, and, they will support you with their hands so that you will not strike your foot against a stone"* (Mt 4:6).

But note that whereas Jesus quoted from the Law, Satan quoted from the psalms (Ps 91:11–12). He quoted poetry as though it were prose. Also

The traditional pinnacle of the temple

Satan omitted one vital phrase: *"For He will give His angels orders con-cerning you,* to protect you in all your ways"* (Ps 91:11, author's emphasis). Satan sought to divert Jesus from His way to Satan's way. The Jews thought of the Messiah as suddenly coming to His temple, perhaps floating down from its pinnacle amid the acclaim of the multitudes.

But Jesus again refused Satan's proposal: *"Do not test the Lord your God"* (Mt 4:7; Dt 6:16). He did not come to found a kingdom upon outward spectacular deeds but upon truth in the inward parts. He would not do so by daring God but by trusting Him.

The third temptation was based upon spiritual ambition. In His mission Jesus challenged Satan's falsely-assumed sovereignty over the earth. He would assert His own sovereignty as seen in His kingdom, and this assertion involved His death for the sins of men.

But from an exceeding high mountain Satan caused the kingdoms of the world and their glory to pass in review before Jesus. And then his proposal: *"I will give You all these things if You will fall down and worship me"* (Mt 4:9). He offered Jesus a short cut to world supremacy.

In the first place, this was not Satan's to give. In the second place, it would have been an empty sovereignty. In the third place, had Jesus succumbed to this temptation the very moral structure of the universe would have collapsed. God would have been defeated, and Satan would have been sovereign indeed.

But Jesus again wielded the Sword of the Spirit: *"Go away, Satan! For it is written: Worship the Lord your God, and serve only Him"* (Mt 4:10; Dt 6:13). Jesus chose to follow God's way, even though it led Him to a cross. It was the longer, harder way, but it was the only true way.

Satan left Jesus for a season, but he would return again and again, even as he has come to men and nations through the ages. Unhappily they have fallen victims to his wiles. But the Son of God came forth from the wilderness in triumph to walk in the ways of His Father, and He calls all men everywhere to follow in His train.

THE FIRST DISCIPLES

In the meantime John the Baptist continued to preach along the banks of the Jordan. When once again he saw Jesus in his midst he clearly identified Him as the Christ, setting forth the divine fulfillment of the sign by which he would recognize Him. In one sentence he foretold the nature of His mission as he said, *"Here is the Lamb of God, who takes away the sin of the world!"* (Jn 1:29). As the result of this proclamation two of John's disciples left him to follow after Jesus. These were Andrew and, probably, John, the beloved disciple. Andrew brought his brother, Simon, later to be called Peter, to Jesus. By implication it may be inferred that John did the same for his brother James.

The next day Jesus left the Jordan valley to return to Galilee. Along the way He called Philip to follow Him, and Philip led Nathanael to become a disciple of Jesus. All of these men had been drawn to John the Baptist, but both by his preaching and the power of Jesus' personality they left the "forerunner" to follow the Christ. Later, as Jesus' ministry broadened, this very fact engendered jealousy among those who still clung to John the Baptist. But ever true to his mission he declared, *"He must increase, but I must decrease"* (Jn 3:30). So John, with his mission accomplished, waned before Jesus as the moon does with the rising of the sun.

THE FIRST MIRACLE

Three days after His return to Galilee, Jesus, His mother, and disciples were guests at a marriage feast in Cana, a village located only a few miles from Nazareth. When the supply of wine was exhausted, Mary called the emergency to the attention of her Son. Mildly rebuking His mother for her implied request that He do something about it, Jesus proceeded to turn water into wine, a wine which the steward of the feast declared to be better than the first.

Four lessons may be drawn from this incident. First, Jesus avowed that, in contrast to John the Baptist's ascetic nature, He would render His ministry as a social being. Second, He respectfully reminded His mother that no longer would He be merely her Son but her Lord. Third, by calling attention to the steward's response, John, the author of the fourth Gospel, mystically suggests that the revelation of God in Jesus is better or more complete than that found in the Old Testament. Fourth, by this miracle the disciples were led to believe fully in Jesus as the Christ. It was the *"beginning of his signs"* (Jn 2:11 ASV), which would show forth His deity.

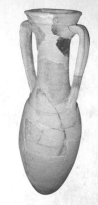

First-century storage jar (Jn 2:1–11)

From Cana Jesus and His company paid a brief visit to Capernaum, the city which later would serve as His headquarters for the Galilean ministry. From here He probably returned to His home in Nazareth where He remained in seclusion for some time.

THE FIRST CLEANSING OF THE TEMPLE

Several months had elapsed since Jesus' baptism, which probably took place in the late summer of AD 26. It was now the Spring of AD 27, just prior to the Passover during the week before what we call Easter Sunday. This was the greatest of all the feasts of the Jews, memorializing Israel's deliverance out of the bondage of Egypt. So Jesus and His disciples journeyed from Galilee to be present for this feast. The Synoptic Gospels (Matt., Mark and Luke) record only one visit of Jesus to Jerusalem, but John, in keeping with his purpose to report portions of His ministry omitted by the others, includes several visits prior to His final one at the close of His ministry.

Apart from a Jew's natural desire to be in Jerusalem for the Passover, Jesus' present journey seems to indicate a greater purpose. A. T. Robertson calls the first year following Jesus' baptism "The Year of Obscurity." It is recorded only in John's gospel. The Synoptic Gospels plunge Jesus immediately into His Galilean ministry. Why this period of "obscurity"? For some unknown reason the Lord delayed what may more likely be called His public ministry. But what more appropriate time could He have chosen to inaugurate it than the Passover, and in Jerusalem itself? It was the feast of deliverance, and Jerusalem was the capital city of the Jewish religion. So He began by challenging the center of Judaism, at the time of year when the Jews were most expectant concerning their Messiah.

He threw out His challenge in the temple itself, the center of Jewish worship. This He did by cleansing the temple. This act was not only a protest against the emptiness of the Jewish religion, but it was directed immediately against merchandising in the temple itself. What had begun as a service to the worshipers had degenerated into a system of defrauding them. This constituted what was commonly called "The Bazaars of Annas," for it was under the control of the former high priest and his sons.

Pilgrims came from great distances to sacrifice in the temple. Therefore oxen, sheep, and doves were kept in the Court of the Gentiles to be sold at exorbitant prices to the worshipers. Furthermore, each adult male Jew was required to pay annually the half-shekel temple tax. Since it must be paid in Jewish coins, moneychangers were set up to exchange foreign coins for this Jewish money. A fee was charged to make this exchange. One has but to visit a modern bazaar in the Middle East to grasp something of the bedlam existing in this "House of Prayer." Not only were the Jews exploited, but it was a scandal to the Gentiles who were permitted in this part of the temple area.

So in righteous indignation Jesus made a scourge of cords and drove the animals out of the temple. He overthrew the tables of the moneychangers and told those who sold doves to take them away. *"Stop turning My Father's house into a marketplace"* (or an *emporium*) (Jn 2:16). Note the sense of divine Sonship once again expressed by Jesus.

Upon learning of Jesus' action, the Jewish religious leaders came to Him with a challenge as to the authority by which He did this. They demanded a "sign" to justify such action. According to their own belief, they were justified in making this demand. For to them only a prophet or the Messiah Himself could exercise authority beyond their own over the temple, and since Jesus did not claim to be a prophet, His act could have but one meaning. It signified that He claimed Messianic authority. The Jewish leaders comprehended the significance of Jesus' deed.

Since Jesus was not yet ready to proclaim His Messiahship openly, He replied with a veiled "sign," which was yet in the future. *"Destroy this sanctuary, and I will raise it up in three days"* (Jn 2:19). He may have pointed to His body as He spoke of His death and Resurrection, but the Jews were in no position at this time to grasp His meaning. They thought only of the material temple. Herod the Great began to build the temple in 20–19 BC. It was now in its forty-sixth year of building and was not finished until AD 64—six years before it was destroyed by the Romans. So Jesus' words seemed preposterous to the Jews. They showed their scorn of this Galilean *peasant* when they asked literally, *"and will You raise it up in three days?"* (Jn 2:20, author's emphasis). Therefore the Jewish leaders as a group scornfully rejected this first challenge of Jesus.

However, many of the people did believe on Him as they witnessed the many miracles He performed. Still Jesus did not commit Himself to them since He knew their innermost thoughts. The time had not yet come for Him to do so.

THE VISIT OF NICODEMUS

But there was one Jewish leader who did not reject Jesus. This was Nicodemus, a Pharisee and a member of the Sanhedrin, the ruling body or Supreme Court among the Jews. He was a man of position, power, wealth, and righteous character. Some suggest that his use of the word "we" indicates that he came to Jesus as the representative of a group of interested inquirers.

At any rate Nicodemus sought out Jesus under the cover of night. It is quite natural that this teacher among the Jews would come to this unknown, unaccredited teacher thusly. He wished to escape the criticism of his colleagues who had rejected Jesus as being of no consequence. In spite of that fact, Nicodemus was convinced by Jesus' signs that He was a teacher come from God.

However, when Nicodemus so stated this, Jesus brushed his compliments aside as He went to the very heart of the matter: *"Unless someone is born again, he cannot see the kingdom of God"* (Jn 3:3). As a good Jew Nicodemus thought that he was already in that kingdom. Furthermore, his mind could go no further than the physical birth. Did Jesus mean that he should experience another such birth? But Jesus told him that he must be born both naturally and spiritually. By his natural birth ("of water") he entered into certain natural relationships. By his spiritual birth ("of . . . the

"The wind blows where it pleases, and you hear its sound, but you don't know where it comes from or where it is going. So it is with everyone born of the Spirit" (Jn 3:8).

Spirit") he would enter into certain spiritual relationships. Thus Jesus clearly declared the nature of His kingdom as spiritual.

That this experience involved a mystery beyond man's natural comprehension, Jesus recognized as He compared it to the mystery of the wind. Both must be accepted by faith based upon the evident results of each.

Nicodemus still did not understand. So Jesus led him to more familiar ground, that of the Scriptures of which he was a master. Citing the incident of Moses lifting up the brazen serpent in the wilderness (Nm 21:8–9) Jesus said, *"Even so must the Son of man be lifted up on the cross; that whosoever believeth may in him have eternal life"* (Jn 3:14–15 ASV). Then there follows John 3:16, the "Little Gospel," and other words of infinite depth and meaning. Some hold these words (Jn 3:16–21) to be comments made by John, but there is no reason why they could not have been spoken by Jesus Himself. Words of such matchless beauty and profundity fall naturally from the lips of the Teacher.

Did Nicodemus at this time believe in Jesus as his Savior? The answer to this question is not given. But, if not then, certainly prior to Jesus' death Nicodemus did make such a commitment.

JESUS' DEPARTURE FOR GALILEE

Following the interview with Nicodemus, Jesus enjoyed a brief but fruitful ministry in Judea. John the Baptist's ministry was on the decline. More and more people were coming to Jesus, who soon was making and baptizing more disciples than the Baptist. John's Gospel points out, however, that Jesus baptized no one, leaving this work to be done by His disciples. Nevertheless reports of Jesus' successful ministry came to the Pharisees, and this increased their hostility toward Him. Furthermore, at this time word came to Jesus that John the Baptist had been imprisoned by Herod Antipas, the puppet king of Galilee and Perea, a region east of the Jordan. John was probably imprisoned at Machaerus, a strongly fortified castle east of the Dead Sea. This would indicate that Herod Antipas also may have been there at this time.

Therefore, because of the rising hostility of the Pharisees in Jerusalem and Herod's show of opposition to John the Baptist, Jesus felt that it was wise to go to the more favorable atmosphere of Galilee. He was not running from opposition, but He would pick His time and place to meet it.

JESUS AND THE WOMAN OF SAMARIA

"He had to travel through Samaria" (Jn 4:4). What did the fourth evangelist mean by these words?

The Samaritans were a hybrid race produced by a union of Israelites and other people sent into the northern kingdom following its conquest by Assyria. Following the Babylonian captivity of the Jews they had opposed efforts to rebuild Jerusalem. These things, plus the long enmity existing between the kingdoms of Israel and Judah, resulted in a strong antagonism between the Jews and Samaritans in Jesus' time.

Partly out of fear of the Samaritans and also their resentment toward them, the Jews avoided their land whenever possible. Therefore, for Jews traveling between Judea and Galilee, it was customary to cross the Jordan River and journey north or south on its eastern side. On occasion Jesus followed this route, though for different reasons. He also traveled through Samaria more than once, as He did on the occasion at hand.

Why was it that *"He had to travel through Samaria"*? Certainly this need was neither physical nor geographical. This was probably one of those times where John wrote words containing a mystical or spiritual meaning. The *need*, therefore, was a spiritual compulsion, for Jesus knew the experience awaiting Him there.

The Samaritan village of Sychar was about twenty-five miles from Jerusalem. Nearby was Jacob's well. It was and still is a flowing spring about one hundred feet deep. One may still visit this well and drink its cool water. It is perhaps the most certain spot in modern Palestine insofar as its connection with Jesus is concerned.

When Jesus and His disciples arrived at this well, the disciples went into the nearby village to purchase food, leaving Jesus to rest. It was the sixth hour, about noon, the hottest time of the day. Usually the women came to draw water in the cool of the evening. A lone Samaritan woman came to draw water. She was a woman who lived a sordid life and could not associate with the decent women of the town. And Jesus proposed to lead her to receive Him and the life which He could give. Shortly before, Jesus had dealt with a man of the upper stratum of Jewish life. Now He is confronted with a woman of the lower stratum of Samaritan society, and His manner of dealing with her provides the classic example in soul-winning.

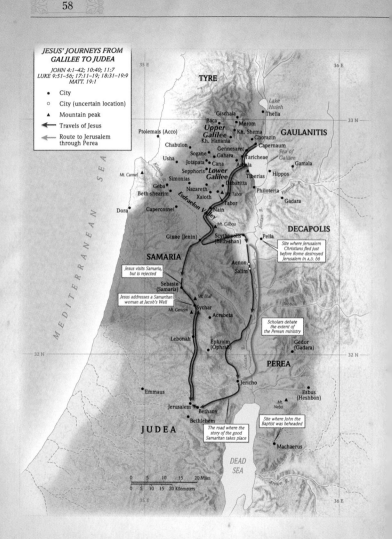

JESUS' JOURNEYS FROM GALILEE TO JUDEA

JOHN 4:1–42; 10:40; 11:7
LUKE 9:51–56; 17:11–19; 18:31–19:9
MATT. 19:1

- ● City
- ○ City (uncertain location)
- ▲ Mountain peak
- ← Travels of Jesus
- ← Route to Jerusalem through Perea

TYRE

Lake Huleh
Thella
Gischala
Baca
Merom
Kh. Shema
GAULANITIS
Upper Galilee
Kh. Hanania
Chorazin
Ptolemais (Acco)
Chabulon
Capernaum
Gennesaret
Usha
Sogane
Gabara
Taricheae
Sea of Galilee
Jotapata
Cana
Arbela
Gamala
Sepphoris
Lower Galilee
Tiberias
Hippos
Simonias
Mt. Carmel ▲
Nazareth
Tabaritta
Philoteria
Geba
Xaloth
▲ Tabor
Beth-shearim
Esdraelon Valley
Gadara
Dora
Capercotnei
Nain
DECAPOLIS
Mt. Gilboa
Scythopolis (Bethshan)
Pella
Ginae (Jenin)
Site where Jerusalem Christians fled just before Rome destroyed Jerusalem in A.D. 66
SAMARIA
Aenon
Salim
Jesus visits Samaria, but is rejected
Sebaste (Samaria)
Mt. Ebal
Jesus addresses a Samaritan woman at Jacob's Well
Sychar
Mt. Gerizim
Acrabeta
Scholars debate the extent of the Perean ministry
Lebonah
Ephraim (Ophrah)
Gedor (Gadara)
PEREA
Emmaus
Jericho
Esbus (Heshbon)
Jerusalem
Bethany
Mt. Nebo
Bethlehem
JUDEA
The road where the story of the good Samaritan takes place
Site where John the Baptist was beheaded
Machaerus

DEAD SEA

0   5   10   15   20 Miles
0   5   10 15 20 Kilometers

MEDITERRANEAN SEA

Jesus began the conversation by establishing a common bond of need. The woman had come to draw water, and Jesus was thirsty, so He said, *"Give me a drink"* (Jn 4:7). She responded by raising the wall of prejudice that to her was so evident between a Jewish *man* and a Samaritan *woman*. Not only did Jews have no dealings with the Samaritans, but Jewish men, and especially rabbis, which Jesus appeared to her to be, had little dealings with women. One of their daily prayers was to thank God that He had not made them a Gentile, a Samaritan, or a woman.

Jesus ignored these prejudices of race and sex. Instead He contrasted the natural water in Jacob's well with the spiritual water He longed to give her. To drink from Jacob's well was to thirst again, but His water quenched thirst completely and permanently. Furthermore, it would become in her an ever-flowing spring of eternal life. Her only interest in such water was that she no longer would have to make the long walk daily to draw water from Jacob's well. She showed no evidence of a sense of spiritual need.

To reveal to her this need, Jesus probed into her personal, sinful life by telling her to call her husband. When she denied having a husband, Jesus revealed to her His knowledge of her five previous husbands. Also He reminded her that even then she was living with a man outside of wedlock. It was then that her flippancy and hostility gave way to admiration as she admitted that Jesus was a prophet.

However, this admission she used only to turn the conversation from her shady personal life toward a theological controversy. Towering high above them was Mount Gerizim where the Samaritans had their place of worship as over against the Jewish worship in Jerusalem. She sought refuge in this age-old dispute, but again Jesus drew her back to the main question by pointing out that God is a Spirit whose true worship depends not upon a place but upon one's spirit in worship.

Headed off again the woman made one last effort to escape. She brought up the question of the Messiah, who when He should come would resolve all questions. And for the first time Jesus clearly declared His Messiahship by saying, *"I am He, the One speaking to you"* (Jn 4:26).

It was at this point that the disciples returned, and the woman used this interruption to return to the village, leaving her water pot behind. But Jesus' words had done their work. For when she came into the village she said to the men, *"Come, see a man who told me everything I ever did! Could this be the Messiah?"* (Jn 4:29). Her question was a veiled admission that He was. Subsequently the men also believed on Him as *"the Savior of the world"* (Jn 4:42). Not of the Jews only, but of the whole world! And for two days they enjoyed the supreme privilege of having Jesus in their village.

From Sychar Jesus went on into Galilee and there He began His great Galilean ministry.

The traditional site of Jacob's Well in the village of Sychar

CHAPTER IV
THE GREAT GALILEAN MINISTRY
THE OPENING EVENTS

Following the first year of comparative obscurity, Jesus launched His more public ministry in Galilee. This period lasted for approximately eighteen months, from the fall of AD 27 until the spring of AD 29. Jerusalem and Judea had clearly demonstrated their hostility to Him, and so it was natural that He would return to the more favorable intellectual and spiritual climate of His own section of Palestine. On one occasion during this period Jesus made a visit to Jerusalem.

THE NATURE OF GALILEE

Galilee was the most northerly of the three divisions of Palestine (Judea, Samaria, and Galilee). It encompassed an area about sixty miles long and thirty miles wide. As one travels across Galilee eastward from the Mediterranean, he passes from rich coastal plains into sloping hills that rise and fall until he comes to the eastern edge where it drops precipitously into the deep trough of the Jordan Valley. There, six hundred and eighty feet below sea level, lies the beautiful Sea of Galilee, stretched out like a large pear, thirteen miles long and seven miles wide at the broadest point.

Unlike the barren hills of Judea, it was a fertile, well-watered land yielding abundant crops of wheat, grapes, olives, figs, and pomegranates. In the semi-tropical climate along the shores of the Sea of Galilee, oranges and other tropical fruits were plentiful. Quite naturally this compact area boasted of a large population. About the time of Jesus, Josephus estimated it at about three million people. In addition to its principal cities such as Capernaum, Bethsaida, Tiberias, and Chorazin, these people were crowded into numerous villages that studded the landscape in every direction. It is no wonder, then, that immense swarms of people followed Jesus wherever He went.

Another characteristic in which Galilee differed from Judea was the nature of the people. Judea was largely Jewish, a people wedded to the temple and its worship. During the period following the conquest of Alexander the Great, they had strongly resisted the encroachment of Greek thought, customs, and religion. Galilee, on the other hand, was made up of a mixture of people. There were many Jews, of course, but they were mingled with other people such as Phoenicians and Greeks. In fact, east of the Sea

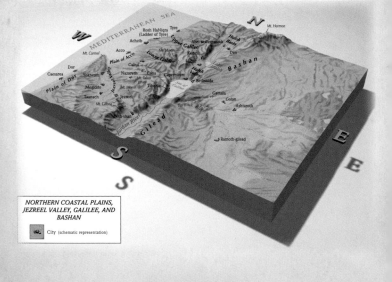

NORTHERN COASTAL PLAINS,
JEZREEL VALLEY, GALILEE, AND
BASHAN

City (schematic representation)

of Galilee, there was a region known as the Decapolis, taking its name from ten Greek cities there. This within itself had a profound influence upon Galilee. The Galilean area had more readily received the Greek culture. Thus the people were less wedded to the orthodoxy of Judea; they were open to new ideas. This fact figured in Jesus' choice to major on Galilee as the base for His public ministry.

SOME PRELIMINARY EVENTS

Jesus returned to Galilee to find that the fame of His miracles and teachings had spread throughout the region. Wherever He went, He echoed the message John the Baptist had preached: *"Repent, because the kingdom of heaven has come near!"* (Mt 4:17).

On His way back to Nazareth He passed through Cana. In Capernaum the son of an official of Herod Antipas was ill. His father, hearing that Jesus was back in Galilee, sought Him out and found Him in Cana. In response to his request that Jesus come to Capernaum to heal his son, Jesus told him to return home, that his son was well. The father did so and found that his son had been healed at the very hour when Jesus had spoken His words to him.

Shortly after Jesus' return to Nazareth, as was His custom, He went into the synagogue on the Sabbath day. It was customary at times, when some notable person was present, for the ruler of the synagogue to request him to read the Scriptures and to comment upon them. On this occasion this privilege was accorded to the hometown Boy who was receiving so much notice. Jesus chose to read from the roll of Isaiah (61:1–2). As was customary He stood up to read and then sat down to speak. The people were astonished to hear Jesus say, *"Today as you listen, this Scripture has been fulfilled"* (Lk 4:21).

And then the congregation began to buzz. *"Isn't this Joseph's son?"* (Lk 4:22). In response Jesus reminded them that a prophet is not without honor except in his own country. He drove this lesson home by citing examples from their own history when foreigners had enjoyed blessings from God rather than His own people because they had rejected God's messengers. The people caught the point, and their wonder gave place to rage. They seized Jesus and rushed out to the edge of the town intent upon casting Him to His death over a cliff (tourists today are shown what is said to be this cliff), but in the confusion Jesus slipped away from them.

Following this rejection by Nazareth, Jesus established His base of operations in Capernaum, a city on the northwestern shore of the Sea of Galilee. While He spent very little time here, He always returned to Capernaum after various journeys throughout Galilee. Some of the most

The synagogue church in Nazareth old city, Israel

Mount Precipice (or Mount Kedumim) is a mountain just outside of Nazareth in northern Israel, where tradition has it an angry mob attempted to throw Jesus off the cliff (Luke 4:16–30).

vital things in the Galilean ministry did take place in this populous and prosperous city, however.

Having established His headquarters for the Galilean campaign, Jesus was now ready to gather about Him certain disciples who would figure prominently in this effort. Already there were those who had received Him as the Messiah, but upon their return to Galilee they had resumed their occupations. Among these were Peter, Andrew, James, and John. These two pairs of brothers were fishermen, along with Zebedee, the father of the latter pair. Fishing was one of the principal occupations about the Sea of Galilee, since fish was a major item on the diet of the people.

Early one day Jesus was walking along the seashore. He saw these men fishing and later washing their nets. The Lord called to these four brothers to leave their occupation and to accompany Him on His mission. From

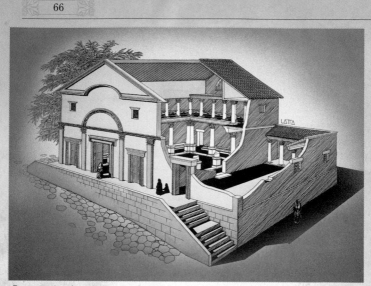

Reconstruction of a typical synagogue of the first century AD showing the large inner room where the men gathered and its loft where the women gathered. This particular drawing is patterned after the synagogue at Capernaum.

fishers of fish He would make them fishers of men. Apparently they had had a fruitless night at fishing. Simon protested when Jesus, a landlubber, told them to try again, but when they let down their nets they brought up a multitude of fish. This so impressed them that the four brothers responded to Jesus' call to follow Him.

This little company returned to Capernaum, and on the Sabbath day Jesus taught in the synagogue. This synagogue was to be the scene of some of His greatest work. Among the ruins of Capernaum today may be seen the remains of a later synagogue that was built upon the site of the one which figured so largely in Jesus' ministry. Unlike the people of Nazareth, those of Capernaum responded favorably to His teachings, noting that He taught with an authority and freshness so different from the rote repetitions of the Jewish scribes.

On this occasion there was present a man possessed by an unclean spirit or a demon. Demon possession is a mystery that has plagued interpreters through the ages. Some explain it as the superstitions of an ignorant, ancient age, but Jesus accepted it as a reality. Given who Jesus is, it is untenable to say that He either did not know better or else that He merely went along with their superstitions. Modern man knows far too little about the spirit world to deny arbitrarily the reality of this phenomenon. As with Satan in the wilderness, it is reasonable to say that evil spirits entered into men even as God was incarnated in Jesus of Nazareth. Furthermore, who can deny that some men today are demon-possessed, only it is described in terminology adapted to modern modes of thought? This would explain the actions of many that are a moral and spiritual puzzle otherwise.

At any rate the Scriptures treat demon possession as a reality. On this occasion the demon even talked to Jesus, probably through the person indwelt by it. But Jesus cast it out of him, and the people were amazed that even demons were subject to Him. It is no wonder that His fame continued to spread abroad.

Going from the synagogue Jesus and His company went to Simon Peter's home, which was probably nearby. Finding Simon's wife's mother ill of a fever, which no doubt was common in this semi-tropical area, Jesus healed her. The miraculous element in this healing is evident in the fact that immediately she was strong enough to prepare a meal for them.

Since it was a Sabbath day, the Jews were forbidden even to bear their sick to Jesus, but at sunset, the end of the Sabbath day, they did bring them to Him. It was a beautiful ending to an eventful day—Jesus moving among this multitude of sick and demon-possessed people in His healing ministry.

Truly they would be reminded of Isaiah 53:4: *"He Himself took our weaknesses and carried our diseases"* (Mt 8:17).

A GROWING POPULARITY

The Galilean ministry was characterized by the growing popularity of Jesus. Not that He deliberately courted it. The very contrary was true, but He found a ready response among these people who were so far removed from Jerusalem. At the same time Jesus experienced the increasing hostility of the Pharisees both in Jerusalem and in Galilee. It was His popularity among the people that inspired the Pharisees' opposition, for they feared that their hold on the multitudes would be broken.

Having chosen His first four disciples, Jesus took them on a tour of Galilee. Wherever He went, the people flocked to Him to hear His preaching and to behold His healing miracles. Jesus' message on the kingdom excited their imagination, even though their concept of a political kingdom was far removed from the spiritual kingdom He envisioned. Nevertheless the people came from Galilee, Decapolis, Jerusalem, Judea, and Perea to hear and to see.

It was during His first tour of Galilee that Jesus greatly excited the people by healing a leper. Leprosy was the most dreaded of all diseases in ancient Palestine, and lepers were forbidden to live among other people. They were not even supposed to come nearer than one hundred feet from those who were free of leprosy. If someone approached them, they were required to give the warning cry, *"Unclean!"* One rabbi boasted of having driven one leper from him with stones.

So when this leper came to Jesus, people might suppose Him to shrink from him. Instead He *touched* him, saying, *"Be made clean,"* and immediately his leprosy was healed. It was obviously a miracle, but even though Jesus ignored the taboos of the Jews, He did not evade divine law. Therefore

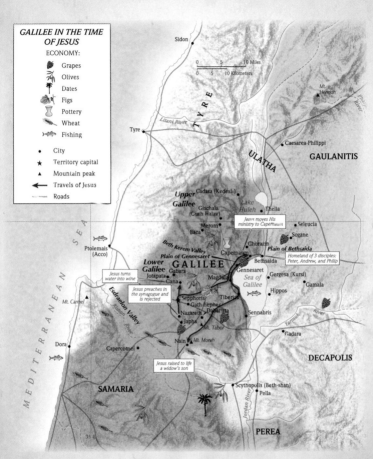

GALILEE IN THE TIME OF JESUS

ECONOMY:

- Grapes
- Olives
- Dates
- Figs
- Pottery
- Wheat
- Fishing

- City
- ★ Territory capital
- ▲ Mountain peak
- ← Travels of Jesus
- Roads

0   5   10 Miles
0   5   10 Kilometers

Sidon

Mt. Hermon

Litani River

TYRE

Tyre

Caesarea-Philippi

ULATHA

GAULANITIS

Cadasa (Kedesh)

Upper Galilee

Gischala (Gush Halav)

Lake Huleh

Thella

Merom

Seleucia

Baca

Sogane

Jesus moves His ministry to Capernaum

Beth Kerem Valley

Chorazin

Plain of Bethsaida

Ptolemais (Acco)

Plain of Gennesaret

Capernaum

Bethsaida

Homeland of 3 disciples: Peter, Andrew, and Philip

Lower Galilee

GALILEE

Jotapata

Gabara

Magdala

Gennesaret

Gergesa (Kursi)

Jesus turns water into wine

Cana

Sea of Galilee

Hippos

Gamala

MEDITERRANEAN SEA

Mt. Carmel

Sepphoris

Tiberias

Jesus preaches in the synagogue and is rejected

Gath-hepher

Nazareth

Dabaritta

Sennabris

Yarmuk River

Japha

Mt. Tabor

Dora

Kishon River

Gadara

Capercotnei

Nain

Mt. Moreh

DECAPOLIS

Esdraelon Valley

Jesus raised to life a widow's son

SAMARIA

Scythopolis (Beth-shan)

Pella

Jordan River

PEREA

Galilee in the time of Jesus

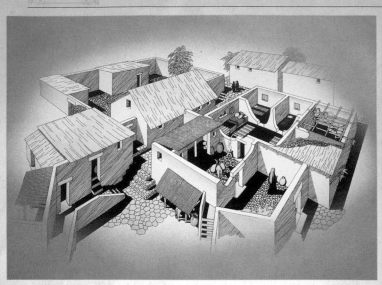

Cutaway reconstruction of a first-century AD house in Israel

He told the leper to go to the priest, make certain sacrifices required by the Mosaic law, and thus be pronounced clean. And despite Jesus' stern admonition that the man not tell of this healing, he did so wherever he went, so much so that the crowds were greater than ever. For some time, because of the rising enthusiasm, it was necessary that Jesus avoid cities. Then the people flocked to Him in the country.

After some days Jesus returned to Capernaum. As the news spread, the people ran to the house where He was staying. Among those gathered there were Pharisees and teachers of the Law (Scribes), not only the Mosaic law, but the multitude of rules of conduct that were interpretations and application of the Mosaic Code in a variety of situations.

As Jesus was teaching four men approached, bearing a paralytic on a pallet. When they could not get into the house because of the crowd, they carried the man to the roof by way of a set of outside stairs. After tearing a hole in the roof, they lowered him into the presence of Jesus, but Jesus did not at once heal the man. Instead He said, *"Friend, your sins are forgiven you"* (Lk 5:20). This was the first record of Jesus having spoken such words. The scribes were horrified, for according to them only God could forgive sin. In their hearts they accused Jesus of blasphemy, but perceiving their thoughts Jesus challenged them. *"Which is easier: to say, 'Your sins are forgiven you,' or to say, 'Get up and walk'? But so you may know that the Son of Man has authority on earth to forgive sins"*—He told the paralyzed man, *"I tell you: get up, pick up your stretcher, and go home"* (Lk 5:23–24). The religious scholars were mute as the man did as he was bidden, but the people glorified God.

The order of Jesus' words is significant. He forgave the man's sins before He healed his body. Four reasons may have prompted this. First, Jesus' primary mission was related to man's sin. Second, this man's physical condition may have been due to his spiritual need. Third, Jesus posed a situation by which to prove His authority to forgive sin. Fourth, by the scribes' claim that only God had such authority, the indirect result was their own unwilling testimony to the deity of Jesus. So the people were amazed and the Pharisees were bewildered.

THE CALL OF MATTHEW (LEVI)

Capernaum was one of the most important cities of Galilee. In a sense it was at the crossroads of the ancient world, for the International Coastal Highway from Egypt to Damascus passed through it. This alone would make it a great center of tax collections. All of the merchandise passing over this segment of the road would have to pay duty as it entered the territory of Herod Antipas.

"INTERNATIONAL ROUTES"

- • City
- —— International Coastal Highway
- —— King's Highway
- —— Sea routes
- ---- Other routes

The Roman system of tax collecting was most unusual according to modern standards. The Roman government auctioned off to the highest bidder the privilege of collecting taxes in a given area. This person, in turn, must so levy taxes as to make a profit. Under him would be lesser officials who did his bidding. These collectors as a class were called *publicans,* a word derived from the Latin word *publicanus,* one who did public duty. But in this case the duty was for private gain, a fact which gave rise to much graft and extortion. Quite naturally the publicans were a hated class among the Jews, not only for their evil practices but because they were regarded as traitors to their people. For personal gain they sold themselves to the Jews' captors as instruments of oppression. It is no wonder, then, that a common phrase was *"publicans and sinners."*

Matthew, or Levi as he is sometimes called, was a publican. He was one of the underling collectors, either under a commercial tax collector or under Herod Antipas himself. At any rate Jesus passed by his *"tax office."* Seeing Matthew He simply said, *"Follow me."* Matthew, like the two sets of brothers, may have known Jesus previously. Certainly he had heard of Him, so he left his tax table to follow Jesus.

It was quite an occasion in Matthew's life, so to celebrate it he gave a feast in honor of Jesus and His disciples. To it he invited his publican friends and others. It was customary for those other than guests to stand about and watch the festivities, and among this group were the ever-present Pharisees and their scribes. They were horrified that Jesus would eat with such a motley crowd. Publicans and sinners, indeed! To the Pharisees this was an immoral act. When Jesus heard their criticism He said to them, *"Those who are well don't need a doctor, but the sick do"* (Mt 9:12). Jesus came not *"to call the righteous, but sinners"* (Mt 9:13).

By their own standards the Pharisees were righteous and needed no repentance as did these publicans and sinners. So taking them at their own word, Jesus turned the tables on them. They felt no need of His spiritual healing. Where else would the physician be but among those who need His ministry?

In this scene one sees the added opposition to Jesus on the part of the Pharisees. First they accused Him of blasphemy. Now they charged Him with immorality. And so the story ever went.

However, the matter did not end there. For among the onlookers was a group of the disciples of John the Baptist; and while the Pharisees licked their wounds, they took up the charge against Jesus: *"Why do we and the Pharisees fast often, but Your disciples do not fast?"* (Mt 9:14).

At least two things may have prompted this question. First, they were perhaps critical because, while their teacher was in prison, Jesus and His disciples were attending a banquet. The Baptist would not have done so under any circumstance. And then there was the matter of fasting itself. The Jews placed a great emphasis upon this practice. Jesus Himself fasted on occasion, but He did so out of preoccupation for His spiritual concern, not as a rote performance as did the Pharisees. In reply to their question, Jesus reminded John's disciples that as long as He was with His disciples they had no reason to fast. There would be a real occasion for them to do so after He was taken from them. Thus He made an indirect reference to His death and return to heaven.

Then Jesus went to the heart of the matter by speaking two parables— of new cloth on old garments and new wine in old wineskins. If an old garment were patched with new cloth, the new cloth would shrink, and the hole in the old garment would be torn larger. In essence, Jesus did not come to patch up the old garment of Judaism but to weave a new garment altogether. Furthermore, if new wine were placed in old brittle wineskins, as the new wine worked it would expand or generate gases that would burst the old skins, thus losing the new wine. In effect, the old forms of Judaism could not contain the new revelation Jesus brought. It must be contained in new wineskins or expressions. To try to pour the Christian revelation into Old Testament forms is to destroy both.

A GROWING OPPOSITION

It was now probably the spring of AD 28. Jesus and His disciples left Galilee to attend the Passover in Jerusalem. While there, Jesus walked by the pool of Bethesda, meaning *the house of mercy*. The ruins of this pool are in the process of being excavated in present time. In Jesus' day this pool was fed by an underground spring that flowed intermittently. Jewish belief held that the water was stirred by an angel, and that the first one to step into the pool at such times would be healed of his disease. Therefore, its five porches were filled with those hoping to be healed. Among these was a man who had had an infirmity for thirty-eight years.

Seeing him Jesus asked if he wished to be healed. The man replied that he did, but that others beat him into the water each time it was troubled. So Jesus simply told him to arise and to take up his bed and walk. The man proceeded to do so. It was on the Sabbath day, and Jewish law forbade one to bear a burden on this day.

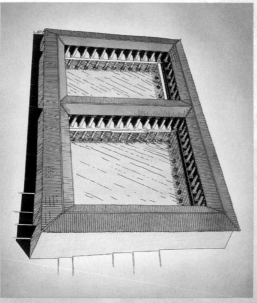

A reconstruction of the Pool of Bethesda in Jerusalem

Jesus' act brought the wrath of the Jewish leaders down on both the man and Jesus. For when they challenged the man for breaking the Sabbath, he related what Jesus had done. Thereafter the Jews persecuted Jesus. He received no thanks for healing the man, only criticism for doing it on the Sabbath. In reply Jesus said, *"My Father is still working, and I am working also"* (Jn 5:17). By this time the Jews were worked into a murderous rage, for to them Jesus not only broke the Sabbath; He also claimed equality with God. Sabbath breaking and blasphemy! So they said.

Then followed one of Jesus' marvelous discourses as recorded in John 5:19–47. He reiterated His relation to the Father, stating that God had accorded Him the right of judgment and made Him worthy of all honor. He challenged these Jews in one of the Pharisees' most precious beliefs, the resurrection of the dead, by saying that at His word the dead would rise. He charged them with refusing to hear John the Baptist, and now they were rejecting Him. Even the Scriptures, of which they claimed to be experts, revealed Him, but they refused Him. He called upon even Moses, whose teachings were their law, to witness against them, because Moses wrote of Him. Then He flung the sharpest javelin of all. They did not even believe Moses, so how could they believe Him of whom Moses wrote?

It should be noted that this opposition to Jesus did not hinge primarily upon His person as much as it did upon the institution of the Sabbath. His person was incidental only in that He claimed authority over the Sabbath, and it was at this point that the Jewish leaders hounded Jesus the most.

Judaism was based upon three things: the Law, the temple, and the Sabbath, and in each of these the Jewish leaders found themselves at odds with Jesus. However, to the Jews, the Sabbath was the most sacred of all. Other religions had their scriptures and temples, but only Judaism had its Sabbath. So it was the Sabbath that particularly made Judaism distinct

Wheat growing in the Asochis Valley.

from all other religions. One can well understand why the Jews would be so sensitive at this point. While Jesus had disregarded their meticulous laws concerning the Sabbath prior to this time, this instance was pivotal, because it happened in Jerusalem itself.

Once again Jerusalem had rejected Jesus, so He and His disciples returned to Galilee. Apparently some Pharisees dogged their steps even then. It was the time of the approaching grain harvest, so on a Sabbath day they walked along a path provided for travel through the grain fields. Being hungry the disciples followed a time honored and permitted custom. They plucked some heads of grain, rubbed the grain free from the chaff and ate it (Lk 6:1). A simple matter, to be sure, but to the Pharisees this constituted harvesting and threshing. And this violated the Sabbath day.

To the modern reader this seems rather foolish, but not to the ancient Pharisees. Someone has estimated that they had devised over twelve hundred ways by which the Sabbath might be broken. God's commandment regarding the Sabbath day forbade work on that day, but what was work? A hen worked laying an egg, so one could not eat an egg laid on the Sabbath. On that day one could not draw a stick along the ground, for that was plowing. Nor could a woman pull a gray hair out of her head, for that was shearing. And so it went. It is understandable, therefore, how the Pharisees should regard the simple action of the disciples as a violation of their rules regarding the Sabbath.

Here then was a continuation of the controversy over the Sabbath that began in Jerusalem, but once again Jesus was master of the situation. In reply to the charge of the Pharisees, He made five statements. First, He cited the historical example of David and his men who, being hungry, entered the tabernacle and ate the sacred bread (Lk 6:3–4; 1 Sm 21:1–6). Thus He spoke of the priority of human need. Second, He pointed out that the priests were guiltless as they served in the temple on the Sabbath. Their service was necessary for divine worship. Third, He quoted from prophecy (Hs 6:6) to show that God desires right spiritual attitudes above rites and ceremonies. Fourth, He declared God's true purpose for the Sabbath. It was made as a blessing to man and not to be a burden. Fifth, He claimed lordship over the Sabbath (Lk 6:5).

This was a tremendous claim, for it meant that Jesus asserted His authority over the most unique institution in Judaism. Already He had demonstrated His authority over the temple, and now this. Soon He would do the same with regard to the Law (Mt 5:17ff.). However, it should be noted that in no instance did Jesus discount these institutions; rather He placed them in their proper perspective.

Shortly after the above instance, Jesus, in the presence of the Pharisees, on another Sabbath, healed a man with a withered hand (Mk 3:1–6). In so doing He pointed out the inconsistencies of their teachings regarding healing on the Sabbath day. Immediately thereafter the Pharisees took counsel with the Herodians as to how they might destroy Jesus. This within itself shows the extent of the Pharisees' hatred toward Jesus. They were arch political enemies of the Herodians. The former were bent upon restoring the ancient kingdom of Israel. The latter were dedicated to the restoration of the kingdom of Herod, a bitter foe of the Pharisees. Yet in their common enmity toward Jesus, these two groups became strange bedfellows.

THE CALLING OF THE TWELVE APOSTLES

At this point the public ministry of Jesus was at approximately the half-way mark (perhaps AD 28), and it seems at this time to take a somewhat new turn. Henceforth Jesus placed a greater emphasis upon teaching as He gradually revealed His person and purpose. It is as though He was beginning to prepare for the climax awaiting Him at the cross.

In this light it is significant that in a special way He chose twelve men who were to bear a particular relationship to Him. These men were called apostles or *the ones sent forth*. Mark gives three reasons for this action: *"to be with Him, to send them out to preach, and to have authority to drive out demons"* (3:14–15). These men were Simon Peter, James, John, Andrew, Philip, Bartholemew (Nathanael), Matthew, Thomas, James the son of Alphaeus, Thaddaeus, Simon the Canaanite (or Zealot), and Judas Iscariot. Previous mention has been made of the first seven; but the last five are mentioned for the first time. Perhaps Jesus had won them in much the same manner as He had the others. For some time certainly some of them had accompanied Jesus in His ministry. From this point on all of them would enjoy the special advantage of His association and teaching. Jesus proceeded to train them for the day when the Bridegroom would be taken from them.

THE APOSTLES AND

Name	Surname	Parents	Home	Business	Writings
Simon	Peter or Cephas = Rock	Jonah	*Early Life:* Bethsaida; *Later:* Capernaum	Fisherman	1 & 2 Peter
Andrew = manhood or valor		Jonah	*Early life:* Bethsaida; *Later:* Capernaum	Fisherman	
James the greater or the elder	Boanerges or Sons of Thunder	Zebedee and Salome	Bethsaida, Capernaum, and Jerusalem	Fisherman	
John, the beloved disciple	Boanerges or Sons of Thunder	Zebedee and Salome	Bethsaida, Capernaum, and Jerusalem	Fisherman	Gospel, three epistles, and Revelation
James the less		Alphaeus and Mary	Galilee		
Jude	Same as Thaddeus and Lebbeus	James	Galilee		
Philip			Bethsaida		
Bartholomew	Nathaniel		Cana of Galilee		
Matthew	Levi		Galilee	Tax Collector	Gospel
Thomas	Didymus		Galilee		
Simon	The Zealot, lit. Cananaean		Galilee, perhaps Cana		
Judas	Iscariot	Simon Iscariot	Kerioth of Judea		

THEIR HISTORY

Bible Facts
Confessed Jesus as Messiah (Mt 16:16); Part of Jesus' inner circle (Mk 5:37), Walked on water (Mt 14:29), Witnessed Jesus' transfiguration (Lk 9:28), Denied Jesus (Lk 22:54–62), Restored by Jesus (Jn 21:15–19), Preached at Pentecost (Ac 2:14–40)
Was a disciple of John the Baptist (Jn 1:40). Introduced his brother, Simon, to Jesus (Jn 1:40). Told Jesus about the boy with loaves and fishes (Jn 6:8), With Philip told Jesus about the Greeks seeking Him (Jn 12:20), one of four to hear Jesus' teaching about what would soon happen (Mk 13:3)
Wanted to call down fire on Samaritans (Lk 9:54), Highly ambitious (Mk 10:35–45), Went fishing after Jesus' resurrection (Jn 21:2); First disciple to be martyred (Ac 12:2)
Highly ambitious (Mk 10:35–45), Witnessed Jesus' transfiguration (Lk 9:28), With Peter prepared Passover meal (Lk 22:8), Reclined close beside Jesus at the Last Supper (Jn 13:23); Entrusted with the care of Mary, Jesus' mother (Jn 19:26–27), Bold witness (Ac 4:14); Exiled on Patmos (Rv 1:9)
Was called James the younger; son of Alphaeus and Mary (Mk 3:18; 15:40)
Asked Jesus how He was going to reveal Himself to the disciples and not to the world (Jn 14:22)
Invited Nathanael to come and see Jesus (Jn 1:43–48); Tested by Jesus about how to feed 5000 (Jn 6:4–7), Approached by Greeks who wanted to see Jesus (Jn 12:20–21), Asked Jesus to show the Father to the disciples (Jn 14: 8)
In prayer with other disciples following Jesus' ascension (Ac 1:13)
Hosts a dinner where his friends could meet Jesus (Mk 2:15)
Encouraged his fellow disciples to returned to Judea with Jesus and there die with Him (Jn 11:16), Asks Jesus where He is going (Jn 14:5), Requires clear evidence that Jesus has been raised from death (Jn 20:25), Jesus gives Thomas compelling evidence of His resurrection (Jn 20:27)
Protested Mary of Bethany's lavish gift to Jesus (Jn 12:5), Stole from the disciples' money bag (Jn 12:6), Satan entered into him at the Last Supper (Jn 13:27), Betrayed Jesus (Lk 22:47–48), Was filled with remorse for his betrayal of Jesus (Mt 27:3), Committed suicide (Mt 27:5)

What a strange and motley group they were! As far as is known they were selected from the common run of people. In this group were at least four fishermen, a publican, and a former member of the fanatical revolutionary party called the Zealots, who were bent upon the overthrow of Roman rule in Palestine. This group finally brought on the Jewish War against the Romans (AD 66–70) that resulted in the destruction of Jerusalem and the Jewish nation. And one of the Twelve was to betray Jesus in the end.

One naturally asks why Jesus chose these particular men. Certainly He did so carefully, for the selection was made after a night spent in prayer. Perhaps as good an answer as any is that in each of these men Jesus saw certain qualities, which if dedicated to Him, would make them valuable servants in the work He was launching: for instance, the enthusiasm of Peter; the depth of spirit in John; the patient plodding of Andrew; the record-keeping ability of Matthew; the heroic devotion of Thomas; the business ability of Judas Iscariot. They were diamonds in the rough, and only one, Judas Iscariot, failed to respond to the Master's confidence in and compassion for them. Still Jesus chose him, knowing that he was a bad one from the beginning. At the proper time in this account, certain things will be pointed out about him, but, even so, he will forever remain a mystery.

THE CONSTITUTION OF THE KINGDOM

After Jesus had chosen the twelve apostles, He took them up into a mountain. However the multitudes followed Him; so finding a level place in the mountain where they might be seated in comfort, Jesus also sat down and taught them. When a rabbi taught officially he was always seated. This custom is still reflected in the term "a professor's chair." When the Pope speaks officially in religion and morals he speaks ex cathedra or "from his seat."

Sea of Galilee from the Church of the Beatitudes built on the site where Jesus is thought to have taught the Sermon on the Mount. This church, built in 1938, is an octagonal structure, representing the eight beatitudes.

Various titles have been given to this sermon. Coming as it did immediately after the selection of the apostles, it has been called "The Ordination Address to the Twelve." Other titles are "The Manifesto of the King" and "The Magna Carta of the Kingdom." Perhaps as good a designation as any is "The Constitution of the Kingdom," for in it the King declared those qualities and practices that should characterize the kingdom citizen. Even though the multitudes heard it, the sermon was given primarily to the disciples of Jesus.

1. The Characteristics of the Kingdom Citizen

Jesus began the Sermon by setting forth the characteristics of those who are in the kingdom of God. Primarily they are described as "blessed" or "happy." These characteristics are called "The Beatitudes." In the Greek version these "blesseds" are used without the verb "to be." Therefore, they may be called absolutes. They set forth the nature of the kingdom citizen.

The Greek word is *makarios,* and its meaning can be determined by noting that it is the word used to denote Cyprus as *he makaria,* the Happy Isle. This island was said to be so blessed with minerals, fertility, water, and climate as to produce everything necessary for the perfectly happy life. So, in effect, by using this word to describe the kingdom citizen, Jesus said that he possesses within himself everything that is necessary to live the full, rich life.

Now what is it that makes possible such a life? In eight terse statements Jesus answered this question (Mt 5:3–12). The *"poor in spirit"* are those who recognize that they are sinners, who possess nothing meriting their approach to God. Therefore, they *"mourn"* as for the dead because of their sins and the sins of others. The *"gentle"* are the teachable ones who submit themselves to God as those who need to be forgiven and to be instructed of God. In this state they are never satisfied with their achievements but constantly *"hunger and thirst"* after the true righteousness. Having obtained mercy they are *"merciful."* This word means to get inside another's skin so as to see his needs as one's own, and as they show this mercy to others they receive it in turn. Such are the *"pure in heart."* They are clean, sincere, and without alloy with nothing between the soul and the Savior, and because of this they have constant access to the presence of God. In Oriental courts the king lived in seclusion for protection from some evil designing enemy. They held intercourse with their subjects through some trusted, single-hearted, loyal official who was always admitted to the presence of the king. The Christian is such a person in relation to God, and such persons will be *"peacemakers"* between God and man, and between man and man. Since God is a God of peace, those who make such peace will be recognized as being *"sons of God"* or like Him. They will, by the world, *"be persecuted for righteousness,"* but they are to rejoice in it, knowing that in Christ they are sufficient within themselves and will be greatly rewarded in heaven for their faithfulness and patient endurance.

Looking back over these "beatitudes" one sees a progression: conviction for sin; repentance for sin; committal to Christ; progressive development in righteousness; mercy toward others; sincerity of heart in constant fellowship with God; evangels of the gospel of peace between God and man and between man and man; and patient endurance and joy as one experiences the enmity of the world.

It is understandable, therefore, that Jesus said such are to be *"salt"* and *"light."* They are to cleanse, season, and preserve society; they are to be the means of giving God's revelation, illumination, and healing to a lost world. This light is not to be hidden from men but shared with them. Thus Jesus commanded His followers to shine before men that they by the Christian's good works will be brought to glorify their Father in heaven.

It is possible that in this tone of teaching, the apostles already were beginning to see the contrast between the principles of the kingdom and the burdensome legality of Judaism. So Jesus warned them *"Don't assume that I came to destroy the Law or the Prophets. I did not come to destroy but to fulfill."* The kingdom citizen will not be gauged by outward conformity to the letter of the Law. He will be measured or weighed by his spiritual understanding of and obedience to the deeper meaning of the teachings of God. In truth more will be expected of him than the demands placed upon him by the scribes and Pharisees. Such is the nature of the kingdom citizenship.

2. The Letter and the Spirit of the Law

Jesus then proceeded to illustrate the superiority of His ethical demands over those of the scribes in their teaching of the Old Testament, and of their oral law by which they sought to explain and apply the Old Testament Scriptures. In so doing He chose six examples: murder, adultery, divorce, oaths, retaliation and love for one's enemies. In each of these Jesus went beyond the overt act to the inner spirit. Already He had claimed authority with respect to the temple and the Sabbath. Here He did the same with regard to the Law. *"It was said . . . but I tell you"* has the finality of divine authority. It is of interest to note that in each case the *"I"* is written out in the Greek text, which gives it an emphatic meaning. It is no matter what the scribes have been saying. The One having authority is now speaking.

Jesus extended the law against murder beyond the overt act to include the entire realm of attitudes toward another person. Anger against a fellowman makes one liable ("in danger of") to the local court of twenty-three people. Contempt for one's intelligence ("Fool!") makes the offender liable before the Sanhedrin, the council of seventy in Jerusalem. And slander against one's character ("you moron") makes one liable to being thrown

A Roman milestone with Latin inscription at Caesarea Maritime, the provincial capital of Judea and home of the Roman procurators after AD 6. One application Jesus made of the command to love one's enemies was going the second mile. A Roman soldier could compel a person in an occupied country to carry his military gear for one mile. Not only are Jesus' followers not to retaliate, they are to work for the good of their enemies.

into the Gehenna of fire, the garbage dump outside the city of Jerusalem. *"Gehenna of fire"* was a figure used by Jesus, and only by Him, to depict the horrors of hell. Into this garbage dump were thrown the unclaimed bodies of executed criminals, and this is probably the meaning of Jesus' words here, although the thought of eternal punishment is also involved.

Murder is in one's heart before it is in his hand. It is a progressive attitude that, if not curbed, will eventually express itself in the overt act. Even if it does not erupt into violence it is a destructive attitude nevertheless, both to its subject as well as to its object. Wrong attitudes toward others even make true worship of God impossible. It is far better to guard the attitudes of one's heart than to regret the bloody acts of one's hands.

The same is true with respect to the law forbidding adultery. The scribes forbade the overt act, but Jesus warned against lust in the heart. Temptation becomes sin at the point of the consent of one's will. If one is held back from the overt act only by a lack of opportunity or from fear of the consequences, he is already guilty of adultery in his heart. The proper safeguard is a correct respect for human personality, both of one's own and that of another.

Jesus' teaching concerning divorce should be considered in the light of the prevailing practice. According to the school of Hillel, a man might divorce his wife for any cause, but Jesus said that it is to be permitted only for *"sexual immorality"* (Mt 5:32). Some interpreters question the genuineness of these words, but there is strong manuscript evidence for accepting them. Near the close of His ministry Jesus will enlarge upon this teaching (Mt 19:3ff.).

The practice of taking oaths was a much abused one among the Jews. So unreliable were they in their dealings with each other that they swore by all sorts of things: their heads, hair; the temple, its altar and sacrifices; by heaven; and by the throne of God. Jesus said that the Christian should be so trustworthy that his word would be his bond. When he says "yes" or "no," that should end the matter. But this is not to mean a prohibition against testifying under oath, for Jesus Himself did that (Mt 26:63–64).

"An eye for an eye, and a tooth for a tooth," said the Law. But Jesus taught that the Christian should suffer wrong rather than to live by the law of retaliation. Furthermore, his love should not stop with his neighbor. He should love his enemies also. What credit is there in the Christian loving only those who love him? Even Gentile and publicans did this. The goal of the Christian should be to emulate the character of his Heavenly Father. In Him alone does one find perfection or completeness.

3. The Practice of True Righteousness

There is no area in the Christian's life so sacred that Satan will not endeavor to pervert it to his own evil ends. So Jesus warned against such a danger. Three of the most religious acts of the Jews were giving alms, prayer, and fasting. Jesus did not condemn these as such, but He did condemn the wrong attitude in doing them.

Those who did their righteous deeds *"to be seen"* by men Jesus called *"hypocrites"* or play actors. *To be seen* renders a word from which comes the word *theater.* So these people were merely putting on a theatrical performance before an audience. They did so for the plaudits of the crowd, and receiving these plaudits they had their reward. They were paid-in-full, and, therefore should expect to receive no reward from God.

The Christian, on the other hand, should act out of a pure heart as unto God and not unto men. Alms should be given out of a heart of compassion. Prayer should be uttered out of a heart of hunger for fellowship with God. Fasting should result from a preoccupation with God's will. Giving no thought to reward, yet such will be rewarded by God.

Since prayer occupies so vital a place in the Christian's life, Jesus dwelt upon this subject. He did not condemn public praying any more than He did public alms giving and fasting, but the motive prompting it must be an inner one. Prayer should not be mere empty repetition that is so common in pagan prayers. Instead it should be the outreach and upreach of a hungry soul toward God. In this connection Jesus gave what is called "The Lord's Prayer." It may more correctly be labeled "The Model Prayer," for in giving it Jesus was not praying but reaching. An analysis of this prayer reveals that it contains in embryo everything for which a Christian should pray. It is also a model for guiding the Christian in prayer because it presupposes a right relationship between God and man, that of Father and child.

This warning of Jesus concerning the three deeds of righteousness flows naturally into His teaching concerning kingdom values. *"Don't collect for yourselves treasures on earth . . . but collect for yourselves treasures in heaven"* (Mt 6:19–20). The *hypocrites* regarded religion in terms of earthly values and rewards. The Christian should place the emphasis upon heavenly values and rewards. The Christian who has a "good" eye, or one in proper focus, will be full of heavenly light, but those whose eyes are "bad," or out of focus, will be full of darkness. One eye is trained on earthly values while the other is pointed toward heaven and its values. The result is a split personality that is torn between heaven and earth. Jesus said that is it impossible to be a slave to two masters, God and mammon. Each demands absolute loyalty—and it is impossible to give this to both. The Christian is not to be unmindful of his physical needs, but his primary concern should be to seek to bring in the rule of God and the practice of the true righteousness of God. This is enough to employ all of his daily energies without being torn apart by the cares of tomorrow, for *"Each day has enough trouble of its own"* (Mt 6:34).

4. The Problem of Judgment

In kingdom relationships one Christian should not set himself up as the judge of others, for judgment belongs to God alone. This does not mean that the Christian should not exercise discrimination. The very opposite is true, as Jesus had shown in the preceding part of this sermon, but he is not to be a self-appointed judge of others.

In vivid oriental fashion Jesus drove home this point—a man with a log in his eye cannot remove a splinter or a speck of dust from another's eye. Does not this suggest that the spiritual sin of censorious criticism outweighs the physical sin of the one being judged? If one Christian brother would help another with his problem, he must come to him in love and not in condemnation.

Now should the Christian become embroiled in the controversies of non-Christians (Mt 7:6)? "Dogs" and "pigs" lack the capacity to appreciate kingdom ethics. The Christian would be far wiser to endeavor to lead them to Christ, else he will himself be destroyed by them rather than lead them to appreciate and practice that which they do not understand. In reality this exhortation climaxed Jesus' teaching about kingdom righteousness and values. The kingdom of God will not be brought in through external reformation but through the experience of inner regeneration. The message of Jesus was *"You must be born again."*

5. The Source of Power

How shall the Christian find the power to live up to the high standards set forth by Jesus in this Sermon? He said, *"Keep asking, and it will be given to you. Keep searching, and you will find. Keep knocking, and the door will be opened to you"* (Mt 7:7). Note the progression: ask, seek, knock.

Sunset over the Dead Sea at Machaerus, Jordan. It is the location of Herod Antipas's fortress palace where John the Baptist was imprisoned and beheaded.

This implies the earnest and continuing effort of the Christian to obtain the power to rise to the standard of righteous living which Jesus set forth, and God will surely give it to the one asking, seeking, and knocking.

Within one's own heart what shall be the determining factor? This Jesus stated in "The Golden Rule" (Mt 7:12). Other teachers had uttered outwardly similar words. For instance, Hillel said, "What is hateful to yourself, do to no other." Confucius said "What you do not want done to yourself, do not do to others." Similar? They miss by the distance between the poles what Jesus said. Their rules are silver. Jesus' rule is golden. Theirs are negative; His is positive. Selfishness alone would enable a pagan to keep theirs. Only a regenerated nature is capable of keeping that of Jesus. Hillel's rule reflects the nature of Judaism. Refrain from doing to others the evil that you do not wish them to do to you. Jesus' rule is the fruit of kingdom righteousness. Think of something good that you would like for someone to do for you, then go and do it for another. Jesus pointed out that this is not merely a new ethic for a new kingdom, it is the very essence of the Law and the Prophets if one reads them with spiritual discernment. Thus He did not come to destroy them or to render them inactive. He came to fill them full of meaning, and that is the essence of the Sermon on the Mount.

6. The Conclusion of the Sermon

Jesus concluded His sermon by driving home its truths in three parables: two gates, two trees, and two foundations. Two gates are open before every man, the broad and the narrow. The former leads to destruction; the latter leads to life. Two trees offer their fruits to every man, the bad tree and the good tree. The good tree, or the ministry of Jesus, yields good fruit. The bad tree, the false prophets of outward conformity, brings forth evil fruit. The one brings life; the other brings death.

The climax of the Sermon pictures two foundations. The one is the man who hears and does the words of Jesus. The other is the man who does neither. Outwardly the structures of the two houses or lives appear the same. The test comes with the storm, and the difference is in the foundations. The life founded upon Christ stands; the other falls.

It is no wonder that the people marveled at these authoritative words of Jesus. Nor is it amazing that when He came down out of the mountain they continued to follow after Him.

AN INQUIRY AND A EULOGY

Jesus and the Twelve returned to Capernaum where, from a distance and by His authoritative word, He healed the servant of a Roman centurion, a commander of one hundred soldiers. Later, perhaps the next day, they visited the village of Nain, and there Jesus raised from the dead a widow's son. Quite naturally news of these incidents spread throughout Galilee, reaching even into Judea.

John the Baptist was still in prison at Machaerus. One day his disciples brought him word of the mighty works of Jesus. Evidently they were still resentful of His rising popularity while their teacher sat in a dungeon. It is possible that they even questioned whether or not Jesus was the Messiah, and this could have caused John to have become confused in his thoughts.

At any rate he sent his disciples to Jesus with an inquiry: *"Art thou he that should come, or do we look for another?"* (Mt 11:3). Literally, "Are You the One who is to come, or should we expect someone else?" "The One who is to come" was an expression used for the Messiah in the Minor Prophets, whose major picture of Him was one of judgment. The Major Prophets presented Him more as a gentle, suffering Servant. Both of these elements were present in John's preaching in the Jordan Valley, although its burden emphasized the former. It is in this light that John's question takes on meaning.

In contrast to his emphasis on the judgment aspects of the Messiah's work, John heard that Jesus was a gentle teacher and healer. So actually John asked Jesus if there were to be two Messiahs. That Jesus was fulfilling the Major Prophet role was quite clear. Would there be another Messiah of a different kind who would fulfill the Minor Prophet role?

Jesus replied by pointing out the work that He was doing—healing and preaching. *"Go and report to John what you hear and see,"* was His answer. In a sense these were some of the things John himself had said that the Messiah would do (Jn 1:29–34). To the modern reader this may appear to be an inadequate answer, but John would see and understand. The day of opportunity must precede the day of judgment. The former was central at this time; the latter would come in due time to those who rejected the opportunity. But even then Jesus' ministry was one of mingled mercy and judgment, as is seen in the woes He pronounced upon the Galilean cities that were even then rejecting Him (Mt 11:20–24). They were being judged within the context of history. So the mission of the Messiah was one—a mingling of mercy and judgment. In His redemptive work Jesus fulfilled the former. In the final judgment the latter will find full expression. But, even so, every man, yes, every nation, stands in a moment of crisis as he/it faces the question as to what reaction to give to Christ.

It is possible that after the departure of John's disciples some of those about Jesus criticized him for his question about the Messiah. But no criticism fell from the lips of Jesus. Instead He delivered a eulogy concerning him. Did anyone think of John the Baptist as a fragile reed shaken by the wind? Or as a pampered freeloader enjoying the gratuities of a king? Quite the contrary was true concerning him. It was not his faith but his under-

standing that had faltered. His present predicament was due to his courage
in daring to challenge the king and his conduct. Should he be regarded as
a prophet? Yes, more than a prophet. He was the forerunner of the Messiah.
There was none born of a woman who was greater than John. Yet even the
least one in the kingdom of heaven is greater than John. Not greater in
stature but in privilege. John was the acme of the old revelation, but everyone in the kingdom who comes after him stands on his shoulders.

And then as though turning upon the Pharisees and lawyers who were
in the group, Jesus turned from praising John to a censure of those who
by violent means tried to force the kingdom of heaven into their own

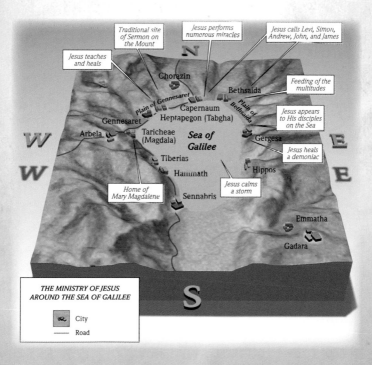

Traditional site
of Sermon on
the Mount

Jesus performs
numerous miracles

Jesus calls Levi, Simon,
Andrew, John, and James

Jesus teaches
and heals

N

Chorazin

Bethsaida

Feeding of the
multitudes

Plain of Gennesaret

Capernaum

Plain of Bethsaida

Jesus appears
to His disciples
on the Sea

Gennesaret

Heptapegon (Tabgha)

Arbela

Taricheae
(Magdala)

Sea of
Galilee

Gergesa

Jesus heals
a demoniac

W

Tiberias

Hippos

W

Hammath

Jesus calms
a storm

E

E

Home of
Mary Magdalene

Sennabris

Emmatha

Gadara

S

THE MINISTRY OF JESUS
AROUND THE SEA OF GALILEE

City

Road

preconceived molds. While publicans and common people were being baptized by John, they held themselves aloof from him. And they were doing the same thing with respect to Jesus. The Lord likened them to children playing in the marketplace, some of which may have been in evidence at the time. It was certainly a common sight. Some said to their fellows, *"We played the flute for you, but you didn't dance; we sang a lament, but you didn't weep!"* (Lk 7:32). They would neither dance nor play funeral. The trouble was that they just did not want to play.

Applying this truth Jesus said that John came as an ascetic, and the Pharisees called him insane. Jesus came as a social being, and they labeled Him a glutton, a drunkard, and a friend of publicans and sinners. They simply did not want to play. Nevertheless, *"wisdom is vindicated by her deeds"* (Mt 11:19). The fruits of the labors of both John and Jesus would prove the reality of their missions.

A STUDY IN CONTRASTS

As if in answer to Jesus' charge concerning the Pharisees' attitude toward Him as a social being, Simon, a Pharisee, invited Jesus to a meal. When they sat down or reclined on couches to eat, a notoriously sinful woman came and performed what seems to present-day people to be a strange act. She stood behind Jesus weeping so that her tears fell on His feet. Then she wiped His feet with her hair as she kissed them profusely. She ended by pouring ointment on His feet. A similar thing was done by Mary of Bethany shortly before the crucifixion. Some would make these two events identical, but the contrast of circumstances and personalities makes this most unlikely.

In the event at hand, the Pharisee in his mind criticized Jesus for allowing this sinful woman to do as she did. To him it was proof that Jesus was not a prophet.

Knowing his thoughts Jesus used the occasion to teach a great lesson in forgiveness and love. A certain lender forgave the debts of two men, one of which owed ten times as much as the other. When asked which of the two would love the benefactor the more, Simon gave the obvious answer. The one who was forgiven more.

Then Jesus applied the lesson. It was evident that the woman loved Jesus more than Simon did because she was to be forgiven the more. The difference between the sinful woman and the self-righteous Pharisee who felt no need for forgiveness was one of compassionate love as over against cold courtesy. Then fitting His deeds to His words, Jesus said to the woman, *"Your sins are forgiven"* (Lk 7:48). The crowd buzzed within themselves that He should claim to forgive sins, but Jesus ignored them as He said to the woman, *"Your faith has saved you. Go in peace"* (Lk 7:50).

Shortly after this incident Jesus and the Twelve made a second preaching tour of Galilee. They were accompanied by certain women who had been healed of evil spirits and diseases. One of these was Mary Magdalene out of whom Jesus had cast seven demons. It is usually held that this indicates that she had been a very sinful woman, but this is not necessarily true. This extreme case of demon possession could have been something else entirely and probably was. Nevertheless, these women, like the one in Simon's house, showed their great love for Jesus by ministering to Him and the Twelve out of their material substance. This little band of women is symbolic of that innumerable caravan of women who have done likewise through the ages. If any group should love Jesus, it is womanhood for whom Jesus did and does so much! And, incidentally, this event suggests the source of livelihood for Jesus and His little band.

THE MINISTRY OF THE PARABLE

The following events all occurred in a single day that A. T. Robertson called "The Busy Day." Doubtless it was one of many such days in the life of Jesus. The happenings of this day took place near and on the Sea of Galilee.

1. A Blasphemous Accusation.

The day began in a house. The crowds awaiting Jesus' ministry were so great that He could not find time even to eat. Such dedication to His work was interpreted by His friends as a form of insanity.

In the course of this morning, Jesus healed a blind and mute demoniac. Seeing this, the people asked, *"Is not this the Son of David?"* (Mt 12:23). This term was avoided by Jesus because to the Jews it carried a highly political Messianic connotation. Such a declaration apparently drove the Pharisees to desperation, for they responded, *"This fellow doth not cast out devils, but by Beelzebub the prince of the devils"* (Mt 12:24). This statement evidently was made to the people and not to Jesus directly. *Beelzebub* was a title of contempt that the Jews applied to Satan. It was a derivative of the name *Baal,* the Canaanite pagan god. The name *Beelzebub* probably means "lord of flies."

Knowing their evil thoughts Jesus called the Pharisees to Him, and in four points He answered their charge. First, if by the power of Satan He cast out demons, then Satan is casting out Satan. How then shall his kingdom of evil stand? Second, the Pharisees' disciples claimed, though falsely, to cast out demons. Did they also work by Satan's power? Let them decide the issue. Naturally they would say that it was by God's power. Third, if Jesus cast out demons by the power of God, then why did not the Pharisees accept Him? Fourth, the very fact that He was casting out Satan proved that Jesus' power was superior to Satan's power. Thus the Pharisees were without a logical answer to Jesus' arguments.

Then Jesus pronounced upon them what is called the "unpardonable sin," or the sin against the Holy Spirit (Mt 12:31–32). This was not a sin of impulse. It was the climax of a deliberate hardening of their hearts against Jesus. Neither was it a sin of ignorance. The Pharisees committed it in the full knowledge of Jesus' miraculous deed. Others saw it and glorified God. The Pharisees saw it and blasphemed or spoke insultingly of the Holy Spirit. They witnessed an obviously good work of God's Spirit, yet they attributed it to Satan's evil spirit. They had lost the power to discern between good and evil. To them good was evil and evil was good. Like Milton's Satan in *Paradise Lost,* they said, "Evil, be thou my good." So like John the Baptist Jesus called them a *"generation of vipers"* or a brood of snakes. Terrible words! But they came from Him who is infinite Mercy to all who will receive it.

As if to prove their spiritual emptiness, the Pharisees sought to counter Jesus' words by asking that He show them a sign of His deity. They ignored completely the "sign" He had just given in casting out the demon. The only sign Jesus promised them was the sign of Jonah, which in effect was His resurrection from the dead (Mt 12:39–40). Because His contemporary generation, of which the Pharisees were a sample, rejected Him, the Ninevites and the queen of Sheba would witness or be evidence against them in the final judgment. For the former responded to the preaching of Jonah, and the latter came from afar to hear the wisdom of Solomon. But a greater than either Jonah or Solomon was among that generation, and they were rejecting Him.

Jesus closed this interview by condemning the entire Pharisaical system. So empty were their teachings that those to whom they sought to minister were left in a worse condition than when they found them. It is a sad picture of the spiritual poverty of those who claimed to be religious teachers. It is no wonder, therefore, that theirs was a generation of unrecognized spiritual poverty.

2. A New Relationship

During all this time Jesus was still in a house. Just at this point someone came to him with word that His mother and brethren were outside wishing to see Him. Why they had come is not stated. It is generally held that, fearing that He was beside Himself, they wished to take Him home. But this is mere supposition. Their coming could have been for any legitimate reason.

At any rate when Jesus heard it, He replied that no longer should they presume upon a family relationship, and then looking about at His disciples He said, *"Behold my mother and my brethren! For whosoever shall do the will of God, the same is my brother, and my sister, and mother"* (Mk 3:34–35). There is every reason to believe that Jesus' mother fell within this category, but His half-brothers did not believe upon Him until after His resurrection. The point of Jesus' words is that the true relationship with Him is spiritual and not genetic.

3. Jesus Teaching in Parables

At this juncture, probably about noon, Jesus left the house and went out to the seaside. The crowds were so great that He got into a boat and pulled away from the shore to enable all to see and hear, and then He began to teach them in parables.

Previously from time to time Jesus had employed this method of teaching, but here He used it altogether. And this is significant. The Pharisees had definitely shown that they were not disposed to heed His teachings but were using His words as a basis of criticism. The people as a whole were so enchanted by the Pharisees' dream of a kingdom of earthly grandeur that they were, for the most part, incapable of understanding the spiritual nature of Christ's kingdom. So Jesus with good reason adopted the parabolic method of teaching by which He might impact truths to His disciples. It was not a deliberate attempt to hide truth, but an effort to depict it in vivid imagery to those who were capable of receiving it.

The parable was a favorite method of teaching among the Orientals. By it they took one central truth and so adorned it in familiar dress that it might be viewed from many angles. The parables of Jesus have been called earthly stories with heavenly meanings. They were handles by which His listeners might pick up truth and take it home with them.

For convenience the parables under consideration may be divided into two groups: those spoken to the larger audience by the seaside and those delivered to the disciples in a house. Each of them depicts some aspect of the kingdom of God.

(1) By the Seaside.

The first parable is called the Parable of the Sower, but more correctly it is the Parable of the Soils, for one sower sowed the same kind of seed in different types of soil with varying results.

To understand it one must recall the situation. A grain field usually has a hard path running through it over which people might travel. Palestine sits on a hard pan of limestone rock. In many places the topsoil is very thin. In a given field there would be deeper, richer soil infested with thorn bushes or other wild growth. Then there was good soil that was free from such. So the scene is fixed.

A sower broadcasts the field with seed. Some falls on the hard path where the ever-present birds eat it. Other falls on the thin soil and takes root. The warmth of the limestone rock causes it to grow quickly in the early springtime, but because it has no firm rootage, it soon withers under the hot sun. Yet other falls on the rich soil infested with thorns. While it grows, it bears no fruit because the thorns choke it out, depriving it of needed nutrition. But that which falls on the good, clean soil bears an abundant harvest.

Privately the Twelve asked Jesus to interpret this parable. The sower may be anyone who scatters abroad the gospel of the kingdom. He is not responsible for the results but for the sowing. Some gospel seed will fall on hard hearts that do not receive it, and Satan immediately takes it away. Other seeds are received enthusiastically but without comprehension of the true meaning of the gospel. Under tribulation those receiving it soon show their true colors as they wilt away. They were never really in the kingdom. Other seeds fall into lives that genuinely receive them, but they are so cluttered up with the cares of the world that, while the plants live, they bear no fruit. However those who are completely dedicated to the Lord bear an abundant harvest in the kingdom.

An Arab farmer near Bethlehem sowing seeds on his land

The same gospel sown in different soils with such varied results! An analysis reveals that these results were and are obtained both among those who heard Jesus and who hear His evangels today. It is no wonder that Jesus said, *"Take care how you listen"* (Lk 8:18).

Another parable deals with the nature of the growth of the kingdom. The seed is sown, and the sower leaves it there. It grows and bears fruit without his knowledge of the process. It is a gradual growth: the blade, the head, and then the ripened grain. Then he knows that the harvest is ready and he reaps.

In like fashion God places His kingdom upon the earth. It does not grow by outward force or adornment. The growth is secret, inward, and gradual. When in His wisdom, not man's, the harvest is ripe, then He will reap.

At first sight the Parable of the Wheat and the Weeds may resemble that of the soils, but it teaches a different truth altogether. In the Parable of the Soils there was one sower, one type of seed, but different soils. In that of the tares there were two sowers, two types of seed and one kind of soil.

Again it is necessary to note certain conditions in order to understand this parable. Tares or darnel (weeds) and wheat were similar plants until the grain formed in the head. Then darnel formed black, inedible grains. It was a common practice for one's enemy to oversow his sown field with darnel.

Jesus drew upon this phenomenon to teach the nature of the kingdom of God. A man's field was oversown with weeds. Later when this was discovered, the owner's servants asked if they should pull up the weeds, but he wisely told them that to do this would injure the wheat. So he left them to grow together until harvest. Then the weeds were burned and the wheat stored in his barn.

Later in the house Jesus interpreted this parable to His disciples. Here the sower of the good seed, or sons of the kingdom, is the Son of man. The enemy is the Devil, and his seed are the sons of the evil one. The harvest is the end of the world, and the reapers are the angels. The point is that while Jesus is sowing down the world with sons of the kingdom, Satan is oversowing the world with his sons. To man's outward judgment they may appear similar, but the harvest time will reveal the difference, and the Son of man knows His own. Men are not to endeavor to remove the sons of Satan lest they injure the wheat. Then the sons of the kingdom will be gathered unto the Son of man, and the sons of the evil one will be cast into hell. *"Anyone who has ears should listen"* (Mt 13:43).

The Parables of the Mustard Seed and the Yeast teach similar truths but with different emphases. Like the very small mustard seed growing into a large plant, so from a small beginning the kingdom of God will grow—to unbelievable proportions. And as a small piece of yeast placed in dough silently works until it leavens the whole lump, so will the kingdom spread until it fills the earth. Some see yeast or leaven as a universal symbol of evil. Thus to them this parable means that evil will permeate the kingdom while it is on earth, but this is an unwarranted position. Leaven was to be put in a certain bread sacrifice prescribed by the Law of Moses (Lv 23:17). Is this also evil? No! Jesus was simply drawing upon a common custom to teach a spiritual truth.

The disciples in keeping with their contemporaries were expecting the kingdom to spring forth full-grown in a day. Jesus says that its growth will be gradual and without outward ostentation. This is a comforting thought after two thousand years. The growth of the kingdom seems to be slow and ineffective, but silently, inwardly, it continues to increase, and its leaven permeates even those elements opposing it.

(2) In the House.

Having finished His teaching by the seaside, Jesus retired into a house. It may have been Simon Peter's house in Capernaum, and there, after explaining the Parable of the Weeds, Jesus spoke four additional parables to the Twelve.

The Parables of the Hidden Treasure and the Priceless Pearl teach the price that He will pay for the kingdom. Some regard it as the price one must pay to get into the kingdom, but man does not buy his way into it. Jesus, and Jesus alone, purchased the kingdom!

In ancient times it was a common practice for one to bury his treasure. It might be a robber, or it might be the rightful owner. At any rate someone buried a treasure, went away, and never returned. Perhaps he died without revealing its location. In due time the land belonged to another who was unaware of the treasure. Someone found it, hid it, and purchased the field, selling all that he had in order to do so.

Some see a moral difficulty here, but it was not so regarded in that day. However, one must not press every point in a parable. The one truth is that finding the treasure, the man "in his joy" sold all that he had and bought the field. Likewise Jesus sold all that He had, His life, in order to purchase the kingdom. This is suggestive of Hebrews 12:2: *"Who for the joy that lay before Him endured a cross and despised the shame."*

The Parable of the Priceless Pearl relates the same truth. A traveling pearl merchant found a pearl of superlative value. To purchase it he sold all that he had. Jesus, likewise, gave His all, even His life, in order to purchase the kingdom.

The Parable of the Net reiterates with a different figure the truth set forth in the Parable of the Tares. It was a common sight around the Sea of Galilee to see fishermen letting down their nets. In them they caught all

"The kingdom of heaven is like a large net thrown into the sea" (Mt 13:47).

manner of fish. The good they kept, but the bad they threw away. Even so, in the net of the kingdom age there will be found true and false confessors, but in the consummation of the age the true will be saved and the false or bad will be cast into hell.

With this, Jesus finished this particular body of His teaching about the kingdom. But one thought remained. Jesus is, in truth, a scribe teaching about the kingdom. He is also teaching the Twelve to become scribes in the kingdom. As such they are to bring out of their treasures of knowledge things "new and old." Like Jesus, they are to teach the old truths, the Old Testament, but they are also to declare the new revelation in Jesus Christ. They are not yet ready to do so, but their time will come.

4. A Visit to Gerasa.

It was probably the middle of the afternoon of "The Busy Day." The crowds still followed Jesus. So for a brief respite He and the Twelve took a boat to go to the eastern shore of the Sea of Galilee. Jesus was tired after a strenuous day, so He lay down to sleep on a cushion in the back of the boat. The valleys on the eastern shore empty into the sea so as to form wind funnels. Sometimes without warning the wind rushes down suddenly turning a placid lake into a seething cauldron. This phenomenon occurred at this time, possibly as the result of an afternoon thunderstorm. The sea rocked as if it were an earthquake. The waves were beating into the boat so that it was in danger of sinking. In their jeopardy the disciples called to Jesus, *"Lord, save us: we perish"* (Mt 8:25). Some of the Twelve were men of the sea, and most likely had done their best to weather the storm, but when all of their skills failed them, they called on Jesus. Fishermen calling to a landlubber for help! This shows their conviction as to the supernatural power of Jesus.

A wave on the Sea of Galilee generated by just a 15 mph wind! The surface of the lake is nearly 700 feet below the level of the Mediterranean, some 30 miles to the west. The nearby hills of Galilee reach an altitude of 1,500 feet above sea level. To the east are the mountains of Gilead with peaks of more than 3,300 feet. To the north are the snow-covered Lebanon Mountains. Because of its location, it is subject to sudden and violent storms that are usually of short duration.

But despite their faith in Jesus, He still rebuked them for their lack of faith. This suggests that they lacked enough faith to believe that God would preserve His Son even in a storm such as this one was.

Then Jesus rebuked the winds and the sea. Here was the Master of nature bidding these elements to behave: *"And there was a great calm"* (Mt 8:26). According to the language this was not a gradual subsiding of the storm's force as would be true in a natural phenomenon. It was a sudden calm, denoting the miraculous element. It is no wonder that the Twelve wondered that even the natural elements were subject to Jesus. Literally, *"the men began to marvel . . . and the sea kept on obeying him"* (Mt 8:27).

Probably late in the afternoon Jesus arrived on the eastern shore of the Sea of Galilee. He was in the region of the Decapolis, which was largely Gentile territory. This particular locality was called the country of the Gadarenes or the Gerasenes. There He was confronted by two demon-possessed or insane men who dwelt among the tombs. They were a scourge to the entire area. Efforts had been made to bind them in fetters and chains, but they broke them in pieces. Night and day they wandered among the tombs and in the mountains, crying out and cutting themselves with stones. Passersby gave them a wide berth.

But when these demoniacs saw Jesus they ran and knelt before Him crying out that He would not torment them, for Jesus had commanded them to come out of the men. The demons themselves were speaking through their victims. They recognized Jesus as the *"Son of the most high God,"* but when they were commanded to come out of the men, they implored Jesus to permit them to enter into a herd of swine feeding nearby. They did not want to be disembodied. When their petition was granted the swine were crazed so that they ran into the sea and were drowned.

Word soon reached the owners of the swine. So they, along with the entire city, came to find the demoniacs clothes and in their right minds. One would think that they would be delighted to find them so, but instead they asked Jesus to leave their land. Was it simply that they preferred swine over souls? Perhaps. But Luke says that they were terrified over the entire matter, and this may suggest another reason for their request. This was pagan territory, and pagans were fearful of their gods. The entire affair, including the confession of Jesus' deity by the demons, suggested to them that a god was among them. So out of fear they asked Jesus to leave.

The Lord granted their request, but He did not leave Himself without a witness among them. For in reply to one healed man's request to be allowed to accompany Jesus, He said, *"Go home to thy friends, and tell them how great things the Lord hath done for thee, and hath had compassion on thee"* (Mk 5:19). This man became an evangel throughout the Decapolis. This within itself brought a happy ending to "The Busy Day."

A FINAL VISIT TO NAZARETH

The next day Jesus and the Twelve returned to Capernaum. There He healed a woman who had been suffering from an issue of blood for twelve years, raised the daughter of Jairus from the dead, and healed two blind men and a mute demoniac. Then He paid a last visit to Nazareth. His home village had failed her first test—so Jesus gave her another.

Again on the Sabbath day Jesus taught in the synagogue. This time there was no violence. They met His words with cold unbelief. True He spoke wonderful words, and they knew by hearsay of His mighty works, but their familiarity bred contempt. Was not this the former village carpenter, the son of Mary and Joseph? And His half-brothers and half-sisters were still their neighbors. So since they knew Him so well He could not be the

Messiah. Apparently they shared with Nathanael the belief that nothing good could come from their town.

Therefore, in light of their cynicism, Jesus spoke words of universal import: *"A prophet is not without honor except in his hometown, among his relatives, and in his household"* (Mk 6:4). Not only His fellow-Nazarenes, but His own family, save Mary, rejected Him. So wondering as to their unbelief, Jesus left Nazareth never to return.

A THIRD TOUR OF GALILEE

However, even if Nazareth would not receive Jesus, the harvest was plenteous elsewhere. So one day he called the Twelve to Him that He might send them on a preaching tour of Galilee. The time had arrived when they should attempt to use what they had been taught. Furthermore, to empower them for their work, He endued them with authority to cast out demons and to heal diseases.

Also Jesus gave them instructions, not only for their immediate journey but for all who would come after them in the preaching of the gospel. W. Hersey Davis divides these instructions according to three periods in the gospel age:

THREE PERIODS IN THE GOSPEL AGE

to the time of the crucifixion	(Mt 10:6–15);
from Pentecost to the fall of Jerusalem	(Mt 10:16–23);
from the fall of Jerusalem to the end of the age	(Mt 10:24–42)

1. To the Time of the Crucifixion.

In this period the apostles are sent to the Jews only, even excluding the Samaritans. In the commission following the resurrection, they are sent

into the whole world with a specific mention of Samaria. But now they
are to proclaim to the Jews that the kingdom of heaven is at hand. Their
work will be authenticated by miraculous works. During this time haste
is essential. Therefore, they are to travel without provisions as men on an
urgent mission, but they are not to go as beggar-prophets. Those to whom
they minister will provide for their needs. Wherever they are welcomed
they are to speak words of peace and blessing, but when they are rejected
they are to shake off from their feet the dust of that house or city as a
judgment against them. This was a typical Oriental gesture, and in the
final judgment it will be more tolerable for Sodom and Gomorrah than
for such cities.

2. From Pentecost to the Fall of Jerusalem.

Here a sudden change of atmosphere is seen. The apostles now are sent
forth as sheep among wolves. They will be persecuted by both Jews and
Gentiles. It was only during this period that the Christians were persecuted
by both of these groups. They will be scourged in the synagogues, and
Davis notes that such has not happened since the fall of the Jewish state
in AD 70.

During such a time they were not to worry about their defense before
governors and kings. The Holy Spirit would give them the words to say.
This was because they had not yet had time or opportunity to hammer out
the terms of faith.

This period in Christian history was characterized by bitter family strife
as Jews became Christians. The most intimate of family relationships were
broken as the members betrayed other members to the persecutors, even
unto death.

Jesus told His apostles that they were not to tarry in one city under
persecution. If one place would not hear them, they were to go to another,

and He said that they would not have gone through *"the cities of Israel, till the Son of man be come"* (Mt 10:23). After the fall of Jerusalem, there were no "cities of Israel." The coming of the Son of man does not necessarily refer to the end of the age. It could also be any cataclysmic event in history. This coming of the Son of man was the destruction of Jerusalem under Titus in AD 70.

3. From the Fall of Jerusalem to the End of the Age.

This period marks the identification of the Christians with Christ. As the world had persecuted and blasphemed Christ, so would it do to His people (Mt 10:24–25). But they were not to fear their persecutors. Rather they were to be fearful of failing to do the will of God. They could be certain that God's care would ever be about them. They were going forth to declare the gospel. There would be varied responses to it, but men must make a choice between Jesus and even the unbelieving members of their families.

Death may await those who proclaim the gospel, so they should be prepared to die in the cause. But in so doing they will have fulfilled the purpose of their being, and that will be life indeed.

4. The Mission of the Twelve.

Therefore, the Twelve went forth to begin their first phase of this age-long mission, and it was a successful mission indeed. It was a glorious experience of preaching, casting out devils and healing the sick. The power which Jesus had given to them really worked!

THE DEATH OF JOHN THE BAPTIST

It was while the Twelve were away on their mission that Jesus received word that Herod Antipas thought He was John the Baptist come to life again. This news marked a definite turn in His subsequent ministry.

John had been arrested by Herod Antipas toward the close of the first year of Jesus' ministry. Herod had visited his brother Philip in Rome. He was a private citizen who is not to be confused with another brother Philip, the tetrarch of Iturea and Trachonitis. The Roman brother was married to Herodias. While in Rome Herod Antipas seduced her and persuaded her to divorce his brother to marry him. Knowing Herodias' character none of these things must have proved difficult. She gladly traded her role as the wife of a private citizen for that of a state of royalty.

This evidently happened during the time of John the Baptist's ministry. So hearing about it he repeatedly denounced this unholy marriage. As a result Herodias had it in for John. Finally, she persuaded her husband to arrest him and throw him in a dungeon in his castle in Machaerus. Josephus takes note of this fact, saying that Herod did so because he feared that John might lead a rebellion against him. This probably was Herod's publicly announced reason for John's arrest, but the true reason is told in the Gospel of Mark.

Apparently Herod was intrigued by John, for he evidently heard him preach often, either in the dungeon or else in his court. Despite Herodias' insistence that he destroy the prophet, Herod by one excuse or another protected him. However, Herodias bided her time until an opportunity presented itself.

It was on the occasion of Herod's birthday. He gave a banquet for the grandees of his realm, and when he was drunk with wine Herodias struck. She connived to have her daughter to dance before Herod in such fashion that he promised to grant her every wish. Following her mother's advice she requested John the Baptist's head on a platter. Even though this shocked Herod, out of pride he granted the wish, and the noble forerunner paid with his life for his loyalty to his commission.

THE HERODIAN RULERS

Ruler	Family Relationships	Realm of Responsibility	Dates of Reign	Biblical Reference
Herod 1 (the Great)	Son of Antipater	King of Judea	37–4 BC	Mt 2:1–22; Luke 1:5
Herod Archelaus	Oldest son of Herod the Great	Ethanarch of Judea, Samaria, and Idumea	4 BC–AD 6	Mt 2:22
Philip*	Son of Herod the Great and Cleopatra of Jerusalem	Tetrarch of territories north and east of the Sea of Galilee	4 BC–AD 34	Luke 3:1
Herod Antipas	Youngest son of Herod the Great; second husband of Herodias	Tetrarch of Galilee and Perea	4 BC–AD 39	Mt 14:1–11; Mark 6:14–29; Luke 3:1, 19; 13:31–33; 23:7–12
Herod Agrippa I	Grandson of Herod the Great	King of Judea	AD 37–44	Acts 12
Herod Agrippa II	Great-grandson of Herod the Great	Tetrach and king of Chalcis	AD 44–100 (became king in AD 48)	Acts 25:13 – 26:32

*Not to be confused with Herod Philip also mentioned in the New Testament. Herod Philip was the son of Herod the Great and Mariamne and was the first husband of Herodias. (See Mt 14:3; Mark 6:17; and Luke 3:19.)

The disciples of John claimed his body and buried it. Then they brought the sad news to Jesus. Evidently at this stage in Jesus' ministry John had been dead for some time. The thing that made a change in the present ministry of Jesus was the fact that the superstitious Herod, when he heard of Jesus' works, said that He was John the Baptist come to life again. This fact posed a threat to Jesus Himself, and since His hour had not yet come, He decided to leave Herod's territory. This among other matters caused Jesus to bring to a close His Galilean ministry. From this time on His ministry took a different turn and was focused on a different purpose. It was ever working toward the accomplishment of God's redemptive will and purpose, for He causes even the wrath of men to praise Him.

CHAPTER V
THE PERIOD OF WITHDRAWALS

It was one year before the crucifixion of Jesus—just prior to the Passover in AD 29. Shortly after Jesus learned that Herod Antipas had cast his designing and superstitious eyes upon Him, the Twelve returned with exciting reports of their successful tour of Galilee. Doubtless they were physically tired and emotionally exhausted. So Jesus said to them, *"Come away by yourselves to a remote place and rest a while"* (Mk 6:31).

Thus there began a period of four withdrawals from Galilee lasting for approximately six months, from the Passover until about the time of the Feast of Tabernacles. This encompassed a period from spring until autumn.

Five reasons may be given for these withdrawals. Jesus withdrew from the jealous superstition of Herod Antipas. He wanted to escape the rising fanaticism of the Galilean crowds. The hostility of the Jewish rulers was deepening. The season of extreme heat around the Sea of Galilee was approaching, so Jesus went to the seashore and the mountains to rest. And He wanted privacy in which to instruct the Twelve. The end was rapidly approaching, and they must be prepared for it. Two things are worthy of note. In each of these withdrawals, Jesus avoided the territory of Herod Antipas and those areas under the direct influence of the Jewish rulers. After each withdrawal He returned to Galilee but only for brief periods, and the teaching of this period centered upon the King of the Kingdom or the Person of Christ. It was one of the most important segments of Jesus' ministry.

THE WITHDRAWAL INTO BETHSAIDA JULIAS

1. Feeding the Five Thousand

Even though it was the time of the Passover, Jesus did not go to Jerusalem for its observance. Instead He and the Twelve took a boat and rowed to the northeastern side of the Sea of Galilee. They landed in the region connected with the city of Bethsaida Julias, so named to distinguish it from the western Bethsaida near Capernaum. It was in the tetrarchy of Philip. Although this was

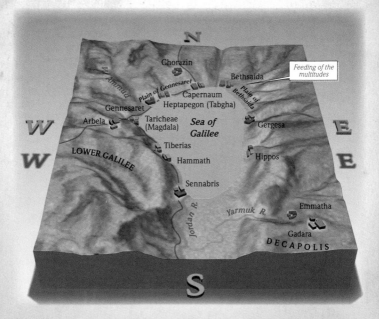

a heavily populated section, the spot chosen by Jesus was a "remote place," not necessarily a desert but a deserted area that promised privacy.

However, it was not to be, for the people, discerning Jesus' destination, ran around the northern edge of the sea. When the little company arrived, they were met by the multitudes; and even though Jesus had come there to rest, His compassion was such that He taught them and healed their sick.

The people had been without food all day. Therefore, late in the afternoon the Twelve came to Jesus with the suggestion that He should send the crowds away into the nearby villages that they might buy food. But Jesus astounded them by saying, *"You give them something to eat"* (Mk 6:37). The disciples had compassion on the people. They recognized their hunger, but it never occurred to them that they should or could do anything about it. They failed to recognize the resources that were at their disposal. How like modern Christians they were! Hungry people must be fed, but let them do it themselves, or else let the government assume the responsibility. Herod Antipas could have said as much, but Jesus still says, *"You give them something to eat."*

Thrown back upon their own resources, the Twelve began to count the cost or to reckon their ability only in monetary terms. They estimated that it would require *"two hundred denarii"* (half a year's wages for an average worker) of bread to feed the crowd, but Jesus told them to search among the people to see what food was available. Finally Andrew reported that he had found a boy who had five barley cakes and two dried fishes. This was the food of the poor. Perhaps it was a lunch the boy's mother had fixed for him. Someone remarked that the greatest miracle that day was not Jesus' multiplying the loaves and fishes but that this growing boy had not eaten his lunch so late in the day. Evidently he was quite absorbed in the events he was witnessing.

At any rate Jesus told the people to sit down in groups of hundreds and fifties. Note Jesus' use of organization to ensure that all would be fed. It was a beautiful sight. At this time of year the grass was green. As the groups clothed in their varicolored robes sat on the green grass, it made a colorful display.

Then Jesus blessed the food, began to break it, giving it to His disciples, who in turn distributed it among the people. It was an awesome occasion, for the supply seemed to be inexhaustible. As the Lord of the harvest had produced the food by the gradual working of His natural laws, so in accelerated fashion He reproduced it by supernatural laws. The result was that five thousand men, to say nothing about the women and children, were fed. Judging by a modern congregation there could have been fifteen or twenty thousand people involved! When all had been fed, Jesus ordered that the fragments of food be gathered. He wasted nothing He had made. The remainder filled twelve baskets. This type of basket was a *cophinus*, a small hand basket used to carry food.

Various efforts have been made to explain this event by natural means. One suggests that the disciples discovered a cache of food stored in a cave as military supplies. A more likely theory holds that Jesus and the Twelve shared their own meager lunch, and this set off a wave of generosity as others shared their food with others. But there is no reason to reject the miraculous element if one believes Jesus to be the Son of God. If God could produce the food in the first place, there is no reason He could not reproduce it in this fashion.

Behind this event is a great spiritual truth. The supplier of the loaves and fishes was only a boy. He did not have very much, but what he had he gave to Jesus; and Jesus blessed it, enlarged it, and with it fed a multitude. What He did with this boy's food He can do with anyone's life.

2. A Revolutionary Effort Rejected

The miracle electrified the multitude, and that which Jesus feared began to take shape. The people were on the verge of trying to acclaim Him their political king. Had they succeeded in doing so, it would have meant rebellion against Rome; and like all such sporadic rebellions, it would have brought the wrath of Rome down upon Jesus and upon the people. The result would be the destruction of the purpose for which Jesus came into the world.

The people were ripe for such a revolution. For it to flame into reality called only for a leader, and in Jesus they thought that they had found one. They had either witnessed or heard of His many past miracles, and now this. With Him as their military leader, they would need no medical corps. He could heal them of their wounds. There would be no need for further recruitment. If a soldier were killed, Jesus could restore him to life, and they would have a ready source of military supplies. With a handful of food Jesus could feed an army.

But there was an even greater cause for their proposed action. One of their favorite messianic prophecies was Deuteronomy 18:15. Moses had said, *"The Lord your God will raise up for you a prophet like me from among your own brothers. You must listen to him."* Certainly Jesus' miracles attested to the fact that God had raised Him up. Most certainly He was a Prophet. He was a Jew, one of their "brothers," and He was a Galilean, one from their very midst. And He was like Moses. Moses had furnished manna and quail in the wilderness, and Jesus had miraculously fed them with loaves and fishes in "a remote place." So they were ready to "listen" to Him.

Note Jesus' actions in the light of this situation. First, He forced the disciples to embark. Second, He dismissed the multitude. Did He send the disciples away or get them out of this revolutionary atmosphere? Or were they the actual source of it? It is entirely possible that the latter was true. So Jesus had to send the Twelve away before He could quiet the multitude. And, third, He went away to the mountain to pray. The recent situation was Satan's temptation all over again.

Jesus needed this communion with His Father, not only for Himself, but also for the Twelve, that they might come to understand fully His Person and purpose.

It was just one year before the crucifixion, and they were still captivated by the Jewish dream of a political kingdom and a political messiah. They had so much to learn before they could go forth as heralds of the kingdom of heaven. Old obsessions die hard, but although He had dull students, Jesus was the Teacher and was possessed of infinite patience.

3. Jesus Walks on the Water

In the meantime the disciples were rowing their way back to Galilee. At this point it is about six miles across the sea. Evidently the sea was running heavy because of a great wind, for by the fourth watch of the night, sometime between three and six in the morning, they were only halfway across. Suddenly

Storm on the Sea of Galilee

they saw what appeared to them to be a phantom walking on the water. It was Jesus coming to them. Failing to recognize Him in the darkness, the disciples cried out in fear. However, their hearts were gladdened to hear Him say, *"It is I; don't be afraid"* (Jn 6:20).

Peter went from fear to joy, as no doubt did all the others, but true to his nature Peter went further. He asked Jesus if he might come to Him on the water. Some may consider this a rash request, but Jesus did not. He told him to do so, and Peter did as Jesus bade him do. It was a miracle to be sure, even as it was for Jesus to walk on the waves, but when one reckons it in the light of Jesus' word and power, there is no reason to question it. This was a picturesque moment as, with his eyes upon Jesus, Peter walked toward Him. But when he shifted his attention to the hurricane-like wind, he became afraid and began to sink. *"Lord, save me,"* he cried, and Jesus did so, reaching forth His hand to him. Presently they were in the boat, and the wind ceased immediately. When a storm abated naturally, it did so gradually, leaving the sea rough for a time. This immediate ceasing was a miracle just as much as walking on the water. Evidently the disciples had not been properly impressed by the multiplying of the loaves and fishes, though it is strange that their hearts were so hardened. But they were deeply moved by the spectacular events on the sea, and it is this fact that suggests why Jesus did the latter.

The miracle of the loaves and fishes had served only to fan the disciples' enthusiasm for their mistaken idea concerning the kingdom, and Jesus had soon cooled their ardor in this regard. Perhaps resentment was in their hearts because they had been so rebuked, but the miracles on the sea reconfirmed their faith that Jesus was the Messiah, although He refused to fill their own expected role. Indeed, their confusion may explain why Jesus permitted Peter to come to Him on the water. It was to teach all of the disciples a lesson. As long as they kept their faith centered in Jesus, they were safe. It was only when they became engulfed in the contrary winds of current Messianic expectations that they were in danger of losing their sense of equilibrium and direction. Apparently for the moment the Twelve learned the lesson, for in the boat they worshiped Jesus, saying, *"Truly You are the Son of God"* (Mt 14:33).

It was a fitting end to a turbulent day. Jesus was in the midst of His small worshiping congregation, and their cathedral was a little boat whose vaulting ceiling was a star-studded night sky. Perhaps as they disembarked, the eastern sky was growing light, heralding the dawn of a new day.

4. The Collapse of the Galilean Campaign

While Jesus and the Twelve were crossing the lake, the crowd was doing the same; and upon their arrival in Capernaum, they found Jesus in the synagogue. Seeking to make conversation, they asked Him when He had returned to Capernaum; but knowing their hearts, Jesus replied, *"You are looking for me, not because you saw the signs, but because you ate the loaves and were filled"* (Jn 6:26). It was breakfast time, and they were hungry again. The words "were filled" render a word which may be translated "were gorged." One classical Greek writer used it of a cow eating its food and gorging its stomach but never saying "thanks" or asking whence came the food or for what purpose it was given. These people had missed the point of the miracle altogether. They sought Jesus now only because they were hungry again. In the wilderness temptation Jesus had refused to be a bread messiah, the very kind of messiah they now wanted Him to be. In effect, the people were saying that if Jesus would not claim their loyalty by leading them in a revolution, at least He might do so by feeding them. But Jesus would do neither.

Instead, in the discourse following He sought to lead them to a spiritual understanding of His person and purpose (Jn 6:27–65). Rather than to labor for physical bread which soon perishes, He challenged them to seek after spiritual bread which results in eternal life. In turn they asked what they should do to work the works of God. They were still thinking on a physical level. Jesus said that they should believe on Him whom God had sent. That He spoke of Himself they realized. Ignoring the sign of the day before, they asked Him for a sign in order that they might believe on Him. Then speaking specifically they cited Moses' sign of giving their forefathers manna in the wilderness. The day before, on the basis of the miracles of the loaves and fishes, they had identified Jesus as the Prophet who would be like Moses, but Moses had given new manna each day. Was this not their subtle way of asking Jesus for more loaves and fishes for this new day? If Jesus wanted them to believe on Him, let Him feed them again.

But Jesus sidestepped their ruse by reminding them that it was God, not Moses, who gave the manna. Furthermore, their forefathers ate it and died, but the bread of God that He offered them would give them eternal life. Like the woman of Samaria was with water, they were ready for that kind of bread. Or were they? Nevertheless, still thinking of their stomachs, they said, *"Sir, give us this bread always!"* (Jn 6:34).

So they wanted bread! Very well, Jesus would offer it to them. But it was hardly the bread which they expected, for He said, *"I am the bread of life. . . . No one who comes to Me will ever be hungry, and no one who believes in Me will ever be thirsty again"* (Jn 6:35). He is both meat and drink, the two primary necessities of life. This multitude stood in the presence of Life but would not accept Him. Jesus "came down from heaven," in keeping with the Father's will, to give them life; but they would not receive it.

The mention of heaven gave the dialogue a different turn. The previous day the crowd was ready to make Jesus a political Messiah because He was one of their brethren, out of their very midst. But now *"the Jews,"* probably Jewish rulers, used that fact to dispute His claim. They said, *"Isn't this Jesus the son of Joseph, whose father and mother we know? How can He now say 'I have come down from heaven'?"* (Jn 6:42). But Jesus pressed His point. *"I am the living bread that came down from heaven. If anyone eats of this bread he will live forever. The bread that I will give for the life of the world is My flesh"* (Jn 6:51). *"How,"* asked the Jewish rulers, *"can this man give us His flesh to eat?"* (Jn 6:52). Failing to rise above the physical level, they saw Jesus' teaching as cannibalism.

The murmuring of the Jewish rulers infected the crowd, so finally they said, *"This teaching is hard. Who can accept it?"* (Jn 6:60). Despite the fact that Jesus insisted that He spoke not in physical terms but in words of "spirit" and "life," the multitudes forsook Him. Never thereafter would Jesus' popularity with the people of Galilee be the same. When He made clear that He would not accede to their own concept of the messiah, they left Him. They were more concerned about their stomachs than about their souls.

Evidently the departure of the crowd made the Twelve themselves uneasy. Were they about to follow the people in forsaking Jesus? So Jesus asked, *"You don't want to go away too, do you?"* And Simon Peter, as usual speaking for the group, replied, *"Lord, who will we go to? You have the words of eternal life. We have come to believe and know that You are the Holy One of God!"* (Jn 6:68–69). They had been disappointed the day before. They did not fully understand Jesus' words now, but they were convinced that He was the true Messiah of God. They did not yet fully comprehend the Person and purpose of Jesus, but they were learning; and anchored as they were by their faith in Christ, they would go on growing in the grace and in the knowledge of the Lord.

The events of these past twenty-four hours had clearly demonstrated Jesus' wisdom. The kingdom of God would not come through mass movements but through decisions of faith and commitment within the individual heart. So Jesus continued to focus His efforts on this little group. Yet even among them was one who did not share their faith and commitment, for Judas was a devil.

Therefore, it is evident that one year before the despicable deed Jesus knew His betrayer by name. Only twelve left out of this multitude, and one of them a devil. Still Jesus ever pressed His way forward.

5. An Unhappy Interlude

Even though the Galilean campaign had collapsed, Jesus remained there for a short period before departing on the second withdrawal. During this interval Pharisees and scribes from Jerusalem, the Jewish rulers, accosted Him with a question: *"Why do Your disciples break the tradition of the elders? For they don't wash their hands when they eat!"* (Mt 15:2). Apparently they had noted that the Twelve ignored this custom, which to Jewish rulers was a sin equal to sexual immorality. The elders taught that before eating a Jew should rinse his hands and arms up to his elbows.

Now this had nothing whatever to do with physical hygiene. It was a matter of ceremonial purity. In a sense it was due to superstition, for it was believed that demons rested on one's hands. Therefore, to eat with unrinsed hands was to permit the demons to enter into the body. But the primary purpose in this tradition was related to racial and social prejudice. A Jew in the marketplace might inadvertently touch the garments of a Gentile or publican. He was then considered defiled; hence the rinsing before eating. Even one's eating utensils might have been touched last by the hands or lips of such. So they also must be rinsed.

When a faithful Jew crossed from Gentile territory into a Jewish land, in contempt he stamped the dust of the former from his feet. So this pride of race held the Jews aloof from the rest of men as being cursed of God. Naturally this prevented them from reaching non-Jews for God, which was their divinely given mission. Why should they bother with the rest of the world? For according to them salvation was for the Jews only.

Of course Jesus held no such attitude. He never disobeyed a law of God nor taught that men should do so, but the empty traditions of the elders were another matter. The Jewish leaders, on the other hand, might have ignored disregard for their traditions on the part of the despised "people of the land" or common herd, but to them it was unthinkable that the disciples of a reputed rabbi should do so. Thus their critical question.

In this light one may understand Jesus' reply. He accused the Pharisees of breaking God's commandments in order to keep their traditions, and then He cited one example. God through Moses had commanded men to honor their parents and that anyone who spoke evil of them should be put to death (Ex 20:12; 21:17). Yet in the face of this, the Jews had a tradition known as Corban. This word was applied to that which had been consecrated to God or to the temple. The treasury of the temple was called by this name (Mt 27:6). On the surface this might appear to be a noble practice, but in actuality it was cruel. By it the son of aged parents might escape responsibility for their care simply by saying that all of his possessions were Corban. This meant that they were dedicated to God and the temple. The man might maintain control over them until his death. Or he might even break the pact of dedication. But as long as it was in force, he was free from the responsibility of caring for his parents. Thus Jesus accused the Pharisees and scribes of setting aside the authority of God's commandments and instead pressing the authority of their own traditions.

Then He turned to the multitude that had been listening. This was probably made up of many who so recently had chosen to follow the Jewish leaders rather than Him. He challenged them to hear and to understand what He was about to say: *"It's not what goes into the mouth that defiles a man, but what comes out of the mouth, this defiles a man"* (Mt 15:11). The word rendered *defiles* means to make common or to desecrate. In the ceremonial sense it meant to defile or to pollute. The Pharisees were concerned about ceremonial defilement. Jesus was concerned about the dignity and worth of the whole man.

This pronouncement of Jesus cut across the entire system of the clean and unclean, which was so great a part of the Jewish teachings and practices. This involved not only their religious forms but also their attitude toward other people. Jesus had already asserted His authority with respect to the Sabbath, the temple, and the Law. Now to this list He added the matter of the teachings of God versus the traditions of men. So the breach between Him and the Jewish leaders was evidenced even more.

With Jesus' words still ringing in the ears of the people, He went from them to enter a house. The Twelve came to Him to remind Him that He had offended the Pharisees. Though Jesus had broken with the Jewish teachers, the disciples were not fully severed from them in their minds. Jesus reminded them that this system of teaching was not of God, and, therefore, should be refuted. They were blind guides leading blind people. The end was the destruction of such leaders and those who insisted upon following them.

The tremendous import of Jesus' words about that which defiles a man is seen in Peter's request for more light on the subject. It was to him a revolutionary thought. So Jesus used a well-known physiological fact to show that what a man eats later passes from the body. Therefore, it is not what goes into a man's stomach that desecrates him. It is that which comes from his heart which does so. Those who were so careful to escape ceremonial pollution were unknowingly being polluted in their hearts and souls. This was a much needed lesson then even as it is now.

THE WITHDRAWAL INTO SYROPHOENICIA

This encounter with the Pharisees prompted Jesus to depart from Galilee on a second withdrawal, and it may even have helped in determining the place

Harbor at Tyre, showing the ancient Phoenician harbor, facing northwest

of retirement. Of course, at that time of year, the cool breezes of the seacoast would prove inviting, but a deeper meaning than that is involved in the Gospel accounts.

Jesus and the Twelve journeyed to the region of Tyre and Sidon, an area on the Mediterranean coast south of modern Beirut, Lebanon. It was Syrophoenician territory and so outside the borders of Israel. Therefore, in going to this Gentile territory, it seems that Jesus did so as a direct challenge to the attitude of the Pharisees. This becomes even more apparent as the story develops.

Shortly after arriving in this area, Jesus was confronted by a woman whose daughter was possessed by an unclean spirit. Over and over the mother cried out to Him for help. Now this woman was not only a Gentile, or non-Jewish, but she was also a Canaanite, a descendant of the despised pagans who had inhabited the land before the Israelite invasion. There could hardly have been one who would be more despised by the Jews and by them to be considered beyond the scope of God's love and mercy. In all likelihood Jesus' foreknowledge that He would meet her had led Him to this region.

This woman had heard of the wonderful powers of Jesus. People from this area had been among the crowds following Him in Galilee, and possibly because of their reports, she believed Jesus to be the Jewish Messiah. At any rate she kept on calling to Jesus, *"Have mercy on me, Lord, Son of David! My daughter is cruelly tormented by a demon"* (Mt 15:22). But Jesus ignored her cries. The disciples were embarrassed by her and asked Jesus to send her away, but He answered them, *"I was sent only to the lost sheep of the house of Israel"* (Mt 15:24).

Why did Jesus ignore the woman? And why did He answer the disciples as He did? Some say that He was testing the woman's faith. Others even accuse Jesus of sharing Jewish prejudice, which was later broken down by the woman's persistence and this in spite of His words to the Pharisees about their traditions. Still others insist that Jesus was not yet ready to enlarge His ministry to include non-Jews, even though He had already done so on occasion.

When all elements of this incident are considered, it seems most likely that Jesus acted as He did in order to teach the Twelve a lesson. What He had taught them by word, He now demonstrated by His actions. In effect this woman was symbolic of the entire Gentile world. It is quite evident that the Twelve still shared the prejudices of the Jews toward non-Jews. It is so easy to be enslaved by a vicious system toward others en masse, but it is quite another thing to see that system in operation against one individual. Therefore, in this event Jesus held up a mirror before His disciples in order that they might clearly see themselves and the entire Jewish attitude toward other people. In effect, He acted that part as an object lesson to them.

Finally, when Jesus continued to ignore the woman, she came and knelt before Him. In reply to her agonizing plea, *"Lord, help me!"* Jesus said, *"It isn't right to take the children's bread and throw it to their dogs"* (Mt 15:26). The Jews regarded themselves as the children of God. To them the Gentiles were dogs or wild beasts. Even though Jesus softened this attitude by using the diminutive "little dogs" or household pets, the disciples would catch the point. And the woman seized upon Jesus' choice of words by replying, *"Yes, Lord . . . yet even the dogs eat the crumbs that fall from their masters' table!"* (Mt 15:27). Let the Jews have the full meal. All that she was asking was for a few morsels that fell from the table. True, she was not a Jew, but she was a personality created by God, and as such she was capable of responding to God's love and grace.

The lesson was over. Therefore Jesus said, *"Woman, your faith is great. Let it be done for you as you want"* (Mt 15:28). And her daughter was healed from that hour. Not because she was a Jew, which she was not. Nor because she was a non-Jewish Canaanite. But because she had faith. If so unlikely a prospect, according to Jewish standards, could believe and share in the grace of God, there was no reason to withhold the gospel of the kingdom from anyone. This was Jesus' way of saying to the Twelve what the Lord later said to Peter alone: *"What God has made clean, you must not call common"* (Ac 10:15). The Twelve had seen a parable enacted. Only later did they grasp its meaning.

THE WITHDRAWAL INTO THE DECAPOLIS

From Syrophoenicia Jesus and His little band traveled north and east until they came to the region of the Decapolis on the eastern shores of the Sea of Galilee, (notice how He avoided the Jewish area and the territory of Herod Antipas), but even here He could not avoid the crowds. They brought their sick to be healed by Jesus, and when He healed them, *"they gave glory to the God of Israel"* (Mt 15:31).

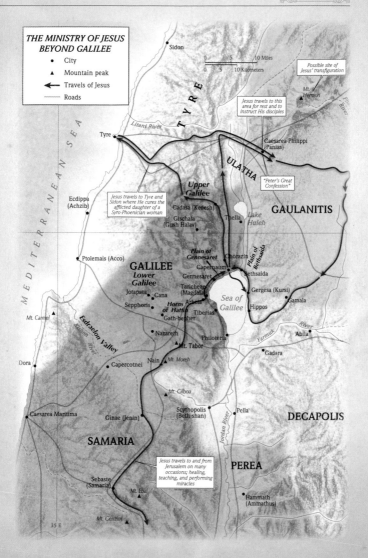

THE MINISTRY OF JESUS BEYOND GALILEE

- • City
- ▲ Mountain peak
- ← Travels of Jesus
- — Roads

Possible site of Jesus' transfiguration

Jesus travels to this area for rest and to instruct His disciples

"Peter's Great Confession"

Jesus travels to Tyre and Sidon where He cures the afflicted daughter of a Syro-Phoenician woman

Jesus travels to and from Jerusalem on many occasions; healing, teaching, and performing miracles

Sidon

0   5   10 Miles
0   5   10 Kilometers

Mt. Hermon ▲

TYRE

Litani River

Caesarea-Philippi (Panias)

Tyre

ULATHA

GAULANITIS

Upper Galilee

Cadasa (Kedesh)

Gischala (Gush Halav)

Thella

Lake Huleh

Ecdippa (Achzib)

MEDITERRANEAN SEA

Ptolemais (Acco)

Plain of Gennesaret

Chorazin

Plain of Bethsaida

GALILEE
Lower Galilee

Capernaum

Bethsaida

Jotapata

Cana

Gennesaret

Taricheae (Magdala)

Sephforis

Horns of Hattin

Arbela

Sea of Galilee

Gergesa (Kursi)

Gamala

Hippos

Mt. Carmel ▲

Esdraelon Valley

Kishon River

Gath-hepher

Tiberias

Philoteria

Yarmuk River

Abila

Nazareth

Mt. Tabor ▲

Dora

Capercotnei

Nain ▲ Mt. Moreh

Mt. Gilboa ▲

Gadara

Caesarea Maritima

Ginae (Jenin)

Scythopolis (Beth-shan)

Pella

Jordan River

DECAPOLIS

SAMARIA

PEREA

Sebaste (Samaria)

Mt. Ebal ▲

Hammath (Ammathus)

Mt. Gerizim ▲

35 E

This is a significant statement. The title "God of Israel" suggests that these people were not Jews but Gentiles. Decapolis was a Gentile or Greek area. So the crowds now following Jesus were most likely Gentile in nature.

At this juncture Jesus performed His second miracle of feeding the multitude, this time about four thousand men, besides women and children. The general pattern of the two feedings was similar, but the details were different. Some interpreters see the account of this latter feeding as a repetition of the former, but the fact that Jesus later referred to both as separate events clearly identifies them (Mk 8:19–20).

Following the feeding of the four thousand, Jesus made a brief visit to Galilee in the area of Magadan (Dalmanutha). No sooner did He arrive back in Jewish territory than He was attacked by the Jewish leaders. But this time something new was added, for along with the Pharisees Jesus was also attacked by the Sadducees. Evidently word had reached Jerusalem that the Pharisees were not doing very well in opposing Him. So reinforcements were dispatched in the form of the rationalistic, realistic Sadducees. This suggests the desperation of Jesus' opposition, for nothing short of that would have produced this coalition of two groups so bitterly opposed to each other. Like the Pharisees and Herodians earlier, so now these widely diverse groups found a common cause in their enmity toward Jesus.

They came to Jesus challenging His messiahship by demanding that He show them *"a sign from heaven."* Earlier the scribes and Pharisees had demanded a "sign" (Mt 12:38). Now the sign must be from "heaven." Quite naturally this additional demand shows the hand of the Sadducees, for they did not believe in signs and especially *"a sign from heaven."* However the Pharisees had a hand in this also. "Signs" on earth were one thing. They believed in them, but *"a sign from heaven,"* perhaps some cosmic disturbance, would be even greater. In neither case did this coalition believe that Jesus could produce such a "sign." Even if the Pharisees believed that He was capable of doing so, since He had refused to work signs on demand, they probably figured that He would not comply this time. In any case their demand would serve to discredit Jesus.

Again the Lord refused to be lured into their trap. Instead, by referring to well-known meteorological facts, He said that they were capable of predicting the weather by reading signs in the heavens but that they were incapable of discerning "the signs of the times." A spiritual revolution was transpiring all about them, but they did not see it.

So once again He gave them only the sign of Jonah, or the sign of His resurrection from the dead. That would be *a sign from heaven* par excellence, but when it came, they did not accept it. Such is ever the reaction of unreasoning prejudice. With these words Jesus left them and departed on His fourth withdrawal.

THE WITHDRAWAL INTO CAESAREA PHILIPPI

This time Jesus took a boat across the Sea of Galilee, landing at Bethsaida Julias. He was passing through the general area of the first retirement on His way to the region of Caesarea Philippi. On the way across the sea, He warned the Twelve against the teachings of the Pharisees and Sadducees and the way of life represented by Herod Antipas. At last Jesus expected some privacy in which to teach the Twelve concerning the King and the kingdom. He would not be an earthly king like Herod, nor would His kingdom fit into the erroneous ideas of the Pharisees and Sadducees. So He prepared for His forthcoming teaching by seeking to negate those contrary systems of life and thought.

1. The Region of Caesarea Philippi

Several reasons probably led Jesus to select this area for His fourth retirement, which probably involved several months of this period. It was now evidently summertime, and the area about the Sea of Galilee is unbearably

Banias waterfall near Caesarea Philippi. Here Jesus gave His disciples an exam concerning His identity.

hot at that time of year. So Jesus led the Twelve into the cool of the mountains. Furthermore this was Gentile territory far removed from the Galilean multitudes who had cast their lot with His enemies. It was outside the domain of Herod Antipas and in that of Herod Philip who had shown no apparent interest in Jesus. It was an area into which Jesus had not gone before. This, plus the comparatively sparse population, promised relief from the crowds and an unbroken opportunity to teach the Twelve. Time was now of the essence.

2. The Testing of the Twelve

For almost three years Jesus had been gradually unveiling Himself as the Christ, the Son of God. Since the calling of the Twelve, He had concentrated more and more on teaching them this truth, and this amid the cross currents of the erroneous concepts of the Jews. How well had the disciples learned their lesson? Examination time had arrived.

Immediately preceding the examination, Jesus had withdrawn from the Twelve to pray. While this was a period of great stress for Him, to the disciples it was vacation time. The region about Caesarea Philippi contained many items of historical interest. It requires little imagination to visualize the Twelve in holiday mood looking at these things and seeking to identify them with certain historical persons. It was probably in such an atmosphere that Jesus came to them with the question, *"Who do people say that the Son of Man is?"* (Mt 16:13). Possibly without turning from their present interest, they replied, *"Some say John the Baptist; others, Elijah; still others, Jeremiah or one of the prophets"* (Mt 16:14). These were the current opinions among the multitudes, but note that they did not mention some of the less flattering opinions.

Then Jesus shocked them into alert attention with the question, *"Who do you say that I am?"* (Mt 16:15). That was quite another matter. The answer was of utmost importance for both them and Jesus. Were they merely a part of the multitudes? Or had they been able to discern the self-revelation of Jesus?

Perhaps the disciples for a moment looked at one another in stunned silence, and then their spokesman replied. Simon Peter said, *"You are the Messiah, the Son of the living God!"* (Mt 16:16). So in the atmosphere of these dead gods, Simon rose to the occasion, and by their silent assent the others passed the examination with him.

No wonder, Jesus exclaimed with joy; *"Simon son of Jonah you are blessed because flesh and blood did not reveal this to you, but My Father in heaven"* (Mt 16:17). Here is that word *blessed* again. So with that faith in Jesus, Simon and the others had within them all that is necessary to live a full and abundant life, and they had not received this faith through the leaven of the Pharisees, Sadducees, or Herod. Neither had it come by man's reason. It was God's revelation that had broken through this variety of opinions to enable them to see God's glory in the face of Jesus Christ. Furthermore, Simon had fulfilled Jesus' prophecy concerning Him. He had indeed become Cephas, a stone (Jn 1:42). *Cephas* is the Aramaic equivalent of the Greek word *petros*. So Simon was now Simon Peter.

With this Jesus made one of the greatest pronouncements of the ages. The Father had revealed one truth. Now Jesus ("and I also say") revealed another: *"And I also say to you, that you are Peter, and on this rock I will build My church, and the forces of Hades will not overpower it. I will give you the keys of the kingdom of heaven, and whatever you bind on earth will have been bound in heaven, and whatever you loose on earth will have been loosed in heaven"* (Mt 16:18–19).

These have become some of the most debated words as to meaning that Jesus ever uttered. Were they spoken to Peter alone or to the Twelve? What did He mean by "Peter" and "rock"? What is the nature of the "church"? And what did Jesus mean by the *"keys of the kingdom . . . bind . . . and loose"*? Quite obviously they cannot be bypassed without some discussion.

Roman Catholic interpreters insist that Jesus spoke to Peter alone. This position is based upon Jesus' use of the singular pronoun *you*. However, it should be recalled that Peter, a person, replied to Jesus' question as the representative of the Twelve. Therefore, it may be inferred that, in turn, Jesus replied to the Twelve through Peter, a person. This position is supported by the fact that later Jesus spoke the words about binding and loosing to the entire group where He used the plural pronoun *you* (Mt 18:18). Indeed, in this latter passage the words were spoken with reference to the action of a local congregation. This within itself enlarges immeasurably the meaning of Jesus' words spoken to Peter.

Furthermore, those who insist that Jesus spoke to Peter alone equate *Peter* and *rock*. Thus they hold that the church was founded upon Peter as the first pope and that to him and his successors in that office are entrusted "the keys of the kingdom" or the power to forgive or not to forgive sins. Let it be said, however, that there is no evidence in the New Testament to support the supremacy of Peter. Nor does early Christian history lend aid to the idea that he was ever a pope, an office which developed much later. The fact that Peter's name always appears first in the list of the Twelve should not so be construed. At best he was first among equals, by virtue of his self-appointed position as the spokesman for the group. To be sure he played a prominent part, along with others, in first-century Christianity, but his contemporaries certainly did not accord to him any place of superiority (cf. Ac 11:1ff.; Gl 2:11ff.). Peter himself regarded his position not as an elder above other elders but as one among them (1 Pt 5:1).

An examination of Jesus' words substantiates these positions. Take, for instance, the words *Peter* and *rock*. The former is the masculine *petros*, a small stone. The latter is the feminine *petra*, a ledge rock or foundation rock. So a *petros* is a small stone broken off of a *petra* and partaking of its nature.

Perhaps when Jesus uttered these words, He was looking at the large ledge rock that was the foundation upon which the city of Caesarea Philippi was built. At least that thought could well have been in the picture. Some insist that Jesus spoke in Aramaic making no such distinction in the word *rock*. Even if this be true, it must be admitted that when he wrote in Greek Matthew had made the distinction evidently portraying Jesus' meaning.

Even in the word *petros* Peter did not regard himself as a rock different from other Christians or the foundation itself. For in 1 Peter 2:5–6 he pictures Jesus Christ as the foundation and believers in Him as living stones (*lithoi*) used in the building of "a spiritual house," the Church.

Now if the "rock" does not refer to Peter, to whom or what does it refer? It is held by some as referring to the faith of the apostles that Jesus is the Christ, the Son of the living God, but this would mean that the Church is built upon the faith of persons. This would be in conflict with the words in 1 Peter 2:5–6 where Christ is the foundation and believers are living stones out of which the "spiritual house" house is built. It is more in keeping with other scriptural teachings to say that Jesus as "the Christ, the Son of the living God" is the *petra* or ledge rock upon which the Church is built. This would explain why Jesus had waited until such a moment to make this pronouncement. Until He was accepted as such by His followers, there was no true basis upon which to found the Church. In a very real sense the Church existed the moment a group of believers received Jesus as Christ, the Son of the living God. But when such a group clearly avowed that faith, as here, Jesus formally pronounced that out of such believers He would build His Church with Himself as its foundation.

However, strange to say, theologians have dwelt so long and ardently upon the identity of the *petra* that the heart of Jesus' statement has been largely lost, for He said, "On this rock I will build My church." In the Greek text *My* is in the emphatic position. Why this emphasis? It is because of the nature of the Church.

The word *church* was not a new addition to man's vocabulary. It was a much used word, *ekklesia*, meaning "the called out ones" or "assembly." In the political sense it was used of the assembly of the citizens of certain Greek cities, granting them the privilege of self-rule by the Roman Empire. It was a local democratic assembly acting within the framework of the laws of the empire. This usage is found in the New Testament (Ac 19:39). Furthermore, in the Greek translation of the Old Testament, it is used to refer to the nation of Israel assembled before God (Dt 31:30), and it is so used in the New Testament (Ac 7:38; Heb 2:12). In this sense the word *ekklesia* speaks of a theocratic assembly or one ruled directly by God. Both of these uses of the word were familiar to the Twelve.

So, in effect, Jesus said, "The Greeks have their assembly and the Jews have their assembly. Now I will build my assembly." In the New Testament, in the Christian sense, *church* is used largely to speak of a local church operating through democratic processes under the lordship of Jesus Christ. But it is also used in the general theocratic sense to refer to all of the redeemed people of God through the ages assembled before Him and under His rule. Comparing Matthew 18:17 with Matthew 16:18, it is evident that Jesus used the word *church* in both senses. So when He spoke of the Church, He referred to that "spiritual house" built out of "living stones" with Him as the foundation. Quite obviously only those who believe in Him as "the Christ, the Son of the living God" can in truth be a part of it in either the local or general sense.

Jesus also spoke of the enduring nature of His Church. *"The forces of Hades will not overpower it"* (Mt 16:18). The word translated *forces* is literally "gates." Hades was the abode of the dead. The word *overpower* means "to have strength against." Gates are to keep one either out or in. Those inside the abode of the dead are trying to get out, and Jesus promised that "the gates of Hades" shall not have strength against His Church (redeemed ones) to keep it in the abode of the dead. It is true that in Christ the Church shall triumph over the powers of evil, but here the Lord's promise is with respect to the resurrection out of the abode of the dead.

Now what did Jesus mean by *"the keys of the kingdom of heaven"*? The answer is found in a literal translation of the words that follow: *"And whatever you bind on earth is already bound in heaven; and whatever you loose on earth is already loosed in heaven"* (Mt 16:19). Thus it seems that heaven has decreed that when certain things are done on earth, they shall have been done in heaven. Now this obviously cannot refer to the power of forgiving or not forgiving sins being conferred upon any person or group of persons, for the Bible clearly teaches that only God can do this. Even He forgives sin on the basis of the gospel of grace through the redemptive work of Christ. In this light, therefore, may it not be said that the gospel is "the keys of the kingdom"? Keys are for either locking or unlocking doors.

Therefore, evidently Jesus was saying that He was entrusting to His Church the gospel of Christ. If the Church binds the gospel on earth by not proclaiming it, heaven has already decreed that it is bound in heaven. On the other hand, if the Church looses the gospel on earth, heaven has already decreed that it is loosed in heaven. Or to put it another way, heaven has already decreed that men can be saved only by believing the gospel. If it is bound, there is no other way by which men can be saved; but if it is loosed, men will believe it, and those who do will be saved. Thus Jesus bestowed upon His Church not only a great privilege but a greater responsibility.

Nevertheless, in spite of the foregoing events, Jesus enjoined the Twelve not to tell any man that He was the Christ. Though they believed Him to be *"the Christ, the Son of the living God,"* they did not yet comprehend the full meaning of these words. They must first learn the true nature of the Christ and of His kingdom before they were ready to use *"the keys of the kingdom."*

3. The Crucifixion and Resurrection Foretold

In the above light one can understand why Jesus chose this particular time to begin plainly to teach the Twelve about His death and Resurrection. For it was through this redemptive work that God would be able to forgive sins or to deal with man on the basis of grace rather than on the basis of law.

This was no new note in Jesus' teaching, for He had alluded to it in a veiled fashion many times. Now He began to speak of it plainly. Only six months remained before His death. Therefore, *"From then on Jesus began to point out to His disciples that He must go unto Jerusalem and suffer many things from the elders, chief priests, and scribes, be killed, and be raised the third day"* (Mt 16:21). The fact that He *"began"* implies that He continued to do so.

That this instruction was needed is seen in the reaction of Simon Peter. He *"began"* to rebuke Jesus for so speaking, insisting that such should never happen to Him. Truly they were not ready to tell any man that He was the Christ. A conquering and reigning Christ, yes! But one who would die—never! They were still wedded to the messianic ideals of their age. Evidently Peter's mind went blank with the words *"be killed."* He seems never even to have heard Jesus say, *"And be raised the third day."*

In response Jesus turned suddenly upon Peter, saying, *"Get behind Me, Satan!"* (Mt 16:23). He was a stumbling block across Jesus' path to the cross. He who had so recently spoken a revelation from God was now the very voice of Satan. He recoiled at the thought of Jesus' dying, but Jesus told him that anyone who proposed to follow Him must be prepared to die also. Any man who sought to save his life by taking the easy way would lose it. Only those who were willing to lose their lives for Jesus' sake would find the true meaning of life.

The disciples were not yet free from the Jewish concept of the Messiah and His kingdom, but that system would soon pass away. Jesus said, *"There are some standing here who will not taste death until they see the Son of Man coming in His kingdom"* (Mt 16:28). Here He looked even beyond His Resurrection, for all of the Eleven lived beyond that point. Obviously Jesus was not speaking of the end of the age, for none of those present lived until then. In Jewish apocalyptic thought any great intervention of God in history was regarded as a *"coming."* The only such event that some, not all, of the Twelve lived to see was the destruction of Jerusalem in AD 70, so evidently it was to this that Jesus referred. It marked the fall of the Jewish nation and of the Jewish system of religion, which was so powerful in Jesus' lifetime. Thereafter Christianity was completely divorced from Judaism, and by the world was regarded as a religion in its own right. It was in this sense that they saw *"the Son of Man coming in His kingdom."*

So the old system is passing away, and the full revelation of God in Christ is rapidly coming to its full fruition. These things Jesus declared in the vicinity of Caesarea Philippi.

4. The Transfiguration of Jesus

One week later Jesus took Peter, James, and John and went up into the slopes of a high mountain, possibly Mount Hermon. It had probably been a week of strained relations between Him and the Twelve. While they regarded Him as the Christ, they still did not understand His nature as such. It is possible that during this week the conversation with Peter about the cross had been repeated many times, for the fact that Jesus "began" to teach and Peter "began" to rebuke Jesus suggests repeated action in this regard.

At any rate in the mountain Jesus *"was praying"* (Lk 9:29). For what He was praying is not stated. Perhaps He was praying that somehow God would give to the three disciples such a demonstration as to His person that it would clear their minds of any mistaken ideas about Him. If so, His prayer was soon answered, for suddenly He *"was transformed in front of them"* (Mt 17:2). In that moment His garments became glistening white, and His face shone as the sun.

Why was He transformed? Some hold that it was to encourage Jesus to go on to the cross in spite of men's thoughts to the contrary. However, there is no evidence that He had ever entertained any idea of avoiding the cross. Therefore, was the Transfiguration for Jesus' benefit or for that of His disciples? The answer may be found in the words *in front of them*. It is possible that in His night vigils as He prayed alone, in perfect communion with the Father, this had happened before with no human being to see. But now He "was transformed *in front of them*" (author's emphasis).

And they saw Him in His glory. This was no light shining upon Jesus from without. It was His deity shining forth from within. Here Jesus is seen in His perfect humanity-deity. It was as if a wick having been turned down low were

Cranes flying over the Hula Valley with Mount Hermon in the background

suddenly turned up to full strength. The deity that had been present in Jesus all the while was suddenly turned up to white heat. Had there been one flaw in His character, this outrushing of deity would have killed Him, even as sudden heat shatters a lamp chimney that has a flaw in the glass.

In this moment Moses and Elijah appeared talking with Jesus. Why these two Old Testament figures? Because in a very real sense they were representative of the Old Testament revelation. "Moses and the prophets" was a common Jewish designation for their Scriptures: Moses symbolized law and Elijah symbolized prophecy. And of what did they speak? The Greek text says that they "spoke of His death, which He was about to accomplish in Jerusalem" (Lk 9:31).

Even though the three disciples were drowsy at the outset, this supernatural phenomenon must have shocked them into a full awareness, and they most likely listened to this conversation. They heard these representatives of the Old Testament talking with Jesus about the thing they had been unable to comprehend. In effect they had a preview in real life of Jesus' words spoken to His disciples after the event. *"These are My words that I spoke to you while I was still with you, that everything written about Me in the law of Moses, the Prophets, and the Psalms must be fulfilled.... This is what is written: the Messiah would suffer and rise from the dead the third day"* (Lk 24:44,46).

However, Peter was so enraptured by the scene that he missed the point of it. For he said, *"Lord, it's good for us to be here! If You want, I will make three tabernacles here: one for You, one for Moses, and one for Elijah"* (Mt 17:4). The Feast of Tabernacles or Booths was approaching, and Peter may have been suggesting that they remain there to celebrate it. During this feast it was customary for faithful Jews to dwell under booths or small brush arbors. This was to commemorate the dwelling in booths of their fathers in their wilderness wanderings.

Even as Peter spoke, a luminous cloud overshadowed them. It was the Shekinah glory of God's presence, for out of the cloud came a voice saying, *"This is My beloved Son. I take delight in Him. Listen to Him!"* (Mt 17:5). As at His baptism, so here, the Son is still well pleasing to the Father. It was His approval of all that Jesus was saying, and they were to hear and heed Him.

But was not this approval of the Son also a rebuke for the disciples? For they were still wedded to the current views of the Christ derived from an erroneous interpretation of their Scriptures. Furthermore, instead of holding Jesus distinct and apart from all others, Peter's suggestion about the tabernacles had proposed that Jesus be but one among three. His proposal placed Jesus alongside Moses and Elijah, not superior to them. He was but another teacher that had come from God, rather than the Teacher who fully revealed both the Old Testament Scriptures and the Father's will. So the Father said that no longer were they to "hear" Moses and Elijah. They were to "hear" Jesus alone as He unfolded the true meaning of the Law and the Prophets.

In stark terror at the voice out of the cloud, the disciples had fallen on their faces. Meanwhile the scene had disappeared, and when at Jesus' touch and reassurance they looked up, *"they saw no one except Him—Jesus alone"* (Mt 17:8). Moses and Elijah had vanished from view—only Jesus remained. This was the lesson of the Transfiguration. The Old Revelation merged into the New with its fulfillment in Jesus. There would still be times when the disciples would have difficulty in this matter, but they never forgot this experience (2 Pt 1:17–18; 1 Jn 1:1–3). Not until after the resurrection of Jesus from the dead would it become clear, and for that reason Jesus commanded that until then they were not to reveal this experience to any man.

5. The Return to Galilee

Shortly thereafter Jesus and the Twelve returned to Galilee. On the way back the Lord continued to teach about His rapidly approaching death and resurrection. Hopefully Peter, James, and John now understood better the meaning of His words. The other disciples who knew nothing of what happened on Mount Hermon certainly did not comprehend them. None of the group dared to question Jesus further about the matter. At least, this time there was no protest from Peter, but they all *"were deeply distressed"* (Mt 17:23) at the prospect.

Back in Capernaum Peter was confronted by those who were supposed to collect the half-shekel temple tax. It was to be paid by every male adult Jew at the time of the Passover. Since Jesus and the Twelve had been out of Galilee since that time, they had not paid it. The collectors asked Peter whether his teacher paid this tax, and he answered in the affirmative. Even though Jesus was the Lord of the temple, He did not ignore this obligation. Therefore, He told Peter to catch a fish in whose mouth he would find a shekel with which to pay the tax for both of them. This was the nearest Jesus ever came to working a miracle for His own benefit, but even this was primarily for the sake of Peter and the collectors, lest He offend the latter.

Throughout the past six months Jesus had focused His teaching upon the King and the kingdom. Therefore during this brief sojourn in Capernaum, the disciples reasoned among themselves about which one should be the greatest in the kingdom of heaven. Using a little child as an object lesson, Jesus taught them that humility, not selfish ambition, was the kingdom criterion of greatness. Possibly their reasoning had erupted into harsh words and hurt feelings, so Jesus taught the Twelve how Christians should settle their differences. The injured party should take the initiative in a personal confrontation with the offender. Rather than to air his grievance to others, he should tell it to the offender alone. Failing there, he was to take one or two other Christians with him. If this failed, the matter should be brought before the local congregation. If the guilty one refused to hear the church, he was to be regarded as a Gentile and a publican. Such an unrelenting spirit would indicate that he

"Unless you . . . become like children" (Mt 18:1–5)

was not himself a Christian in the first place. This power of discipline Jesus deposited in the church, and when it acted in His spirit, He assured the body that He would be present with them in the action.

This teaching brought the inevitable question from Peter. *"Lord, how many times could my brother sin against me and I forgive him? As many as seven times?"* (Mt 18:21). The rabbis taught that one should forgive three times, so Peter thought that he was being generous. But Jesus punctured his ego by saying, *"Seventy times seven"* (Mt 18:22). It is hardly conceivable that one would offend another so many times, so, in effect, Jesus taught unlimited forgiveness. Forgiveness should not be measured by a mathematical formula but by one's spirit.

The Feast of Tabernacles was drawing near, so Jesus' brethren, His half brothers, suggested that He should go to Jerusalem. Any man who wanted public recognition in Palestine should not confine His wondrous works to Galilee. In their unbelieving state they were either unaware of or else chose to ignore the fact that Jesus had already performed many miracles in Jerusalem with little appreciable results.

For the time Jesus chose to remain in Galilee. His brothers proposed to tell Him how to do His work, but His time to challenge Jerusalem fully had not come. However, after His brothers had departed for Jerusalem, probably in a caravan, Jesus also went to the feast in secret or traveled only with the Twelve.

So approximately six months before the Crucifixion, Jesus ended His ministry in Galilee and its environs. Henceforth, possibly with one brief interval, He concentrated on Judea, Perea, and Jerusalem. The opposition to Him, which had been growing from the beginning, finally would rise to a mighty crescendo of hate. The hour of the power of darkness was drawing ever nearer, and when it finally arrived, Jesus' hour would come.

CHAPTER VI
THE LATER JUDEAN MINISTRY

This phase of Jesus' ministry covered about three months, from the Feast of Tabernacles until the Feast of Dedication. The time was the fall and early winter of AD 29. This period began in Jerusalem and continued in Judea. At one point Jesus visited Bethany, and then at the close of this ministry He returned to Jerusalem for the latter feast. It was a period marked by a growing and sharper conflict between Jesus and the Jewish rulers.

THE FEAST OF TABERNACLES

The Feast of Tabernacles was the most popular of all the Jewish feasts. As Pentecost, held fifty days after the Passover, was the feast of the first fruits and marked the beginning of the wheat harvest, Tabernacles was the feast of the general harvest marking the end of the harvest season. It was held early in October and was a time of great rejoicing, something akin to an American Thanksgiving. This feast was also called the Feast of Booths. It commemorated the wanderings of Israel in the wilderness and God's care for His people. The feast lasted for eight days, the first and last days being days of holy convocations.

JESUS COMES TO THE FEAST

At the beginning of the feast, Jerusalem was buzzing with excitement. Jesus had not yet made an appearance, but it was generally expected that

He would do so. It had been about eighteen months since He had visited Jerusalem. The Jewish rulers' hostility in His previous visits had demonstrated their unwillingness to believe in Him. Indeed, on the last visit before this time, they had sought to kill Him because He had healed a man on the Sabbath, so Jesus had deliberately avoided Jerusalem.

However, the Jewish leaders through their emissaries had kept in touch with Jesus' work in Galilee. Their hostility had continued to mount, and so some kind of crisis was anticipated at this feast. Therefore the Jewish rulers were searching diligently for Him throughout Jerusalem.

The multitudes themselves were not immune to the tense situation. Fearing their rulers, they did not dare to discuss Jesus openly, but they whispered among themselves about Him. Some championed His cause as a good man. They had either seen or heard of His good works, but others, having listened to their leaders, accused Him of leading the people astray.

About the middle of the week, Jesus suddenly appeared in the temple area teaching the people. In the listening crowd were some of the Jewish leaders, maybe some of their professional teachers. They wondered at Jesus' learning, and so they raised the question as to the source of His knowledge since He *"hadn't been trained"* (Jn 7:15). Here was a peasant carpenter who had attended none of their schools. Yet He posed as a rabbi. What is more, He was doing so great a job as to cause the professional rabbis to wonder. Since they did not teach Him, He must be self-educated. Nevertheless they accused Him of not being an accredited rabbi.

Jesus replied by disclaiming that He was self-taught. But He made a greater claim. He was taught of God. Furthermore, if any man would follow His teaching, He would discover that it had God for its source. A self-taught teacher presented his own ideas and aspired for recognition and glory, but Jesus sought only to glorify God. Then He pressed His argument by turning the tables on His accusers. They claimed to be authorities in the Law of Moses. Yet they did not keep that Law. As proof He cited their efforts to kill or murder Him on His previous visit to Jerusalem. In response the Jews denied any knowledge of such an attempt. *"You have a demon! . . . Who wants to kill You?"* (Jn 7:20), they asked. In essence they called Him insane.

However, Jesus' accusation had its effect on the crowd. Even though their rulers sought to kill Him, they were allowing Him to teach openly and were doing nothing about it. Could it be that the rulers knew that Jesus was the Messiah? On the other hand, so they reasoned, this could not be. For according to their popular, but unscriptural, theology, when Christ should appear no one would know from where He came—and they knew that Jesus was from Nazareth. Even if their theology had been correct, they apparently were ignorant of the place of His birth. Jesus replied that even though they did know some things about Him, they were ignorant of the God who sent Him. This angered the multitude so that some in mob violence sought to seize Him, but since His hour had not yet come, they were unable to do so. Jesus would die according to a divine plan and purpose, not by means of mob violence. The immediate occasion of this unsuccessful attempt was a division within the crowd itself. Some raised the question as to whether even if Jesus were not the Messiah, the Messiah Himself would do greater things than Jesus was doing!

This reaction of some of the crowd alarmed the Pharisees who heard it. Therefore they sought the aid of the chief priests (Sadducees) to silence Jesus. Once again this unnatural and infamous coalition occurred. A detachment of temple police was sent to arrest Jesus and bring Him for trial before the Sanhedrin. Apparently He had won the crowd to a hesitant belief that He could be the Christ, so evidently there was a delay in carrying

Recently discovered pool of Siloam in Jerusalem. As part of the annual Festival of Booths, water was drawn from the pool of Siloam and poured out on the altar as an offering.

out the order to arrest Jesus. The temple police bided their time waiting for the right moment to do so.

Finally the last or eighth day of the feast arrived. One of the major features of the celebration was that each day for seven days the priests brought water in golden pitchers from the Pool of Siloam, through the city and into the temple. This pool may still be seen today just outside the east wall of the city. Originally its water flowed down the valley, but for military purposes Hezekiah had dug a tunnel bringing the water inside the city walls. In modern times this tunnel has been excavated, revealing on its walls an inscription telling of the digging of the tunnel.

When the priestly procession arrived in the temple, the water was poured out in commemoration of the water God had provided in the wilderness and to remind the people of the prophecies concerning the coming of God's Spirit upon His people. During this procession the priests chanted

Isaiah 12:3, *"You will joyfully draw water from the springs of salvation."* However, these promises had not yet been fulfilled, so as a reminder of this on the last day of the feast, during a holy convocation, the priest repeated this ritual. Only this time their pitchers were empty. Salvation, the water of life, and the Spirit of God were still a hope for the future.

Jesus was standing and watching this ceremony. Suddenly the proceedings were interrupted by His cry: *"If anyone is thirsty, he should come to Me and drink! The one who believes in Me, as the Scripture has said, will have streams of living water flow from deep within him"* (Jn 7:37–38). He proclaimed Himself as the fulfillment of the promises and the prophecy. Judaism ran into a dead end of frustration, but in His death men should find the water of salvation. And He would send the Holy Spirit upon them. As in Galilee He had proclaimed Himself to be Bread for the hungry, so in Jerusalem He offered Himself as Water for the thirsty. It was a momentous occasion indeed!

Jesus' cry electrified the crowd. Immediately some of them declared Jesus to be *"the prophet"* promised by Moses; others plainly said that He was the Messiah. But others, parroting the words of the Jewish rulers, once again raised the question as to Jesus' origin. He was a Galilean, and the Scriptures plainly taught that the Messiah would be out of the seed of David and from Bethlehem. They were still ignorant of the facts concerning Jesus' birth. So the people were still divided concerning Him.

This division did not help the temple police in their mission to arrest Jesus, but their failure to do so was for quite another reason. Later when asked by the chief priests and Pharisees why they did not do so, they said, *"No man ever spoke like this!"* (Jn 7:46). This upset the Pharisees. Jesus had captivated the multitude, and now the temple police. Was it possible that some of the Sanhedrin were secret believers? Or any of the ultra-orthodox

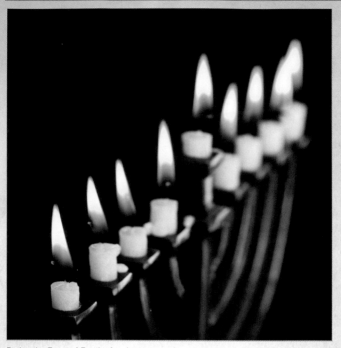

During the Feast of Booths four large menorahs set up around the temple courts burned each night.

Pharisees? One could expect no better of the ignorant, accursed multitudes, but was Jesus even making inroads among the intelligentsia? That the Pharisees were hopeful this was not the case is seen in their question: *"Have any of the rulers or Pharisees believed in Him?"* (Jn 7:48). (The Greek text invites a negative answer.)

Whether one had done so, at least one was approaching that point. Nicodemus was both a Pharisee and a Jewish ruler, a member of the Sanhedrin. He may at this time have been a secret disciple of Jesus. At any rate he spoke directly on Jesus' behalf: *"Our law doesn't judge a man before it hears from him and knows what he's doing, does it?"* (Jn 7:51). Actually he said *"the man"* not "a man." Jesus had the right to be heard in His own defense. The others had no answer for this simple plea for justice. Their only answer was to ridicule Nicodemus: *"You aren't from Galilee too, are you? . . . Investigate and you will see that no prophet arises from Galilee"* (Jn 7:52). This was not true, of course, for Galilee had produced many prophets. It was a matter of their senseless rage and also an expression of Judean pride.

So the Feast of Tabernacles came to a close, and Jesus and the Jewish rulers were farther apart than ever before. Jesus continued to adhere to the Father's will; they stubbornly clung to their own empty system of religious thought. And except for Nicodemus and Joseph of Arimathea, it continued this way until the end.

THE WOMAN TAKEN IN ADULTERY

New Testament scholarship for the most part is agreed that this event (Jn 7:53–8:11) is not a genuine part of John's Gospel. It does not appear in the oldest and best manuscripts but appears first in one of the later ones. Some put it at the close of John's Gospel, and some even include it in Luke. Nevertheless, since it is such a true picture of Jesus, it is generally regarded as a genuine event out of His life. And it is so treated here.

The day following the Feast of Tabernacles, Jesus was teaching in the temple area. While He was so engaged, the scribes and Pharisees brought to Him a woman whom they had caught in the act of adultery. Reminding Him that according to Moses' Law she should be stoned to death, they asked for His judgment. Under ordinary circumstances she would have been executed immediately, but they used her situation as bait by which to entrap Jesus. To them this was more important than punishing the woman.

It was one of those situations into which the Pharisees delighted to place an adversary, for according to them either way Jesus answered, they had Him. If He counseled mercy, they could accuse Him of condoning her deed. If He agreed that she should be stoned, they could accuse Him of being unmerciful.

Jesus did not answer them immediately. Instead He stooped down and wrote on the ground. This is the only time that He is mentioned as writing. It is idle speculation as to what Jesus wrote on the ground, but while He did so, the accusers continued to demand His decision. So rising up, He simply said, *"The one without sin among you should be the first to throw a stone at her"* (Jn 8:7). He challenged such a person to be the executioner. Did Jesus mean only the sin of adultery? According to Him any one of them who had ever looked on a woman lustily was guilty of such in his heart. But Jesus did not specify the sin. He simply said, *"The one without sin."* It could be any sin.

Then leaving the accusers to ponder this matter, Jesus again stooped down and continued to write on the ground. One can imagine the furtive glances passed among these men. Then one by one, the oldest first, they slipped away. Jesus and the woman were left alone. He arose and asked her, *"Woman, where are they? Has no one condemned you?"* (Jn 8:10). *Condemned* means to find guilty and sentence to death. No man did so. And neither did Jesus. He did not condone her sin, but with an admonition to sin no more, He sent her from Him. She called Him *"Lord."* Did she really trust Him as such? It can only be hoped that she did.

THE LIGHT OF THE WORLD

The language of Jn 8:12 naturally follows Jn 7:52. The remainder of John 8 could very well have happened on the last day of the Feast of Tabernacles, but it makes just as good sense to regard it as an event on the day after the Feast and following the matter of the woman taken in adultery. In either case it teaches a tremendous truth regarding the Person of Jesus.

Jesus was still in the temple area, the exact place being the Court of the Women in which were placed the treasury chests to receive the gifts of the worshipers. During the Feast of Tabernacles this court was brilliantly lighted by candelabra. This commemorated the fact that God, during the wilderness wanderings, was Israel's pillar of cloud by day and of fire by night, but now the candelabra were not lighted. This condition corresponds to the empty water pitchers that evoked Jesus' claim to bring the water of life. So now He said, *"I am the light of the world. Anyone who follows Me will never walk in the darkness, but will have the light of life"* (Jn 8:12). Thus to His claims to be Bread and Water, He adds that of Light. These can only be understood as claims to deity, and the Pharisees so comprehended them.

Therefore, once again a debate ensued between them and Jesus. They accused Jesus of bearing false witness since the law required two witnesses to establish a truth. Jesus countered that both He and His Father bore witness to His Person. The Pharisees asked Him to identify His Father. In reply Jesus said that they did not really know Him or His Father. If they knew in their souls who He was, they would also know the Father in like manner. But they knew neither because of their sins; and unless they believed in Jesus, they would die in their sins. They had asked for proof as to Jesus' true identity, and as He had done twice previously in Galilee, so here He cited His death (and resurrection) as proof. Furthermore, He said that they were the ones who would lift Him up on the cross. This Jesus had spoken to the Twelve, but here for the first time He says it to the Jewish leaders.

These words brought a twofold reaction among the Pharisees. Some of them began to believe in Him. To them Jesus said that if their faith were genuine they would in truth be His disciples. They would know the truth that would make them free, but others of the Pharisees were angered at Jesus' words. They asserted that they were Abraham's seed and had never been in bondage to any man. On the surface this was a ridiculous claim, for Israel's history had been one bondage after another. Even then they were a captive nation under the Romans. To give the Pharisees credit at this point, however, they did not recognize this bondage in their hearts.

However, Jesus brushed aside the political implication, declaring that they were slaves to their sin. It was freedom from this that Jesus promised, and then taking up the matter of Abraham, He said that they were not even a true seed of Abraham for they did not the works of Abraham. Because He spoke the truth, they were seeking to kill Him, something Abraham had not done. No, they were doing the works of their father the Devil. They could not answer this charge, so they resorted to slander. As an obvious slur upon Jesus' birth, they said, *"We weren't born of sexual immorality. . . . We have one Father—God"* (Jn 8:41). Jesus replied that if God were their Father they would love Him. Then pressing home His charge, He added, *"You are of your father the Devil, and you want to carry out your father's desires. He was a murderer from the beginning and has not stood in the truth, because there is no truth in him"* (Jn 8:44). Jesus called them liars, murderers, and tools of the Devil. Note the growing intensity of the conflict between Him and the Pharisees.

Stung by these strong words, the Pharisees proved that they were the children of the Slanderer, the Devil. They said that Jesus was a Samaritan and had a devil. In plain language they called Him an insane Samaritan. The Lord denied the charge, stating that He sought to honor God while they dishonored Him. Jesus did not turn back but pressed His point even more strongly. Said He, *"If anyone keeps My word, he will never see death"* (Jn 8:51). In derision the Pharisees replied that now they knew Jesus was insane, for both Abraham and the prophets had kept God's Word, yet they were all dead. They demanded to know if He placed Himself above them.

Jesus answered with a tremendous claim: *"Your father Abraham was overjoyed that he would see My day; he saw it and rejoiced"* (Jn 8:56). He looked for Messiah's day and rejoiced in it. That day was before their very eyes, and they were angry. Not to be outdone, the Pharisees mocked Jesus: *"You aren't fifty years old yet, and You've seen Abraham?"* (Jn 8:57). But they were stunned by His reply: *"I assure you: Before Abraham was, I am"* (Jn 8:58), literally, *"before Abraham was born, I always am."* This was a claim to eternal being or to deity, and the Pharisees so interpreted it; for them this was blasphemy. So they took up stones, intent on stoning Him to death. Mob violence without a trial! When they could not answer His arguments, they had but two choices—believe in Him or destroy Him, and they chose the latter course. This was not the first or the last time they would face this alternative, and their choice was always the same.

But Jesus' time had not yet come, so He left them in the temple area with murderous stones in their hands. However, these stones were but outward symbols of the murder that was in their hearts.

ANOTHER SABBATH CONTROVERSY

While Jesus remained in Jerusalem, His actions caused the old Sabbath controversy to break out again. It was probably the Sabbath after the Feast of Tabernacles, and Jesus met a man blind from birth. Jesus healed him by anointing his eyes with clay and telling him to rinse it off in the pool of Siloam. Having done so, the man returned with his sight. The matter was brought to the attention of the Pharisees, and upon their inquiry the man told them how his blindness had been healed. They had no concern about it except that it had occurred on the Sabbath.

They endeavored therefore to discount the whole thing. Some of them simply said that Jesus could not be from God since He broke the Sabbath, but others asked if a sinner could do such a miracle. Thus divided, they sought to deny that a miracle had taken place. It was simply a trick to deceive the people. To prove this the rulers sought out the man's parents. They confirmed the fact that their son had been born blind, but they avoided the question as to how the healing had occurred. They feared the Jewish rulers who had already agreed that anyone confessing Jesus as the Messiah should be put out of the synagogue. A Jew might be put out of the synagogue for thirty days, sixty days, or indefinitely. Apparently the third is meant here. It was to them a terrible thing akin to excommunication today. They were regarded as dead and, therefore, could have no dealings with other Jews. Furthermore, they were cut off from the congregation of the Lord. It is little wonder that the parents sidestepped this question.

Instead they told the Pharisees to ask their son because he was of age, and the son handled himself quite well. When asked if Jesus were a sinner, he replied, *"Whether or not He's a sinner, I don't know. One thing I do know: I was blind, and now I can see!"* (Jn 9:25). He did not know about their theology, but he did know about his experience. It is impossible to argue against results.

When the Pharisees continued to bombard the man with questions, he made sport of them. Why were they so persistent? Did they also want to become disciples of Jesus? In reply they avowed that they were disciples of Moses but disavowed any knowledge about Jesus, and the man taunted them all the more. They were supposed to be up on such matters, yet here was a Man who healed blind eyes, and they did not know about Him. Then he seized upon a bit of their own theology. They asked if he thought that Jesus was a sinner. Very well, said the man, *"We know that God doesn't listen to sinners; but if anyone is God-fearing and does His will, He listens to him. Throughout history no one has ever heard of someone opening the eyes of a person born blind. If this man were not from God, He wouldn't be able to do anything"* (Jn 9:31–33). With a slur that he was born in sin and yet proposed to teach them, the Pharisees drove this upstart from their presence. Apparently they did not cast him out of the synagogue, since this required a meeting of the Sanhedrin. But the incident ended on a beauti-

A shepherd holding his staff

ful note. Jesus found the man, led him to believe on Him, and forgave his sins.

However, Jesus was not rid of the tenacious Pharisees. They continued to attack Him with their words, so Jesus called them false shepherds of Israel. They posed as the shepherds of the people, but their only purpose was to ravage them to their own gain. By contrast, in a series of mixed metaphors, Jesus described Himself as the true Shepherd and the Door to the sheepfold. As the good Shepherd He will lay down His life for His sheep to protect them from the wolves that seek to devour them. The wolves of sin were destroying the sheep. The false shepherds were concerned only for their own safety and power, but the good Shepherd will die to save the sheep—not only the sheep in Israel but also the sheep in the whole world.

The Pharisees were seeking to kill Jesus, but they could not take His life from Him. He will lay it down of Himself. He declared that He had authority within Himself to lay it down and to take it up again. This did not mean that Jesus would raise Himself from the dead but that both His death and resurrection would be within His Father's will. Until God is ready, it is useless for the Pharisees to try to carry out their evil purpose. So Jesus departed from Jerusalem, leaving the Jewish rulers to squabble among themselves.

THE MINISTRY IN JUDEA

Following this latest controversy with the Pharisees, Jesus spent the greater part of three months in a brief but intensive ministry in Judea but outside of Jerusalem. At the close of this period, He returned to the city for the Feast of Dedication. This phase of the later Judean ministry is recorded only by Luke (10:1–13:21). One should not be surprised to encounter events similar to some that took place in Galilee. This is a distinct entity in Jesus' ministry among a different people. He did not propose to deprive them of the witness given to Galilee.

1. The Mission of the Seventy

In Galilee Jesus sent the Twelve on a preaching mission. Here in Judea He chose seventy other disciples and sent them on a similar one. As in

Galilee and Samaria so in Judea the harvest was great, but the laborers were so few.

Before sending these forth two by two, He gave them instructions similar to those given to the Twelve, only the instructions given here were limited to their immediate mission. Previously in instructing the Twelve, Jesus had looked beyond the present to the mission beyond His resurrection and extending unto the end of the age, but this present mission was for the immediate need only.

The seventy did as they were told, and they returned rejoicing that even demons were subject to them in Jesus' name. It was a happy time for Jesus also, for in their triumphs He saw the eventual overthrow of Satan's power. This was not to be through the work of *"the wise and prudent,"* such as the Jewish rulers, but through these simple "babes" who were willing to submit unto Him. Satan's power would be broken through Jesus' death and resurrection, and this victory would be proclaimed by His followers and be realized in salvation in the experience of those who believed the proclamation.

Jesus shared this joy with the Twelve, for privately He said to them, *"Blessed are the eyes that see the things you see! For I tell you that many prophets and kings wanted to see the things you see, yet didn't see them; to hear the things you hear, yet didn't hear them"* (Lk 10:23–24).

What a refreshing experience this was for Jesus! After the sophisticated resistance which He had encountered in Jerusalem, this was as a shower in the desert.

2. The Parable of the Good Samaritan

Even though Jesus had left Jerusalem, the Pharisees continued to dog His steps, so on one occasion one of their number, a lawyer or one skilled in interpreting the Mosaic Law, tempted Jesus with a question. He addressed Him as *"Teacher,"* asking what he must do to inherit eternal life. (Apparently Jesus had been teaching on this subject at the time.) Since the man was a specialist in the Law, Jesus threw his question back upon him by asking him what the Law said. Without hesitation the lawyer quoted what the Jews considered to be the heart of the Law: *"You shall love the Lord your God with all your heart, with all your soul, with all your strength, and with all your mind; and your neighbor as yourself"* (Lk 10:27).

Jesus commended him for his answer, saying that if he did these things he would live. The trouble was that the lawyer could not do them perfectly, and that was the point of Jesus' answer. Jesus did say that if one kept the Law perfectly, always, and without one slip he would inherit eternal life, but because of man's sinful nature, this is an impossibility. It is in this fact that Jesus' redemptive work became a necessity.

The lawyer did not wait long to reveal the flaw in his record. Evidently he saw Jesus' point, and so trying to hedge on the stringent requirement of the Law, he asked, *"And who is my neighbor?"* (Lk 10:29). This was a typical hairsplitting trick of religious leaders. They saw no way to hedge on their attitude toward God, but they sought an outlet in the matter of their neighbor. They excluded from this group all Gentiles and especially all Samaritans. It was no matter to them that the word *neighbor* means "the one who is near." The Jews made exceptions on the basis of race. So the lawyer thought that he had found a loophole in the Law.

Jesus quickly plugged up the hole as He related the Parable of the Good Samaritan. This parable related a common experience for those who traveled the highway of blood from Jerusalem to Jericho. It was an area infested with highwaymen, who beat and stripped their victims of money and clothing, leaving them half dead. Obviously the victim in the story was a Jew, and without pressing every detail of the parable, one sees Jesus'

A traveler along the Jericho road to Jerusalem riding on a donkey while his other donkey leads the way. This 12½ mile stretch is the setting for one of Jesus' most famous parables—the Good Samaritan. The road is steep, descending from 2,500 feet above sea level at Jerusalem to 1290 feet below sea level at the Dead Sea. The winding road provides an abundance of blind spots where robbers could hide.

condemnation of the entire Jewish religious system as He pictured the priest and Levite passing by the poor man without rendering aid. But the bombshell in the story was the character whom Jesus made the hero. A despised Samaritan! The last person who would have been expected to render aid to a helpless Jew! (One wonders whom Jesus would pick in a contemporary setting!)

At any rate He described the man's merciful ministry in detail, including his taking the victim to an inn and providing money to pay for his care until he was well. Having completed the story, Jesus let the lawyer himself apply its lesson. Obviously the neighborly man was the Samaritan who showed mercy on the poor Jew. One's neighbor, then, is anyone who needs his help, regardless of his race or of any other difference between men. So

Woman making bread on a tabun (oven)

Jesus said, *"Go, and do the same"* (Lk 10:37). This is a lesson as much in need today as it was then.

3. Jesus Visits Martha and Mary

As Jesus and the Twelve traveled about Judea, they came one day to a certain village called Bethany. It is located just over the crest of the Mount of Olives less than two miles east of Jerusalem. In this village lived two sisters, Martha and Mary, and their brother, Lazarus. Lazarus was probably not at home at this time, since no mention is made of him. In all likelihood this was Jesus' home when He was in the vicinity of Jerusalem. Tourists are shown the possible ruins of this home even today.

As was probably His custom, Jesus visited with the two sisters on this occasion. The scene is quite vivid. Mary sat alongside and somewhat in front of Jesus' feet as she drank in His every word. It was probably late in the afternoon, and Jesus had been walking all day. So Martha, ever the practical one, was busy preparing a meal for Him. It seems never to have occurred to Mary that while man does not live by bread alone he must have bread.

On the other hand Martha was distracted in her anxiety to prepare a sumptuous meal for the occasion. Suddenly she burst in upon the conversation between Jesus and Mary. The language of the text (Lk 10:40) indicates that she reproached Jesus for keeping Mary from helping her with the meal. This speaks for the friendly relations between Him and His friends. He was at home with them, and they enjoyed His company. So Martha's reproach was of a friendly sort.

It requires little imagination to see a friendly smile on Jesus' face as He, in turn, chided Martha. *"Martha, Martha, you are worried and upset about many things, but one thing is necessary. Mary has made the right choice, and it will not be taken away from her"* (Lk 10:41–42). In effect, Jesus said that only one dish was necessary for the meal rather than the many about which Martha was fretting. Mary had chosen the best dish, that of fellowship with Jesus, and it would not be taken from her. Clearly in this incident Jesus sided with Mary.

One's character should not be judged by one incident alone. From this one account Martha has been labeled as a "cook" only, while Mary is pictured as a spiritually gifted woman, but time was to prove the deep faith of Martha. It is possible to be a practical person and one of great faith as well.

4. A Busy Interval

The following weeks were busy ones for Jesus. In the interval between His visit to Bethany and His return to Jerusalem for the Feast of Dedication, He went about Judea teaching and healing. On one occasion after Jesus had ended a season of prayer, one of His disciples asked that He teach them to pray, as John the Baptist had taught his disciples. Jesus had taught them to pray, as in the Sermon on the Mount, but evidently they had not learned their lesson or else had forgotten it. Jesus replied by giving them the substance of the Model Prayer, followed by a parable designed to teach God's great desire to grant prayers that were prayed within His fatherly will.

However, not all of the events were as pleasant as this one. On one occasion Jesus healed a dumb demoniac, and as in Galilee His enemies accused Him of doing so by the power of Beelzebub. Some students would equate this with the incident in Galilee, but there is no reason to suppose that this accusation would not be made in Judea as in Galilee where it occurred twice. In this latter incident Jesus answered the charge in much the same manner as in Galilee except for one major exception. In Judea He said nothing of the unpardonable sin. Instead He used this as the occasion to point out the emptiness and failure of the Jewish religious system.

He pictured one who by the teaching of the Pharisees had been cleansed of an evil spirit. Later the spirit returned to find his life *"swept and put in order"* (Lk 11:25). It was swept clean morally and adorned with rite and ceremony, but it was left empty. The Pharisees gave the man nothing with which to fill his life, so the evil spirit brought into his life seven others, more evil than it was. Thus the latter state was worse than the former. The man had tried Judaism only to find it empty. In his frustration he would be less likely to respond to any other form of religion.

Jesus was ever alert to seize upon an event of the moment to teach a great spiritual truth. On one occasion a man requested that He should make his brother divide the family inheritance with him. Evidently this request came from the younger of two brothers. It seems that the younger wanted an equal share, but Jesus refused to be an arbiter in this family fuss. He never sided forcibly with one sinner against another sinner. He preached to both the will of God, great moral and spiritual principles, leaving them to apply the truth to their own lives. In this situation He did not say to one or to the other what he should do. Instead, *"He told them, Watch out, and be on guard against all greed, because one's life is not in the abundance of his possessions"* (Lk 12:15). The trouble with both brothers was the sin of covetousness. So Jesus said, *"Look out, and guard yourselves against it!"* for even if one's abundance overflows, that is not life indeed.

To illustrate this truth Jesus gave the parable of the Rich Fool. So abundant was the yield of his fields that his barns could not contain it. He then determined to tear them down and build greater ones, and in selfish indulgence said, *"You have many goods stored up for many years. Take it easy; eat, drink, and enjoy yourself"* (Lk 12:19). Jesus did not accuse the man of dishonesty or of unfair labor practices. Neither did He condemn him for being wealthy. His sin was his desire for more that he might indulge his own selfishness. He had no sense of stewardship. Instead of recognizing God as the source of his blessings, he spoke of *"my crops," "my barns," "my goods," "myself."* He thought to feed his soul on things.

"But God said to him, 'You fool! This very night your life is demanded of you'" (Lk 12:20). Literally, *"This night they [things] are requiring your soul of you."* How sad, yet how universally true. It is no wonder that Jesus concluded this interview with a warning to be ever watchful. God provides, but man receives all things as a steward of God, and he is held responsible for his stewardship.

Current events also provided Jesus with teaching situations. Just as He finished His previous discourse, some of His listeners came to Him with the news that Pilate's soldiers had slain some Galileans who were engaged in making sacrifices in the temple. Their own blood had been mingled with that of their sacrifices. No mention of this event is found in any other record outside of Luke (13:1–3), but it is true to Pilate's record nevertheless. In all likelihood these were revolutionaries who had been slain in the temple itself.

Doubtless His informers expected Jesus to express horror at such an act, a feeling which He most surely felt, but His comments were along an entirely different line. He turned it into a lesson on the necessity for repentance. Were these Galileans sinners above that of other Galileans? *"No, I tell you; but unless you repent, you will all perish as well!"* (Lk 13:3).

Then He brought the lesson nearer home. Apparently it was common knowledge that the tower of Siloam in Jerusalem had fallen killing eighteen people. So Jesus added this incident to His lesson. Were these poor people greater sinners than others in Jerusalem who were spared this tragedy? He again answered in the negative, calling upon all to repent.

Before returning to Jerusalem Jesus had one more run-in with the ruler of a synagogue over the Sabbath question. In the synagogue on the Sabbath, He healed a woman who had had a curvature of the spine for eighteen years. She glorified God, but the ruler was angry with Jesus for violating the rules regarding the Sabbath. He cared more for his rules than for this poor woman, but even though he was angry with Jesus, he rebuked the multitude gathered about Him. Evidently he had heard how difficult it was to get the best of Jesus. Therefore, he ordered the people to come for healing on weekdays, not on the Sabbath. Evidently others, perhaps Pharisees, agreed with the ruler, and so Jesus showed him the same courtesy that had been accorded Him. He spoke to the others through him: *"But the Lord answered him and said, 'Hypocrites! . . .'"* (Lk 13:15). He accused them of treating their animals better than they treated people. On the Sabbath they led their animals to water but denied to Him the right to heal this poor woman on that day. Once again He had bested His adversaries, and the multitude rejoiced at both the healing and His putting the hypocrites in their places.

This prompted Jesus to repeat the Parables of the Mustard Seed and the Leaven. He had made small beginnings in establishing the kingdom of God, as was shown by the response of the people, and it would grow until it filled the earth.

THE FEAST OF DEDICATION

The middle of December had arrived, and it was time for the Feast of Dedication. This was one of the lesser feasts among the Jews. It commemorated the dedication of the temple in 164 BC by Judas Maccabeus. Antiochus Epiphanes had defiled the temple by sacrificing a sow on Jahweh's altar.

Model of Solomon's Porch

This along with other atrocities had precipitated the revolt that led to his defeat, so Judas Maccabeus, the hero of the revolution, had led the now free nation in cleansing and rededicating the temple. For the most part this feast was observed in the local synagogues with great rejoicing much like that associated with the Feast of Tabernacles, but since Jesus was in Judea at the time, He attended the feast in Jerusalem.

John notes that *"it was winter"* (10:22) and Jesus was walking along Solomon's porch in the temple area. This was a colonnaded area on the eastern side of the temple formed by a sort of balcony built out over the slopes going down into the valley below. Since it was a covered area, it was usable in any kind of weather.

As Jesus walked along, He was accosted by the Jewish rulers. Apparently they were exasperated by Jesus. They had tried repeatedly to trap Him into an admission as to His true identity. So surrounding Him, they asked, *"How long are you going to keep us in suspense? If You are the Messiah, tell us plainly"* (Jn 10:24).

The point of their demand was *"plainly."* For the sake of argument they assumed that He was the Messiah, so they demanded that He say so in plain words, "I am the Messiah." Jesus had refrained from using this word "Messiah" to them because of the political connotation they put on it. Had they been able to trap Him into using the word, they would have accused Him of plotting a rebellion against Rome, as indeed they did when He later admitted under oath to being the Messiah. So Jesus continued to avoid the word in His dealings with others.

However, He did answer their question about holding them in suspense. He reminded them that repeatedly He had claimed to be the Son of the Father and they had not believed Him. This title had no political meaning however, and so they were not satisfied. Jesus continued by citing the works He did in the Father's name, but they did not believe them because they were not of His sheep. His sheep heard His voice and followed Him. He insisted that He gave them eternal life, they would never perish, and no one was able to snatch them out of His hand. Furthermore, His Father who gave them to Him is greater than all, and no man is able to snatch them out of His Father's hand. Then Jesus claimed oneness with the Father: *"The Father and I are one"* (Jn 10:30).

This last claim was more than the rulers could take. They knew that Jesus plainly claimed identity with God, and to them this was blasphemy— so they reached for their stones. Mob violence all over again! But Jesus stood His ground, asking them for which of His good works they proposed to stone Him. Not for good works, said they, *"but for blasphemy, and because You—being a man—make Yourself God"* (Jn 10:33).

There are those who insist that Jesus never called Himself God, but the Jews so understood Him, and so He did. Taking them at their word, Jesus challenged them that even if they would not believe Him at least they should recognize His works as benevolent ones, and so the works of God: *"This way you will know and understand that the Father is in Me and I in the Father"* (Jn 10:38).

But His words were wasted on them, for their only response was once again to try to arrest Him. However, once again He escaped their clutches, and Jesus left Jerusalem not to return until a few months later when He made His final challenge to the city and its rulers. The die was cast, but still His hour had not yet arrived.

CHAPTER VII
THE PEREAN MINISTRY
THE MINISTRY OF THE GREAT PHYSICIAN

From Jerusalem Jesus traveled eastward, crossing the Jordan River into Perea. Here He entered again into the territory of Herod Antipas, but for the time being He was out of Judea and away from the center of power of the Jewish rulers. It was late in December of AD 29. About three and one-half months remained before the Crucifixion. The records of this period are rather sparse, but they picture Jesus continuing His ministry of teaching and healing, and this He carried out in a more favorable atmosphere than that of Judea. It must have been refreshing to Jesus to find that in Perea many people believed on Him because they had heard John the Baptist preach concerning Him. What a compliment it is to one's preaching about Jesus that men recognize Him thereby!

A WARNING AGAINST HEROD ANTIPAS

At any rate in His reply, Jesus showed His contempt for Herod Antipas. He called him a *"fox,"* indicating that He was aware of his cunning cowardice and of his evil designs toward Him, but He let it be known that Herod would not succeed in his purpose. Jesus' work must continue until He had reached the final time and purpose of His coming, and He wanted the Pharisees to realize this. Jesus did not court danger, but neither did He run from it. His life was held in the Father's will, and besides, *"it is not possible*

PALESTINE IN THE TIME OF JESUS

- City
- City (uncertain location)
- Decapolis city
- Decapolis city (uncertain location)
- ★ Administrative capital
- ▲ Mountain peak
- Major roads
- Other roads
- First procuratorship
- Territory of Antipas
- Territory of Philip
- Syrian territory

Coponius was named the first prefect and established the administrative capital at Caesarea Maritima

ABILENE
Sidon
ITUREA
Damascus
Pharpar R.
Mt. Hermon
Caesarea Philippi (Panias)
Tyre
PHOENICIA (TYRE)
Kadasa (Kedesh)
Gischala (Gush Halav)
GAULANITIS
King's Highway
Raphana
BATANEA
Ptolemais (Acco)
GALILEE
Capernaum
Bethsaida
Jotapata
Sea of Galilee
Gergesa (Kursi)
Sepphoris
Geba
Nazareth
Tiberias
Hippos
Gamala
Mt. Carmel
Xaloth (Chesullothi)
Mt. Tabor
Abila
Adraa (Edrei)
Dora
Legio (Megiddo)
Jezreel Valley
Gadara
Caesarea Maritima (Strato's Tower)
Scythopolis (Beth-shan)
Ginae (Jenin)
Pella
Dion
DECAPOLIS
Aenon
Salim
SAMARIA
Sebaste (Samaria)
Mt. Ebal
Mt. Gerizim
Neapolis (Shechem)
Gerasa (Jerash)
Apollonia
Antipatris (Aphek)
Coreae
Amathus
Joppa
Alexandrium
MEDITERRANEAN SEA
Ephraim (Ophrah)
Gedor (Gadara)
Philadelphia (Amman)
Lydda
JUDEA
Archelais
PEREA
Jamnia
Jericho
Esbus (Heshbon)
Azotus (Ashdod)
Emmaus (Nicopolis)
Jerusalem
Cypros
Medeba
Ascalon (Ashkelon)
Bethany
Hyrcania
Mesad Hasidim (Qumran)
Betogabris (Beth-guvrin)
Hebron
DEAD SEA
Machaerus
Callirrhoe (Zereth-shahar)
Gaza
En-gedi
Masada
IDUMEA
Raphia
Beersheba
Malatha
Arad
Arnon R.
King's Highway
NABATEA
Arabah
Khirbet Tannur
Zered R.

for a prophet to perish outside of Jerusalem" (Lk 13:33). His destiny lay not in Perea but in Jerusalem.

The mention of Jerusalem evoked from Jesus the first of three laments He uttered over the city. *"Jerusalem! Jerusalem! The city who kills the prophets and stones those who are sent to her. How often I wanted to gather your children together, as a hen gathers her chicks under her wings, but you were not willing! See, your house is abandoned to you. And I tell you, you will not see Me until the time comes when you say, 'Blessed is He who comes in the name of the Lord'!"* (Lk 13:34–35).

Jesus' heart was at the point of breaking as He foresaw the end of the city so dear to the heart of every Jew. He saw the storm of her destruction coming. Repeatedly He had offered Himself as her Savior, only to be rejected. He would not enter the city again until His final visit at the beginning of Passion Week. It is worthy of note that although Luke up to this time has not recorded any visit of Jesus to Jerusalem during His public ministry, he anticipates the record of John's Gospel written years after Luke wrote his.

JESUS IN THE HOME OF A PHARISEE

The friendly attitude of some Pharisees toward Jesus is further evidenced by the fact that early in the Perean ministry He was the dinner guest in one's home who was a ruler among the Pharisees. The same thing had occurred one time in Galilee (Lk 7:36–50), although on the former occasion the host himself was critical of Jesus. Of further interest is the fact that both of these instances are told by Luke (14:1–24).

Clearly, however, in the Perean incident the Pharisee who was the host had apparently invited other *"lawyers and Pharisees"* also. As the story develops, evidently they were not friendly toward Jesus; for as they were eating, they were watching Him out of the corners of their eyes.

It was on a Sabbath day. Suddenly a man who had dropsy entered. Seeing him, Jesus asked these watchful lawyers and Pharisees if it was lawful to heal on the Sabbath. When they refused to answer, Jesus healed the man and let him go, and, as once before, He reminded them that they were kinder to their animals than they were to their fellow human beings.

Jesus had noted that when the guests had arrived they had sought out the chief reclining places at the table. They all wanted to be at the head table. Therefore, using this as the basis, Jesus taught them a lesson in humility, a subject about which they knew very little. If one seeks out the chief reclining place and a more honorable person comes, he may be shamed by being asked to give his place to the honorable person. It would be far better to take the least honorable place. It is possible, however, that the host may ask him to take a better place and thus he would be honored before his friends. *"For everyone who exalts himself will be humbled, and the one who humbles himself will be exalted"* (Lk 14:11).

Furthermore, Jesus used the occasion to teach a lesson in true hospitality. He had noted that the host had invited only his own kind to the dinner. Therefore He said that instead of inviting his friends, relatives, or rich neighbors, who in turn might invite him to a dinner, he should invite the poor, lame, and blind to whom he owed no social obligation and from whom he expected no invitation in return. For such an act he would receive no social favor, but he would receive a far greater spiritual blessing.

Jesus' words about a blessing deeply impressed one of the guests, so he exclaimed, *"The one who will eat bread in the kingdom of God is blessed!"* (Lk 14:15). But knowing these Pharisees' attitude toward the kingdom, Jesus cooled his ardor with a parable that was very much to the point. The Pharisees regarded themselves as especially favored of God, so Jesus said that a certain man gave a dinner. He sent invitations to many, for it was customary to invite guests ahead of time. The story presumes that they had accepted the invitation. When the meal was ready, the host sent his servant to tell the guests to come, but they all began to make excuses as to why they could not come. One had bought a field and must go to inspect it. Another had purchased five yoke of oxen and must go to prove them. Imagine making such purchases without first knowing their value! A third said that he had married a wife and could not come. At least he had some excuse!

The point was that none of them really wanted to come, and the host was angered at their refusals. Therefore, he sent his servant into the street to gather poor unfortunates to eat with him. Still there was room. Then he sent his servant to invite chance passersby to come, but none of those who were first invited and excused themselves would taste of the supper.

Obviously the point of the story was that these Pharisees thought they were the privileged of God. They had in their own thoughts accepted God's invitation to be a part of His kingdom feast, but when the kingdom was ready, they refused to participate. So God will invite those who were despised and neglected by them. Because of their obstinate attitude the Pharisees would miss their opportunity.

ANOTHER GROUP OF PARABLES

Throughout His ministry Jesus placed great emphasis on parabolic teaching. At times, as on one occasion in Galilee, He used only parables, but there is scarcely any extended teaching of Jesus in which He did not use one or more vivid pictures in order to make truth live. The fact that so many of His teachings are remembered in connection with some parable shows how effective this method was in presenting truth in living color.

Jesus continued to employ parables in Perea as He had done in other areas where He ministered. Some of them are repetitions as He unveiled

God's revelation to different audiences, but in a rather brief span of time He added new ones that have become some of His best remembered and most beloved parables. Whether by a set purpose or not, Jesus presented them in three groups of three.

The first group was designed to test the sincerity of the multitudes following Him. Jesus never made a play for the crowds. He was concerned about genuineness of purpose rather than the glamour of numbers, so He ever impressed upon men the price they must pay in order to follow Him. This is seen clearly in an incident in Perea.

On one occasion *"great multitudes"* followed Him. Turning to them, He said that to be His disciple a man must choose Him above love for family or even life itself. He must be willing to be a cross bearer, or one on the way to his execution, if he would be a follower of Jesus. He urged these people to count the cost before making their commitment. Then He used the three parables.

Before a man begins to build a tower, he would be wise to sit down and figure the cost to determine whether he can complete it. Or a king would do well to do likewise before he starts a war. If he knows that he cannot win, he would be wise to negotiate with his enemy in order to reach the terms required for peace. *"In the same way, therefore, every one of you who does not say goodbye to all his possessions cannot be My disciple"* (Lk 14:33). Then to drive home His lesson, Jesus repeated the figure of salt. Salt is good or useful provided that it be salty. Otherwise, it is useless and fit only to be cast out, probably to make a roadbed or footpath. Such is the fate of those who are superficial in their commitment to Christ.

This is a necessary truth for every age. If it were followed, it would decrease the quantity of those who profess the faith, but it would certainly

Jesus asked, *"For which of you wanting to build a tower, doesn't first sit down and calculate the cost to see if he has enough to complete it?"* (Lk 14:28).

increase the quality of those who seek to practice it. It is no wonder that Jesus said, *"Anyone who has ears to hear, should listen!"* (Lk 14:35).

The second group of parables was given in response to the criticism of the Pharisees and scribes because Jesus was receiving publicans and sinners and even eating with them. These stories contrast their attitude with that of God regarding such people. While they rejected and despised them, God was ever seeking them to draw them unto Himself in repentance.

The first of these parables was that of the lost sheep. This is one of the most beautiful of all of Jesus' parables, one having been illustrated in both art and music. A shepherd had one hundred sheep, but one was lost from the fold. So he left the ninety-nine to go in search of the one lost sheep, and when he had found it, in true shepherd fashion, he placed it on his shoulder and with rejoicing brought it back to the fold.

Quite obviously the ninety-nine suggest the self-righteous Pharisees who regarded themselves as being safe in God's fold. The one lost sheep corresponds to the publicans and sinners whom the Pharisees regarded as being outside the fold of God. But Jesus concluded the parable by saying

A shepherd caring for a single sheep

that there is more rejoicing in heaven over one repentant sinner than over the many who do not regard themselves as needing to repent.

The second parable was like unto the first. It pictured a woman who had ten pieces of silver but had lost one of them. Jesus portrayed the diligent search of the woman until she had found the lost coin, and He repeated the lesson derived from the first parable.

The third parable, however, took on quite a different turn. Whereas the first two emphasized heaven's joy over finding one lost person as over against those who did not consider themselves to be lost, the third parable contrasted the Father's attitude toward the lost with that of the Pharisees. It is commonly called the Parable of the Prodigal Son, referring to the lost one. Actually Jesus placed His emphasis upon the merciless attitude of the elder brother.

The story is too familiar to need recounting, but certain elements will bear emphasis. The younger son, chafing under the father's discipline, went into a far country where he wasted his inheritance in foolish living. The degree of his degeneracy is seen in that he wound up feeding swine which were not his own. Imagine a Jew in such a predicament! Finally he realized what a mess he had made of his life, and in abject repentance he determined to return to his father's house. In unparalleled art Jesus pictured the yearning heart of the father. The son had determined to request, not that he be restored to as a son, but that he simply be allowed to be as a hired servant. Before he could finish his repentant request, his compassionate father restored him to full sonship. Actually in the father's heart he had never ceased to be a son or the object of his father's love. It was only that his sin had separated him from his father's grace. His forgiveness and restoration waited only upon his repentance, and to celebrate the lost son's return, the father made a great feast.

At this point the true lesson of the parable emerged. The elder brother, instead of rejoicing over his brother's return, sulked because even though he had served his father well he had never been so royally treated. He was not moved by his brother's need but was concerned only with what he considered to be his rights by virtue of his good works. However, the father said to him, *"'Son,' he said to him, 'you are always with me, and everything I have is yours. But we had to celebrate and rejoice, because this brother of yours was dead and is alive again; he was lost and is found'"* (Lk 15:31–32).

There are many truths to be derived from this parable, but as in all parables one should not press every item unduly. The one great truth Jesus taught was the elder son had a self-righteous attitude toward the sinful brother. In stern reality the Lord placed a mirror before the Pharisees to enable them to see themselves and their unmerciful conduct toward all sinners who are still the object of God's love.

The third group of parables deals with the subject of stewardship, and it may have been suggested by the wasteful attitude of the younger son in the preceding story. If so, the first of this third group may imply Jesus' censure of his lack of stewardship. But its meaning affords a much wider application, for it was spoken to Jesus' disciples.

The first parable is usually called that of the Dishonest Manager, but it is nearer to Jesus' lesson to call it the parable of the shrewd manager. A manager or steward owned nothing in his own right. He was a slave who had been entrusted with his owner's property. The word for *steward* really means the overseer of an estate.

A steward who had wasted his owner's goods was called to an accounting, being told that he had lost his position of trust. What could he do? He was not strong enough to do menial toil, and he was too proud to beg. So he decided on a plan to ensure his own future. Going to his owner's debtors, he dishonestly reduced their indebtedness. His purpose was to feather his own nest, reasoning that when he was dismissed from his stewardship those who had benefited by his unjust acts would befriend him in turn. When his owner discovered what he had done, he did not condemn him. Instead he commended him for having acted shrewdly.

It is obvious that if every point of this parable be pressed, then one is in difficulty, for it makes Jesus approve of dishonesty. But He was not dealing in details. He was simply drawing a word picture, which could have been true to life, and then from that picture He brought forth one great truth. While the man still had control of his owner's goods, which were soon to be taken from him, he used them in such fashion as to ensure his own future.

Jesus' lesson is introduced with one phase: *"'For the sons of this age are more astute than the sons of light in dealing with their own people.' Then He added, 'And I tell you, make friends for yourselves by means of the unrighteous money, so that when it fails, they may welcome you into eternal dwellings'"* (Lk 16:8–9). Man, at best, is but a temporary steward of God's possessions. The time will come when "it" will fail or man through death will no longer have these possessions to manage. In the meantime he should so use them as to ensure for him a welcome into heaven by those who preceded him by virtue of his proper stewardship. There is no thought here of one purchasing salvation, but he can so use material possessions as to enable others to receive eternal life. Here are evangelism and missions at their best. Man can best lay up treasures in heaven by investing them in people who are going there. Man cannot serve God and money, but he can serve God through money or through material wealth.

The Pharisees, being lovers of money, scoffed at the whole idea. So to them Jesus uttered the Parable of the Rich Man and Lazarus. The rich man, living in mirth and splendor every day, was their idea of the better life. His very wealth was to them an evidence of God's approval, but the poor, diseased beggar was to them an object of scorn, one whom they considered to be under God's judgment. However, by a sudden turn of events, Jesus pictured these two men in God's sight. For both of them died or entered into Hades, the abode of the dead; and there the positions were reversed. Lazarus was in Abraham's bosom, a Jewish symbol of heaven, but the rich man was in torment. Note that each entered into his condition immediately upon death.

Furthermore, whereas in this life Lazarus had begged for the crumbs from the rich man's table, now in Hades the rich man begged Abraham to send Lazarus to him to dip his finger in water, just a drop, and with it to cool his parched tongue. But Abraham reminded him that whereas in the world there existed between him and the beggar a social gulf of his own creation, in the afterlife there was also a gulf—one of God's creation. Eternity evened up the inequities of time, only everlastingly so.

Then Jesus made the primary point of His lesson. When the rich man found no relief for himself, he requested Abraham to send Lazarus to warn his five brethren not to make the same mistake that he had made. But Abraham reminded him that they had Moses and the prophets. Let them hear them. The rich man said, *"'No, father Abraham,' he said. 'But if someone from the dead goes to them, they will repent.' But he told him, 'If they don't listen to Moses and the prophets, they will not be persuaded if someone rises from the dead'"* (Lk 16:30–31).

So with consummate skill Jesus drove home His lesson. The Pharisees in their smug complacency refused to heed their Scriptures. The end that awaits them is certain, and they will not even hear Him when He rises from the dead.

After a brief interlude, Jesus spoke to the disciples the Parable of the Unprofitable Servant. Lest they should think that through the right use of their stewardship they could purchase the favor of God, He declared that grace is not for sale. After working all day in the field, a slave is ordered to prepare the evening meal for his owner, but the owner does not thank the slave for doing that which is expected of him. Even so, when a man has done his duty, he should expect no special merit or credit. His only hope is in the grace of God, not in his own faithful works.

THE RAISING OF LAZARUS

Suddenly the scene shifts back to Bethany. Lazarus was seriously ill, so Mary and Martha sent a messenger to Jesus in Perea asking Him to come to them. Even though Jesus loved these friends, He delayed going for two days. He knew that soon in Bethany He would glorify God through His greatest miracle and that He also would be glorified thereby. But it would also result finally in Jesus' Crucifixion by which both Father and Son would receive the greatest glory.

When finally Jesus prepared to return to Judea, His disciples warned against it. They remembered the Jews' efforts to stone Jesus, but He reminded them that He would not die before His appointed time. For the moment, *"Our friend Lazarus has fallen asleep, but I'm on My way to wake him up"* (Jn 11:11). Seizing upon this thought, the disciples suggested that if Lazarus was sleeping he must be getting better. Jesus plainly said that Lazarus was dead but that He was glad for His disciples' sake because it afforded an occasion to increase their faith in Him. Thomas then rose to heights of heroism when he suggested that if Jesus were going to

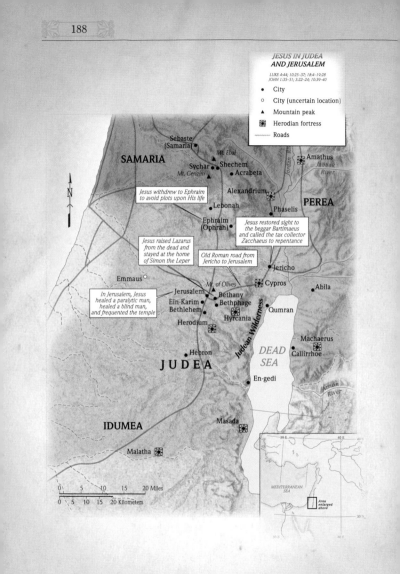

JESUS IN JUDEA AND JERUSALEM

LUKE 4:44; 10:25–37; 18:4–19:28
JOHN 1:35–51; 3:22–24; 10:39–40

- • City
- ○ City (uncertain location)
- ▲ Mountain peak
- ⊞ Herodian fortress
- — Roads

Sebaste (Samaria)

SAMARIA

Mt. Ebal

Sychar   Shechem

Mt. Gerizim   • Acrabeta

Alexandrium

PEREA

Jesus withdrew to Ephraim to avoid plots upon His life

Lebonah

Phaselis

Ephraim (Ophrah)

Jesus restored sight to the beggar Bartimaeus and called the tax collector Zacchaeus to repentance

Jesus raised Lazarus from the dead and stayed at the home of Simon the Leper

Old Roman road from Jericho to Jerusalem

Jericho

Emmaus

Mt. of Olives   Cypros   • Abila

Jerusalem   ▲ Bethany

In Jerusalem, Jesus healed a paralytic man, healed a blind man, and frequented the temple

Ein-Karim   Bethphage

Bethlehem   Hyrcania   Qumran

Herodium

Judean Wilderness

DEAD SEA

Machaerus

Callirrhoe

Hebron

JUDEA

En-gedi

IDUMEA

Masada

Malatha

0   5   10   15   20 Miles

0   5   10   15   20 Kilometers

Amathus
Jabbok River

Arnon River

MEDITERRANEAN SEA

Area enlarged above

what the disciples considered to be certain death, they should go and die with Him.

When they arrived in Bethany, Lazarus had been buried for four days. Friendly Jews from Jerusalem had come to console the bereaved sisters during the seven days of mourning. As Jesus neared the village, He was met by Martha, but Mary remained in the house. Martha, ever the practical one despite her grief, was in charge of things; but Mary was helpless in her sorrow.

There was a note of both rebuke and faith in Martha's voice when she greeted Jesus: *"Lord, if You had been here, my brother wouldn't have died. Yet even now I know that whatever You ask from God, God will give You" (Jn 11:21–22).* Jesus assured her that her brother would rise again, but in her present grief, while it offered comfort in the overall, she still thought in terms of the final resurrection. Then in words which have ever been the pillar of faith upon which bereaved hearts have rested, Jesus said, *"I am the resurrection and the life. The one who believes in Me, even if he dies, will*

View of the ancient village of Bethany, where Mary, Martha, and Lazarus lived. Located on the Mount of Olives' eastern slope, Bethany sat "about two miles" southeast of Jerusalem.

live. Everyone who lives and believes in Me will never die—ever. Do you believe this?" (Jn 11:25–26).

At this point the practical Martha rose to the superlative heights of faith, for she made the greatest confession ever made as to Jesus' Messiahship. Yes, even greater than Peter's. He made his from the exhilarating mountaintop of Jesus' wondrous deeds, but Martha made hers out of the depths of disappointment and grief. Insofar as she could see at the moment, Jesus had failed her. She had sent for Him in her hour of greatest need, and He had not come. In spite of all of this, despite her lack of understanding, out of her pit of frustration, she still declared, *"Yes, Lord, . . . I believe You are the Messiah, the Son of God, who was to come into the world"* (Jn 11:27).

Presently Martha called Mary. When Mary came to Jesus in abject grief, she fell at His feet, saying, *"Lord, if You had been here, my brother would not have died!"* (Jn 11:32). But unlike Martha she uttered no expression of hope. Jesus then asked to be shown the tomb, and amid all the sounds of grief, Jesus also *"burst into tears."* He shared the grief of His friends. Truly He was touched with the feelings of their human weakness, but even in such a tender scene unbelief raised its evil head. Some of the Jews questioned why One who had opened eyes of the blind could not have prevented the death of His friend.

By this time they had arrived before the tomb. Martha protested when Jesus ordered that the stone sealing the tomb be rolled away. By this time Lazarus' body had begun to decompose, for he had been dead for four days.

There is significance in this note of time, for according to one Jewish tradition, the soul hovered about the body for three days in hope of reentering it. On the fourth day the soul departed. There is no evidence that Martha believed this, but in all likelihood the unbelieving Jews did. At any rate there must be no question about what Jesus proposed to do. It would seem, therefore, that Jesus had deliberately timed His miraculous act so as to remove any possibility of denying it. Lazarus was truly dead with no earthly hope of living again upon this earth.

Now Jesus thanked the Father for granting the miracle even before it was performed. Absolute faith of the Son in the Father's will and power! Then with a loud voice He cried, *"Lazarus, come out!"* (Jn 11:43). And he

The traditional site of the tomb of Lazarus in Bethany

did so, still bound in the grave clothes in which he had been entombed. There was absolutely no reasonable room for doubters to deny the miracle, and at Jesus' word they unwound the grave clothes, and Lazarus lived again.

Was this a resurrection? Not in the true sense of the word, for Jesus Himself will be the firstfruits out of the realm of the dead. One is resurrected never to die again. Lazarus was raised but would die once more. In truth this was a resuscitation or the bringing back to life of one who truly had been dead. So Jesus is *"life"* as He is also the *"resurrection."*

What strange and diverse reactions there were to this miracle! Some who saw it believed in Jesus, but others, unmoved by it, simply hastened to nearby Jerusalem to tell the Pharisees what Jesus had done. Since the Pharisees believed in the resurrection of the dead, one would think that this would have been an occasion for rejoicing. But so blinded were they by their hatred for Jesus, the miracle was lost on them—instead it only called them to diabolic action.

THE APPROACHING PASSION

Apparently Jesus intended that the raising of Lazarus should be a direct challenge to the Jewish authorities, and particularly to the Sadducees who through the high priest controlled the Sanhedrin. On two previous occasions He had raised the dead, but these occurred in Galilee. It was always possible for the Sadducees to discount these reports as the idle tales of an ignorant people, but for Jesus to raise a man from the dead within two miles of Jerusalem and the temple was another matter indeed. How could the chief priests deny this fact when it became common knowledge at the very center of their domain? The people of Jerusalem flocked to nearby Bethany to see this man alive who was known to have died. So when Jesus performed this miracle, He sealed His doom insofar as the Sadducees were concerned. He must be done away with.

Whether the Pharisees alone would ever have put Jesus to death is open to question. On several occasions they had been enraged to the verge of mob violence, but even then they evidently lacked the resoluteness to carry out their evil purpose. They might have argued Jesus to death, but killing Him was another matter. On the other hand the Sadducees were realists. Up until this time they had joined with the Pharisees in opposing Jesus, but it was not until He dared to violate their position of denying the resurrection from the dead that they took charge of the situation with a firm resolve to put Jesus to death.

Therefore, when the Pharisees reported the raising of Lazarus to Caiaphas, the high priest, he immediately called the Sanhedrin into session. One senses their exasperated rage in their words: *"What are we going to do since this man does many signs? If we let Him continue in this way, everybody will believe in Him! Then the Romans will come and remove both our place and our nation"* (Jn 11:47–48). They were concerned about their place first, and then their nation. If they did not do something to stop Jesus, they feared a revolution against Rome, which to them would result only in defeat for the nation and their removal from power.

Then Caiaphas took charge. In their excited murmuring the Sanhedrin was finding no solution to their problem. So in coldhearted realism this wily politician reminded them that it was expedient that one man should die for, or as a substitute for, the people rather than to have the nation destroyed. He was perfectly willing to sacrifice Jesus to save his own skin, but he spoke more than he knew. Actually he prophesied the very nature of Jesus' forthcoming death. He used the word *for (huper),* which means a substitute. It was used of one throwing his own body over another to take the blow intended for him. Jesus Himself had used this word when He spoke of the Good Shepherd dying for the sheep.

So they had the solution. It was either Jesus or them, and they all voted for Jesus to be the Substitute. From that moment they took counsel among themselves as they plotted His death.

Did Jesus hear about this conspiracy? Whether or not actual news of it came to Him, He knew the response that might be expected to His challenge. So until such time that He was ready for them to carry it out, He left the vicinity of Jerusalem. He planned to return to the city, but together with His disciples He took a roundabout journey consuming the time until His hour had arrived.

JESUS IN SAMARIA AND GALILEE

The time for the Passover was only a few weeks away. Pilgrims from Galilee would soon be leaving for Jerusalem by the usual route through Perea and thence through Judea to the city. It was probably Jesus' purpose to join such a group. Therefore, He and the Twelve traveled northward out of Judea through Samaria into southern Galilee.

Shortly after arriving in Galilee, they entered into a certain village. There Jesus was accosted by ten lepers pleading that He would have mercy on them and heal them. So again, in keeping with the law concerning lepers, Jesus told them to go and show themselves to the priest. Even though at that moment they had not actually been healed, they had faith to believe that Jesus would comply with their request. They started for the priest, and instantly they were cleansed of the dreaded disease. So eager were they to get the priest to pronounce them healed, nine of them rushed away without even thanking Jesus, but one did turn back, glorifying God as in gratitude he fell upon his face at Jesus' feet. Evidently the nine were Jews, for Luke notes that the one was a Samaritan. In a wistful note Jesus commented on the fact that only this *"stranger"* or alien had returned to give glory to God. Then He added, *"Get up and go on your way. Your faith has made you well"* (Lk 17:19). The words *has made you well* may be rendered "has saved you." It would seem, therefore, that whereas the nine received only physical healing, the one Samaritan, in addition also received forgiveness of his sins, the leprosy of the soul.

Some ever-present Pharisees must have witnessed this miracle. Such a display of power prompted them to ask Jesus when the kingdom of God should come. He replied that it does not come through outward observation, for it is not some outward phenomenon, but an inward experience: *"The kingdom of God is among you"* (Lk 17:21). Then there followed a discourse in which Jesus warned against current errors regarding the coming of the Son of Man. Later, on the Mount of Olives, He repeated much of these same teachings to His disciples.

Why Jesus should suddenly give two parables on prayer is not clear. But He did. One was apparently directed to the Twelve, and the other was aimed at the Pharisees. The disciples were soon to be subjected to great trial. (This may have been the reason for the former parable.) So Jesus *"told them a parable on the need for them to pray always and not become discouraged"* (Lk 18:1). The word *discouraged* means "to give in to evil, to turn into a coward or lose heart, or to behave badly." Any of these meanings makes sense here. They are warned not to do any of these things, and the following weeks reveal how timely was this exhortation. Instead of doing these things they were to pray.

The following parable emphasized that their prayers would surely be heard by God. A widow continually pleaded with a judge to give her justice against an adversary, and after so long a time, even though the judge neither feared God nor had respect for man, he granted her request merely to get rid of her. Then came the lesson. If such a man will grant a poor, helpless widow's request, how much more will the righteous God give heed to the repeated prayers of His own. However, when the Son of Man comes, will He find such a persistent faith on earth? This is a question for every child of God to ponder.

Then Jesus turned His attention to the Pharisees. Perhaps this latter parable was due to the fact that they had asked about the kingdom of God, and because of their self-righteousness they considered themselves to be a part of it. They regarded others nonentities.

Two men went into the temple to pray. One was a proud Pharisee; the other was a despised publican. The Pharisee's prayer was a self-congratulatory soliloquy as to his own soul. He recited his many virtues. Though he addressed God in a formal sort of way, his prayer actually was to himself. It contained no fellowship with God. Not a note of repentance was heard. The only sins he confessed were the sins of others. His only word of praise was thanksgiving that he was not like other men, and especially not like this publican. What a wonderful man this Pharisee considered himself to be. He fasted twice a week, and tithed his entire income—even before taxes! God should be proud to have such a man even condescend to pray before Him. One is amazed that in so few words Jesus could sketch so devastating a picture of the self-righteous man.

With equal skill He portrayed the publican. What a sense of unworthiness he had. Not worthy to approach the altar. Not worthy even to lift his eyes heavenward. In utter despair he beat upon his breast and cried out for mercy: *"God turn your wrath from me—a sinner"* (Lk 18:13). It is actually, *"the sinner,"* as though he were the only sinner in the world. The Pharisee thought of others as sinners; the publican regarded no one as a sinner but himself.

What was the result of these prayers? The publican went home justified or declared just in God's sight. The Pharisee? Well, had not the Roman general Titus destroyed the temple, his prayer might still be beating an empty echo against its walls. It certainly was not heard by God: *"because everyone who exalts himself will be humbled, but the one who humbles himself will be exalted"* (Lk 18:14).

A QUESTION ABOUT DIVORCE

The time arrived when Jesus began His last journey toward Jerusalem, so in company with the Twelve, and probably other pilgrims, He left Galilee. They crossed the Jordan River and headed south through Perea. Great crowds followed Jesus as He both taught and healed on the way.

On one occasion a group of Pharisees came to Him with a knotty question concerning divorce. It was a much debated question among the Jews and provided a most convenient trap into which they might ensnare Jesus. Their question was, *"Is it lawful for a man to divorce his wife on any grounds?"* (Mt 19:3).

To understand this question it is necessary to recall the current teachings on the subject. Among the Jews there were two schools of thought. One teacher, Shammai, taught that divorce and remarriage were permissible only on the one ground of adultery, but another, Hillel, insisted that such was allowable "on any grounds." He based his position on the liberal interpretation of Deuteronomy 24:1—*"If a man marries a woman, but she becomes displeasing to him because he finds something improper about her, he may write her a divorce certificate, hand it to her, and send her away from his house."* This "something improper" was indecent behavior short of immorality, but Hillel placed his emphasis upon "becomes displeasing to him." This he interpreted to mean anything that offended the husband. It might be loss of beauty, boredom in her company, unruly conduct, or even burning his meal.

Quite naturally this was the more popular of the two positions. Evidently the Pharisees expected Jesus to reject it, and thus they would discredit Him with the people. But once more He evaded their trap.

In His reply Jesus ignored both schools of thought. He went back to God's original purpose in marriage. In Genesis 1:27 it was recorded that God had made both male and female, and in marriage they became *"one flesh." "Therefore what God has joined together, man must not separate"* (Mt 19:6). By the words *"male and female"* and *"one flesh"* Jesus pointed to the physical union in marriage. Of course, the spiritual and social aspects of marriage were implied or assumed, but the matter of *"grounds"* is the question related to adultery as over against lesser reasons.

The Pharisees, in turn, countered with another question. If no man was to sever the bonds made by God, why did Moses provide for a bill of divorcement? Jesus pointed out that Moses did not command divorce. He simply improved upon the current practice among the ancient Israelites. Prior to his provision a man simply sent his wife away. The lawgiver merely sought to protect the woman's rights, but, even so, Jesus said that he did this because of the hardness of men's hearts. He insisted that this was not God's original intent in the institution of marriage.

Then Jesus said, *"Whoever divorces his wife, except for sexual immorality, and marries another, commits adultery"* (Mt 19:9). So in this statement as in the Sermon on the Mount, Jesus clearly allowed one cause for divorce and remarriage. In such a situation the innocent party could remarry, but the guilty one could not.

Some interpreters question the genuineness of the exception in these two passages, but the manuscript evidence is strong for their acceptance.

It is objected that Luke 16:18 and Mark 10:11–12 do not include it, but in logic the argument from silence is the weakest of arguments. The question of *"grounds"* was not in the context of Luke's passage. Nor can it be contended that Mark's statement parallels that in Matthew. In the latter Jesus was answering the question of the Pharisees about *"on any grounds,"* but Mark clearly says that the statement in his Gospel was made to the disciples *"in the house"* (10:10). Jesus had already dealt with the matter of grounds, and His remark in Mark 10:11–12 must be read in that light. It is even argued that this exception is not genuine because it makes Jesus side with Shammai against Hillel. Why not, if Shammai agreed with Jesus? But Jesus went behind Shammai to the original nature of marriage as given by God in the beginning.

Why did Jesus permit this one cause for divorce and remarriage? In its very nature marriage consists of spiritual love, a social contract, and physical union, and in that order. To break a marriage in God's sight it must be in the reverse. One can be *"one flesh"* with only one person. Paul later warned against becoming one with a harlot (1 Co 6:15–16). As long as the oneness of flesh remains, the marriage cannot be broken; but when that basic provision (Gn 1:27) has been destroyed, the innocent party is free to dissolve the other phases of the marriage relation if he so chooses. So when Jesus gave this one exception, He planted a safeguard to society, the home, the family, and the individual.

Apparently the disciples themselves were in sympathy with the popular view of Hillel, for they said to Jesus that in the light of His words, it is good or expedient not to marry. Jesus replied that for various reasons marriage is not the best option for some, but the monogamous marriage is still the ideal for man and woman.

JESUS AND CHILDREN

In the wake of this discussion on marriage and divorce, certain parents brought little children to Jesus that He might put His hands on them and pray, but the disciples rebuked the parents. Maybe this was out of concern for Jesus that He not be unduly burdened. More likely they resented the interruption, since they wanted to hear more on the subject under consideration. At any rate they reflected the current trend to discount the importance of children.

However, Jesus was indignant at their action. By contrast He took the little ones into His arms and blessed them, saying, *"Leave the children alone, and don't try to keep them from coming to Me, because the kingdom of heaven is made up of people like this"* (Mt 19:14). It was a brief but beautiful interlude, for Jesus was not only concerned about the home and marriage. He loved and blessed little children who are the crowning blessing of both.

THE RICH YOUNG RULER

While Jesus was still in Perea, a most touching incident occurred. Suddenly out of the crowd a young man ran and kneeled before Him. *"Good Teacher, what must I do to inherit eternal life?"* (Mk 10:17), asked the young man. His concept of *"good"* was inadequate. So leading him as a teacher does a pupil, Jesus reminded him that this quality in its absolute sense belongs only to God. By implication Jesus, however, accepted the tribute, for He Himself was/is God.

In reply to the question, Jesus told him to keep the Commandments; and when the young man asked, *"Which?"* (Mt 19:18), Jesus quoted the last six, substituting for *"covet"* its larger sense of love for one's neighbor (Mt 19:18–19). The young man said that from his childhood he had kept these, yet something was lacking. Then Jesus put His finger on the man's problem—his possessions, for he was wealthy. *"If you want to be perfect, . . . go, sell your belongings and give to the poor, and you will have treasure in heaven. Then come, follow Me"* (Mt 19:21).

This should not be construed to mean that to become a Christian one must take the vow of poverty. Jesus was dealing with this man's particular besetting sin, love for his possessions. With another it may be quite a different sin. It is anything that replaces supreme allegiance to God.

When Jesus quoted the Commandments, He mentioned only those having to do with one's relation to other men. He said nothing of those relating one directly to God, namely, the first four. This omission was by design. The young man made a good score in his dealings with men, but what

"It is easier for a camel to go through the eye of a needle than for a rich person to enter the kingdom of God" (Mt 19:24).

about his relation to God? Thus Jesus' prescription to him becomes understandable. Unknowingly he had broken the first four commandments by making his wealth his god. So Jesus told him to put this god of mammon out of his life, for no man can be a slave to God and to mammon.

On this score the young man failed the test. He went away sorrowful, but, nevertheless, he went away from Jesus. There was sorrow in the heart of the Savior also, not only for him but for all who trust in their wealth instead of God. For this reason it is difficult, though not impossible, for a rich man to enter into the kingdom of heaven. Jesus said, *"It is easier for a camel to go through the eye of a needle than for a rich person to enter the kingdom of God"* (Mt 19:24). This picturesque statement troubled the disciples, for like their contemporaries they regarded wealth as an evidence of God's favor toward a man. If a rich man cannot be saved, *"Then who can be saved?"* they asked. Jesus replied that while it is impossible for man to enter heaven by virtue of his wealth, it is possible for God so to change his nature that he will give his supreme allegiance and love to God.

This thought of forsaking one's wealth for God suggested another problem to the Twelve. They had forsaken all to follow Jesus. So what would be their reward? Evidently some of them felt that such reward should be gauged by their length of service rendered to Jesus. Those who had followed Him from the first should receive more than those who came later. Jesus reminded them that they would surely be rewarded. However, the terms and degrees of that reward were in the wisdom and grace of the Father. Heaven's standards are different from those of earth. Therefore, *"many who are first will be last, and the last first"* (Mt 19:30).

To illustrate this truth Jesus spoke the Parable of the Laborers in the vineyard. Early one morning a man employed laborers for his vineyard. They agreed to work for a denarius, the going rate for a day's labor. At

A vineyard in northern Israel, near the Lebanese border

intervals throughout the day, the man hired other workers, telling them that he would pay them a just wage but specifying no figure. Finally, at the eleventh hour, probably one hour before sundown, he hired still others. To them nothing was said about wages.

The Mosaic Law required that poor laborers should be paid at the end of each day. So when the hour arrived, the owner paid the last group first, and to each he gave a denarius, the same amount that he gave to all of the others. The first group complained bitterly about this. Since they had worked all day in the heat, they felt that they should receive more. But the owner reminded them that they had made a bargain, and he had abided by it, so they had no basis of complaint. The money was his, and he could do with it as he chose. The other laborers had trusted him to deal fairly with them. The last group said nothing whatever about wages, but if he rewarded their faith in him, that was his business.

The lesson was quite clear. If one chooses to work for God on the basis of rewards, God will keep His bargain. The disciples need not worry at that point, but the fact is that a sovereign God rewards a man on the basis of grace rather than works. That the Bible teaches rewards in heaven is true, but, even so, grace is God's impelling motive. For when the Christian does all that is required of him, he is still an unprofitable servant. He and all that he has belong to God in the first place.

THE REQUEST OF SELFISH AMBITION

The burden of the approaching passion rested ever more heavily upon Jesus. However, as though He were eager to meet it, He walked ahead of His disciples. Every step brought Him closer to Jerusalem and His final *"rendezvous with destiny."* The Twelve were both amazed and afraid as they noticed the strange look on Jesus' face. Finally He took them aside from the other pilgrims and once again reminded them of that which awaited Him in Jerusalem, but strange to say they were still unable to comprehend His words. Despite Jesus' repeated instructions the disciples still thought in terms of a political kingdom.

This fact was quite evident in the request that James and John made to Jesus through their mother. Jesus' words about His coming suffering had been wasted on them, but they had seized upon His recent promise that the Twelve would sit upon twelve thrones to judge the tribes of Israel (Mt 19:28). So they came to Jesus asking that He should command that these two brothers should sit one on His right hand and the other on His left in His kingdom. They wanted the two chief seats of power.

What was involved in this request? It has been suggested that Peter had been demoted since his rebuke of Jesus near Caesarea Philippi (Mt 16:22), and so the mother of James and John wanted these principal seats for her sons. However, Peter's demotion is pure conjecture. A more reasonable explanation is possible—Was it not that they sought to gain an advantage because of a family relationship? Since their mothers were sisters, James, John, and Jesus were cousins. So, in effect, this request was a proposal that the seats of power in the coming kingdom should be kept within the family circle. The other ten disciples resented this request. Their resentment probably was not due to the fact that they had made this request at such an inopportune time. For none of them in their present state was fully capable of being sympathetic toward Jesus' passion. It more likely was resentment that James and John had beat them to the request and had sought an unfair advantage because of the family relationship.

What was Jesus' reply to the request? He told them that they were unaware of what they were really asking. Were they able to share the cup which He was to drink or to be baptized with the baptism awaiting Him? These, of course, had reference to His passion, but unaware of this, James and John glibly responded, *"We are able"* (Mt 20:22). There was no martyr spirit in their reply. Jesus replied that indeed they would do so, even though at the time they were ignorant of the fact. However, it was not Jesus' prerogative to assign these chief seats. This had already been determined by the Father. And what was the basis of this determination? Not selfish ambition but selfless service.

To illustrate this truth Jesus related a parable. In doing so He contrasted the pagan standards of greatness with those of the kingdom of God. Among the pagan Gentiles their rulers lorded it over their subjects, and their high officials exercised authority over them. But in the kingdom of God one who aspires to greatness must become the most menial servant, and if one would be first in the kingdom, he must become a slave to his brethren. In essence, pagan greatness was determined by the number of people who served a person, but Christian greatness was to be determined by the number of people one served. Jesus Himself is the prime example of the latter, for the Son of man did not come to be served by menial slaves but to render such service to others and to give His life as a ransom for many. Truly the selfish ambition of the disciples appeared all the uglier when it was subjected to the pure light of self-renunciation on the part of Jesus.

THE HEALING OF BLIND BARTIMAEUS

Following this incident Jesus resumed His journey. With His company He traveled across the Jordan River into Judea. They had passed through the old town of Jericho and were nearing the new or Roman Jericho built by Herod the Great. Alongside the road sat two blind beggars, one of them named Bartimaeus. From the crowd accompanying Jesus they heard the name of Jesus, so they began to cry out, *"Lord, have mercy on us, Son of*

New Testament Jericho

David!" (Mt 20:30). They had heard how Jesus had healed the blind, and so they wished to make the most of their one opportunity. The crowd without mercy sought to silence them, but they simply cried out all the more.

Hearing their cries, Jesus stopped and called them to Him. His own interest in the blind men prompted others to lead them to Him. It was a pathetic moment as Jesus asked what they wished of Him. They had but one request, that they might receive their sight. Therefore, in compassion Jesus touched their eyes, and they saw. What a glorious experience it must have been for them, for the first thing that they saw was the glory of God in the face of Jesus Christ. It is no wonder that they praised God and followed Jesus in the way.

THE CONVERSION OF ZACCHEUS

At this point in His journey Jesus was passing through Roman Jericho. This city was not only a tropical winter resort but also an important trading center for balsam and other items. Located as it was near the entrance to Judea from the east, it was a tax-collecting point not only for transient trade but for the local commercial enterprises.

Evidently Zaccheus was the head of tax collections, something like a tax commissioner. Under him were other publicans serving in subordinate positions. Quite naturally Zaccheus was a rich man, made so by his oppressive methods of tax collecting, and for this reason he was a hated and despised man among his neighbors.

Zaccheus was also low of stature. He wanted to see this notable man, Jesus, but because of the crowds he was unable to do so. Luke in vivid language says that *"he kept on seeking to see Jesus"* (19:3, literal translation). He ran from one spot to another trying to find an opening in the crowd, but because of his stature he was unable to locate one through which he might peep. Finally, he ran ahead. He saw a sycamore tree whose low branches made it possible for him to climb into it and to get a vantage point.

When Jesus came to this tree, He looked up at Zaccheus, telling him to come down quickly because He proposed to visit the chief publican in his home. Overjoyed he did as Jesus had said, but as they entered into his house, the crowd became as a hive of buzzing bees. They were shocked that Jesus would enter into the home of so notorious a sinner. The people of Jericho must have been especially indignant, for there probably was not a man among them who had not suffered injustice at Zaccheus's hand.

The publican heard this grumbling. So as soon as he and Jesus were in the house, he said, *"Look, I'll give half of my possessions to the poor, Lord! And if I have extorted anything from anyone, I'll pay back four times as much!"* (Lk 19:8). This was quite a confession of guilt, for the original language assumes that he was guilty of extortion. The Mosaic law required that such a person should return fourfold the amount so taken, and Zaccheus was prepared to do it. This was quite a change of character for him, but in addition he proposed to give half of his wealth to the poor. From a dishonest money-grubber he suddenly became a philanthropist. Such a change could only come from a changed nature.

In response to such evidence Jesus said, *"Today salvation has come to this house . . . because he too is a son of Abraham"* (Lk 19:9). He was a Jew by birth; he had become a true son of Abraham, the father of the faithful, by the new birth.

Apparently the multitude had stood just outside the house so as to hear the proceedings. Apparently, therefore, Jesus said to them, *"For the Son of Man has come to seek and to save the lost"* (Lk 19:10). This was Jesus' answer to their grumbling. Thus they could understand His reason for daring to show such a benevolent interest in a despised chief publican, and in so doing not only had He saved a lost man; He had served society as well. Now in place of an extortioner they had a child of God for their commissioner of taxes. This was ever Jesus' method. He proposed to save society by placing redeemed men and women in society, and nowhere is this more clearly seen than in His dealings with Zaccheus.

Furthermore, the work Jesus did He expects His people to do. This is the sense of the Parable of the Pounds which He related on this occasion. Like the king in the story, Jesus will soon leave His people. During His absence He will leave His work in the hands of His subjects. They are to use it for His purpose, and eventually there will come a day of reckoning. In keeping with how they attend to affairs, either they will be rewarded or else will be deprived of such. Faithfulness or the lack of it in their task will be evidence as to their true relation to Him. Blessed are they who are His true disciples! Woe upon those who are not!

With this Jesus departed from Jericho, traveling through the wilderness of Judea up the steep and winding road leading to Jerusalem.

CHAPTER VIII
THE FINAL PUBLIC MINISTRY

For three and one-half years the drama of divine redemption had been moving toward a grand climax. It was fitting that it should come in Jerusalem, and at what more appropriate time could it have occurred than in connection with the Feast of the Passover? This feast commemorated God's redemption of His people from Egyptian bondage, and that through the slaying of the paschal lamb.

Furthermore, the Passover was the most largely attended of all the feasts. Every male adult Jew living within twenty-five miles of Jerusalem was required to attend. Voluntarily they came from everywhere. No matter where a Jew lived in the world, it was his hope at least one time to celebrate the Passover in Jerusalem. Understandably, Jesus chose such a time for the dramatic finale to His redemptive ministry, for it was the season involving not only the largest but also the most representative group of Jews, which might be assembled in one place.

JESUS' ARRIVAL AT BETHANY

The year was AD 30. The season was springtime. The day was Friday before the Passover. Already Jerusalem was bustling with pilgrims who had arrived early in order to perform certain purification rites before the Passover began. Among them was one major topic of conversation:

Jesus, and whether He would come to this feast. Most people knew that the Jewish rulers had given orders that anyone knowing of His whereabouts should report it to them, for they purposed to head off any crisis by arresting Him on sight.

Jesus arrived in the vicinity on Friday, but instead of going into the city, He stopped at Bethany where He probably spent the night and Saturday with Martha, Mary, and Lazarus. Word soon spread that He was there. As a result, many people flocked to Bethany not only to see Jesus but Lazarus also. This man whom Jesus had raised from the dead was quite a curiosity, in fact so much so that the chief priests had now determined to put him to death along with Jesus. It was their only answer to a fact which they could not deny but would not accept.

THE ROYAL ENTRY

Finally Sunday morning arrived. The time for Jesus' final challenge to Jerusalem and the Jewish rulers was at hand. Jesus' entrance into Jerusalem on this occasion is commonly called His "Triumphal Entry," but as it turned out, it was everything but triumphant. The term *triumphal entry* suggests a king returning triumphantly to his capital city after a war. Such was done in great pomp and splendor with the king riding on a white horse followed by his trophies of victory. Jesus' Triumphal Entry was His arrival back into heaven following His Resurrection and Ascension (Eph 4:8).

The Lord's entrance into Jerusalem may more appropriately be called His "Royal Entry," for He came as a King of peace. On previous occasions He had entered the city quietly and without any show of publicity, and while at those times He had taught and had demonstrated that He was the Son of God, even indirectly had admitted to being the Christ, He had refused to make such a claim "plainly." Now the situation was quite differ-

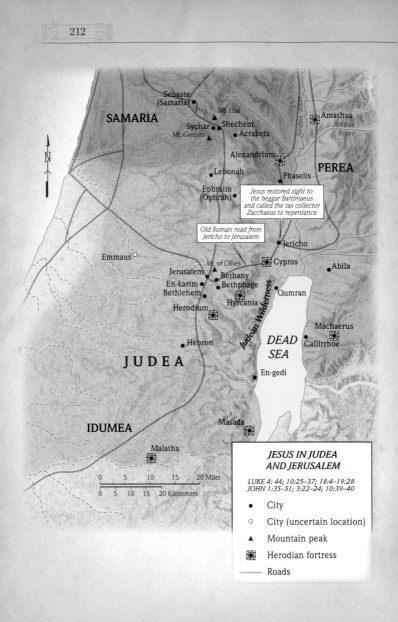

Sebaste
(Samaria)
Mt. Ebal
SAMARIA
Amathus
Jabbok River
Sychar
Mt. Gerizim
Shechem
Acrabeta
Alexandrium
PEREA
Lebonah
Phaselis
Ephraim
(Ophrah)

Jesus restored sight to
the beggar Bartimaeus
and called the tax collector
Zacchaeus to repentance

Old Roman road from
Jericho to Jerusalem

Jericho

Emmaus
Mt. of Olives
Cypros
Abila
Jerusalem
Bethany
En-karim
Bethphage
Bethlehem
Hyrcania
Qumran
Herodium
Judean Wilderness
Hebron
Machaerus
DEAD SEA
Callirrhoe
JUDEA
En-gedi

IDUMEA

Masada

Malatha

| 0 | 5 | 10 | 15 | 20 Miles |
| 0 | 5 | 10 | 15 | 20 Kilometers |

JESUS IN JUDEA
AND JERUSALEM

LUKE 4: 44; 10:25–37; 18:4–19:28
JOHN 1:35–51; 3:22–24; 10:39–40

- City
○ City (uncertain location)
▲ Mountain peak
▣ Herodian fortress
— Roads

ent, for an examination of His entry into Jerusalem on this occasion clearly demonstrates that with deliberate purpose He challenged the city and her religious leaders with the fact that He was their Messiah and King.

Hebrew prophecy taught that when Zion's King came, He would not come as a mighty warrior riding upon a white charger. Instead He would come as King of peace, *"gentle, and mounted on a donkey, even on a colt, the foal of a beast of burden"* (Mt 21:5; cf. Zch 9:9). Jesus rode into Jerusalem in such a fashion.

In order to do so He had made definite but secret plans. Knowing the orders of the Jewish rulers about His arrest and being aware one year earlier that one of His own disciples would betray Him, He did not dare to take even the Twelve into His plans. He arranged with a man, probably in Bethany, to provide the necessary animals. In all likelihood, however, He did not tell the man what use He proposed to make of them. Instead, He arranged a secret sign by which he might recognize those whom Jesus would send for them. The sign was the words, *"The Lord needs them"* (Mt 21:3).

So early on Sunday morning He and the Twelve were at Bethphage, a village near Bethany, where they probably had gone to join the multitude of pilgrims headed for Jerusalem. Jesus sent two of His disciples for the animals, which were by prearrangement tied in a nearby village. As they were untying the ass and her colt, the owner asked what they were doing. They said, *"The Lord needs them,"* and hearing these words, the man let them take the animals to Jesus.

The disciples placed their outer garments on the colt, and Jesus mounted it to ride into Jerusalem. John later reflected that at this point the Twelve did not understand the significance of this (12:16). He probably meant that the full meaning of it was not comprehended until after Jesus' resurrection,

Jerusalem in the Time of Jesus

1. The temple (Herod's temple)
2. Women's court
3. Court of the Gentiles
4. Eastern Gate (Golden Gate)
5. Antonia Fortress
6. City of David
7. Garden of Gethsemane
8. Mount of Olives
9. Kidron Valley
10. Gihon Spring
11. Pool of Siloam
12. Herod's Palace
13. Sheep Pool
14. Traditional Golgotha
15. Traditional tomb of Jesus
16. Pool of Bethesda
17. Hinnon Valley
18. Road to the Dead Sea
19. Road to Samaria

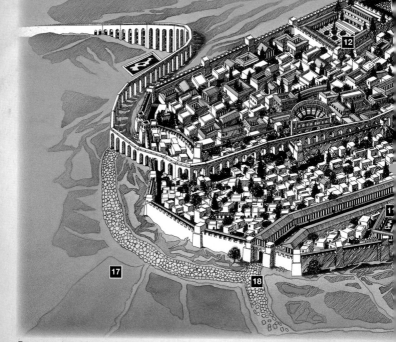

Reconstruction of Jerusalem at the time of Jesus

but it is evident that the multitude did see in it as a messianic act. They knew the prophecy of Zechariah, so they began to spread their garments in the path of the colt to provide a royal carpet. When the colt had walked over them, they ran and placed them before it again. Others cut branches from the palm trees, and with them did the same. And as they went along with Jesus, they were crying, *"Hosanna to the Son of David: Blessed is He that comes in the name of the Lord; Hosanna in the highest"* (Mt 21:9). This showed that they were aware of the meaning of this Royal Entry, for these were messianic proclamations, and Jesus did not stop them.

The Pharisees also recognized the significance of the event. Things had gotten out of hand. Jesus had bested them again. Their plan to arrest Him had been thwarted. It seemed to them that the whole world had gone after Jesus. Therefore, they did the only thing that they could do. They called on Him to stop the whole thing. His only reply was that if He silenced them,

Panoramic view of Jerusalem from the Mount of Olives

the very stones would cry out the same thing, for His hour was approaching, and the machinations of mere men could not delay it.

At this point the procession reached the crest of the Mount of Olives. Before them the city was spread out in all its beauty, a beauty which was crowned by the beautiful Herodian temple; and seeing it, Jesus burst into tears. Once again He lamented over the fate of the city and nation. He knew that soon they would reject Him. Rebellion was in the hearts of the people. The day would come when it would break out into a consuming conflagration. The Romans would besiege Jerusalem and utterly destroy her. This came to pass in AD 70, and all because she knew not the time of her visitation. When she rejected her Prince of Peace, she was doomed in the throes of war.

The procession going down the mountain was met by one coming out of the city, and the two converged to usher Jesus into Jerusalem. Naturally this demonstration stirred the entire city. People ran from every direction to determine its cause. It is hardly conceivable that the dwellers in Jerusalem did not know Jesus, but the city was overrun with pilgrims from outside Palestine. Probably some of these asked, *"Who is this?"* (Mt 21:10). Those about Jesus replied, *"This is the prophet Jesus from Nazareth in Galilee!"* (Mt 21:11). It was quite a different answer from what they had been saying on their way into the city. They had clearly proclaimed Him to be the Messiah, but now they called Him *"Jesus the prophet of Nazareth of Galilee."* Furthermore, they said that He was from the despised village of Nazareth, and the Jewish rulers had said that no prophet came out of Galilee. It was probably out of fear for them that the crowd toned down their answers about Jesus. Everything that the multitude said about Jesus on this occasion was true, but they left unsaid so much more of the truth so as to water down their testimony that it lost its greatest meaning. They missed their greatest opportunity to proclaim Jesus as the Messiah.

Jesus went into the temple area where He healed some blind and lame people, but the chief priests and scribes were unmoved by these wondrous works. Some children had been caught up in the spirit of the occasion. Even though their elders feared the rulers, the children were evidently immune to such. For right under the chief priests' noses they were crying, *"Hosanna to the Son of David!"* (Mt 21:15). This only added to the rulers' anger. *"Do You hear what these children are saying?"* (v. 16) they asked Jesus. They wanted it stopped right then, but Jesus asked them if they had ever read the messianic psalm that said, *"You have prepared praise from the mouths of children and nursing infants"* (8:2). What their elders failed to do these children did. And with this Jesus left Jerusalem and returned to Bethany.

A SECOND CLEANSING OF THE TEMPLE

Early on Monday morning Jesus returned to Jerusalem and to the temple. Entering the Court of the Gentiles, He once again found it filled with the bedlam of a marketplace. Those who sold sacrificial animals and doves and the moneychangers were once again doing a land-office business. The Bazaars of Annas were still engaged in profiteering at the expense of the worshipers. Therefore, as at the beginning of His public ministry, so at its close Jesus drove them from the temple. Instead of making God's house a house of prayer, they had turned it into a den of robbers. Like attracts like, and it has even been suggested that thieves were using this sacred place as one where they met to plot their crimes.

Some interpreters insist that there was but one cleansing of the temple and that this is the same incident as the one reported by John at the outset of Jesus' ministry. However, there is no reason to question that this is the latter of two cleansings. In both cases the Messiah declared His authority over the temple.

Following this outburst a quieter atmosphere prevailed as Jesus continued to teach in the temple area. However, when word of His authoritative action reached the chief priests, they plotted all the more how they might destroy Him. Their initial plans had gone awry, since the people hung on Jesus' every word, but the rulers plotted and waited for the opportune moment to carry out their nefarious purpose.

A VISIT OF CERTAIN GREEKS

Sometime during the day on Monday, an incident occurred that deeply disturbed Jesus. Some Greeks had come to Jerusalem for the Passover. They were probably God-fearers, Greeks who were studying Judaism but who had not yet accepted it as their religion. No doubt they had heard about Jesus, and learning that He was in Jerusalem, they wanted to see Him. So approaching Him they said to Philip, one of His disciples, *"Sir, we want to see Jesus"* (Jn 12:21). Philip told Andrew, and together they relayed the request to Jesus Himself.

Upon hearing that they wished to interview Him, Jesus was deeply moved in His spirit. He had previously said that His fold would contain *"other sheep"* than Jews (Jn 10:16). Apparently in these Greeks He saw the promise of the multitude of Gentiles who would believe in Him, and this realization brought down upon Him an increasing burden of His passion. His predestined hour truly was rapidly approaching. For only through His death on the cross could Greeks be brought to Him with full understanding of His saving work and power. So using the figure of a grain of wheat, Jesus described His own alternative. An unplanted grain could bear no fruit. It would abide by itself alone. Only as it fell into the earth and died to its own self could it bear a harvest. Even so, if Jesus saved His own life,

He would defeat the purpose of His Incarnation. He would bear no fruit. To save a lost world He Himself must die.

In this disturbed state Jesus communed within His own spirit. The *"hour"* was before Him. He had anticipated it from the beginning, but now that He faced it, what should He say? *"Father, save me from this hour"* (Jn 12:27). What did He mean by this statement? Was it a prayer for deliverance from the cross? Or was it a soliloquy within His soul? It depends upon how one punctuates it. If it ends in a period or a colon, then it becomes a prayer. But if it be ended with a question mark, it becomes a soliloquy. There is some manuscript evidence for either, but the context seems to favor the latter. Thus Jesus very likely did not pray to escape the cross. Instead He said, *"What should I say—Father, save Me from this hour? But that is why I came to this hour. Father, glorify Your name!"* (Jn 12:27–28). Not for one moment did Jesus seek to escape death! As will be seen later, even in Gethsemane His prayer related to some-thing else.

His prayer to glorify God's name received an immediate answer. The people heard a noise, and some thought that it had thundered. Others said that an angel spoke to Jesus, but He, ever attuned to the Father's will, heard His voice: *"I have glorified it, and I will glo-rify it again"* (Jn 12:28). That Jesus did not pray to escape the cross is seen in the fact that He said that this voice came not for His sake but for the sake of the people.

A fig tree at Bethphage in early May

THE BARREN FIG TREE

During the early part of Passion Week, Jesus was in Jerusalem during the daytime; but His nights were spent outside the city, probably in the home of His friends in Bethany. On Monday morning about daybreak He and the Twelve were on their way back into the city. This was the hour of the first meal of the day among the Jews. It appears that they left Bethany before breakfast, and so they were hungry. Seeing a fig tree in full leaf, Jesus came to it expecting to find some figs with which to satisfy His hunger. According to Mosaic Law it was permissible for a passerby to pluck figs from another's tree in order to relieve his hunger, but Jesus found no figs.

A fig tree bears two crops each year. In Palestine the former comes in June, and the latter comes in September, but a unique thing about fig trees is that the fruit begins to form before the leaves appear. When the leaves are full, one expects to find figs. Now obviously, since this incident occurred in April, it was before the normal season for ripened figs, but here was a tree ahead of the season as seen by its leaves. However, it had no fruit. So finding none, Jesus cursed the tree, saying, *"May no fruit ever come from you again!"* (Mt 21:19). And the tree began to wither.

Herein lies a difficulty. Why did Jesus perform a destructive miracle? Furthermore, why did He curse a fruitless tree before the normal season for such fruit? However, the point in this incident is that the tree gave evidence of fruit yet produced none. It was promise without performance. It is generally agreed that this was an acted parable. The tree was symbolic of the Jewish nation. With all of its religious pretensions, it was bearing no fruit in God's purpose. Therefore, because of its promise without performance, it too was under the condemnation of God. Within a generation it would wither away as did the fig tree.

This thought gives meaning to the sequel to this event, for on Tuesday morning, as they were again going into the city, the disciples called Jesus' attention to the withered fig tree. He exhorted them to have faith in God. If so, they could say to *"this mountain"* for it to be taken up and cast into the sea, and it would be done (Mt 21:21). Then there followed Jesus' assurance that believing prayer would surely be answered.

Did this mean that by faith the disciples could literally remove mountains? If so, it is strange that Jesus Himself never did this. More likely Jesus spoke in hyperbole. What was *"this mountain"*? Could it be Mount Moriah, the mountain on which stood the temple, the symbol of Jewish religious power? If so, then the symbolic meaning of the barren fig tree is continued. The temple and its power will fall. This obstacle to the progress of the kingdom of God will be utterly removed, and if Jesus' followers have faith in God, in both prayer and effort, they will see all other obstacles to the ongoing of the kingdom of God removed as they go from victory unto victory. It was a glorious promise then and throughout the ages.

A DAY OF CONTROVERSY

The time was Tuesday of Passion Week. The place was the court of the temple. It marked the close of Jesus' public ministry other than His words and deeds at the trial and Crucifixion, and significantly it occurred in the temple. In all likelihood, since this day of controversy ended in the Court of the Women in which were placed the treasury receptacles, it was in this court that the day of controversy occurred.

Since His royal entry Jesus had been the hero of the multitudes. Therefore, if the Jewish rulers were to accomplish their evil purpose concerning Him, it was necessary that they should discredit Him before the people. So one by one different groups of them confronted Jesus with situations designed to do so. In each case they posed a question for Him to answer.

1. The Question of Authority.

The first groups to challenge Jesus were the chief priests and scribes. They asked Him by what authority He dared to teach. According to their system they were in their rights to raise this question. For one to be an authorized rabbi, he must have been taught in one of their schools or by some accredited rabbi, and he should be authorized by the rabbi, a group of rabbis, or by the Sanhedrin. The rulers knew that they had not so authorized Jesus. Therefore, they asked Him to name the person or group who had given to Him this authority.

Jesus countered with His own question, which, if they would answer, He, in turn, would answer theirs. Was the baptism of John the Baptist from heaven or from men? In effect, under whose authority did he do his work? The rulers saw immediately that Jesus had turned the tables on them. If they said *"from heaven,"* then He would ask why they had not followed John. They were afraid to say *"from men"* because the people regarded John as a prophet. So they sought refuge in agnosticism, saying, *"We don't know"* (Mt 21:27). Thus they admitted that they were incapable of judging a man's authority. If they did not know about John, how could they sit in judgment on Jesus? Therefore, Jesus refused to tell them the source of His authority.

But the effect of this encounter was to suggest that Jesus' authority was from heaven. At least this was the result with the multitudes, for they regarded John's authority as being from God. John had baptized Jesus and had heralded Him as the Christ. So if the Jewish rulers or the people were consistent, they must reckon John as the only possible man who could have authorized Jesus for His work. Therefore, in the minds of the people, His authority must ultimately be regarded as being from heaven itself. Rather than to discredit Jesus with them, the rulers only served to consolidate His hold on the multitude. However, He did not let the matter end there. Instead, in three parables He condemned the Jewish rulers and scribes before the people and in God's eternal purpose.

The first parable concerned the attitudes of two sons. Their father told them to go and work in his vineyard. One son refused, but later he regretted his decision and went and did as his father had said. The other readily agreed to go, but he did not do as he agreed. Then Jesus asked, *"Which of the two did his father's will?"* (Mt 21:31). The rulers gave the only obvious answer, the first. Jesus then continued, *"I assure you: Tax collectors and prostitutes are entering the kingdom of God before you! For John came to you in the way of righteousness, and you didn't believe him. Tax collectors and prostitutes did believe him, but you, when you saw it, didn't change your mind later to believe him"* (Mt 21:31–32). To place publicans and harlots before these self-righteous religious leaders was to them a bitter

Reconstruction of a first-century wine press

dose indeed, and they might well have wanted to break off the debate at this point. But Jesus was not through. Not only did they reject John—they were even then planning to kill Him, and so He compounded the first parable with another.

A certain man planted a vineyard. He prepared it with the greatest of care. He planted a hedge fence about it, made a winepress, and fortified it with a watchtower. Then he rented it to some tenant farmers and went away to a distant land. (Jesus' listeners probably recalled Isaiah 5.) When the time for grapes was drawing near, he sent various servants to collect his rent, but the tenants beat one, killed another, and stoned still another. The owner sent other servants with the same results. Finally, he sent his son, thinking that the tenants would honor him in his request. Instead they reasoned that if they killed him, the heir, they would be able to keep the vineyard for themselves. So they killed him.

Then Jesus drew the lesson. He asked the Jewish leaders what the owner of the vineyard would do to these wicked men. Again they gave the obvious answer. He would miserably destroy them and rent out his vineyard to those who would render to him the fruits of it. Jesus asked if they had never read in the Scriptures, *"The stone that the builders rejected, this has become the cornerstone. This cornerstone came from the Lord, and is wonderful in our eyes"* (Mt 21:42; cf. Ps 118:22 23). And then the roof fell in on these rulers, for Jesus said, *"Therefore I tell you, the kingdom of God will be taken away from you and given to a nation producing its fruit"* (Mt 21:43).

Thus He ended the covenant of service God had made with Israel (Ex 19). Repeatedly God had sent His servants to call her to honor this covenant, but she had refused, mistreating and killing those whom God had sent. Soon they would kill His Son. God rejected them only after they had completely rejected Him and refused to honor the conditions of the covenant. He, therefore, was under no obligation to fulfill His promise to Israel. Later Peter would show, in language employing the terminology of both Exodus 19 and Matthew 21, that this new *"nation"* is the Christian people (cf. 1 Pt 2:4–10).

The chief priests and Pharisees got the point, for *"they knew He was speaking about them"* (Mt 21:45) and through them to the nation they represented. If it wasn't for their fear of the multitude, they would have arrested Jesus on the spot.

However, Jesus not only stood His ground; He attacked again. This time He related the parable of the king's marriage feast for his son. The details were similar to the previous parable of the king's supper (Lk 14:15ff.), but the point of this new parable was that when one guest showed up at the marriage feast without the proper wedding garment, he was cast into outer darkness. The lesson is that the Father is preparing a marriage feast for His Son as He takes unto Himself His bride, the Church, but these self-righteous people will be no part of it. They came clothed in their own righteousness and not in the righteousness of God in Christ Jesus.

2. A Question about Tribute.

The first skirmish was over. While the chief priests and scribes retreated in disorder, the Pharisees sent some of their prize students, together with

A Roman denarius.

some Herodians, to try their hand against Jesus. (Note how these various groups had merged in their common cause.) However, on at least one point the Pharisees and Herodians were in agreement—they were both opposed to paying taxes to the Romans. Therefore, they asked Jesus, *"Tell us, therefore, what you think. Is it lawful to pay taxes to Caesar or not?"* (Mt 22:17).

This was one of those loaded questions designed to condemn one no matter how he answered it. Had Jesus said, *"No,"* they would have accused Him of treason against Rome. Had He said, *"Yes,"* they would have charged Him with treason against His own people. This position most certainly would have offended most of the Jews, but there was a deeper and subtler element involved. For had Jesus counseled paying Roman taxes, to the Jews it would have been a virtual denial of His messianic claims, because they said that the Messiah, being a King Himself, would not countenance the payment of taxes to another king.

However, Jesus evaded all of these pitfalls. He asked them to show Him the tribute money. Note that He asked them for it. Roman taxes could be paid only in Roman coins. The very fact that these Pharisees and Herodians had such a coin indicated that they were subservient to and dependent upon Rome. Furthermore, on one side of the coin was the image of Tiberius Caesar; the other side bore his superscription. When Jesus asked His questioners to identify these, they said, *"Caesar's."* Then He said, *"Give back to Caesar the things that are Caesar's, and to God the things that are God's"* (Mt 22:21). A man has obligations to both and should honor them each in his own sphere. Not only did Jesus answer His immediate questioners—He also spoke the words that have become the fountainhead of the principle of separation between Church and State.

The Pharisees and Herodians made no reply. They heard it, wondered about it, left Jesus, and went their way, but they left Jesus still in command of the field.

3. A Question about the Resurrection.

It was the Sadducees' or chief priests' turn again. They did not believe in the resurrection, and so they asked Jesus to solve a problem, probably one of their favorites in their continuing debate with the Pharisees.

Here was their problem. Moses had commanded that if a man died childless his brother should marry his widow and thereby raise up seed unto his brother. Now the Sadducees imagined a case in which there were seven brothers. The first died childless. Then the other six in turn married the widow, each of them also dying without having a child. Finally the woman herself died. In the resurrection whose wife would she be?

Jesus answered their question by reminding them that they did not even understand their own Scriptures; neither did they know the power of God, for in the resurrection there is no such thing as the institution of marriage. All will be one big family of God.

Now did Jesus let them get away with their denial of the resurrection? He cited God's own words, *"I am the God of Abraham and the God of Isaac and the God of Jacob"* (Mt 22:32). He did not say, *"I was"* but *"I am."* These three patriarchs still lived. So God is not the God of the dead, but of the living.

The Sadducees were silent, but the people were astonished at Jesus' teaching. Naturally the Sadducees were unhappy, but there were some happy people in the crowd. For the scribes (Pharisees) said, *"Teacher, You have spoken well"* (Lk 20:39). Even if they could not get the better of Jesus, at least He had put the Sadducees in their place, because they did not dare to ask Him any more questions.

4. A Question about Law.

Now the Pharisees must try their hand again. This time they sent one of their experts in the Mosaic Law. He asked Jesus, *"Teacher, which commandment in the law is the greatest?"* (Mt 22:36). Or as Mark relates it, *"Which commandment is the most important of all?"* (12:28). Jesus answered with the words which were dear to every Jewish heart. He quoted the Shema (Dt 6:4–5): *"Listen, Israel! The Lord our God, the Lord is One. Love the Lord your God with all your heart, with all your soul, with all your mind, and with all your strength. . . . Love your neighbor as yourself."* (Mk 12:29–31). On these, said Jesus, hang all the law and the prophets. The lawyer could only compliment Jesus for His answer. In turn Jesus said of the lawyer that he was not far from the kingdom of God. Not far—but not in. It is to be hoped that he did enter the kingdom of God, not through compliments but by faith in Jesus.

5. A Question about Christ.

It was now Jesus' turn to ask the Pharisees a question, and it concerned their opinion about the Christ: *"What do you think about the Messiah? Whose Son is He?"* (Mt 22:42). They replied that He is the Son of David. Jesus quoted from the Messianic Psalm 110:1—*"The Lord declared to my Lord, 'Sit at My right hand until I put Your enemies under Your feet.'"* Then He asked that if the Christ were his Son, how was it that David called Him his Lord? The Pharisees had no answer for this. Neither did they dare to ask Jesus any other questions. The Teacher had completely silenced His critics.

6. Jesus' Last Public Discourse.

Jesus then turned to the multitude and to His disciples. He recognized that the scribes and Pharisees sat in Moses' seat. They were the accredited teachers of the Jews. Insofar as they really sat in Moses' seat or taught in accord with Moses' Law, they were to be revered and followed. But the people were to be on guard of the multiplicity of rote rules which they devised, and especially of their own example in them, for they said but did not. They could always find ways to circumvent their own teachings. Furthermore, they laid heavy and grievous burdens on the people but did not even extend their fingers to help them to bear the burdens. They were good at prescribing, but they could not impart the power to enable their patients to live up to the prescription. Their only purpose was to impress others with their piety and to gain recognition for themselves. They unduly broadened their phylacteries and enlarged the hem of their garments in order to appear more pious than others. They loved the prominent place at the feasts and the chief seats in the synagogues. It was music in their ears to be greeted in public places and especially to be called rabbi, or *"my great one"* or *"master."*

Therefore, Jesus warned the people, and especially the disciples, against such vainglory. If someone called them *"rabbi,"* that was one thing, but they were not to seek the title. One Jewish teacher said of this office that *"men should love the work, but hate the rabbi-ship,"* but Jesus said that among His people there should be the equality of *"brethren."* Neither should they call any man their father or the source of their spiritual being. Only God is such. Nor should they set themselves up as supreme spiritual authorities, for this authority belonged only to Christ. If any one of them aspired to greatness, he should become a menial servant to others.

Then from warning the crowd and His disciples, Jesus turned upon the Pharisees, and in seven *"woes"* He excoriated them with the most merciless words that ever came from His lips (Mt 23:13,15–36). They are all the more terrible since they came from Him who is the very essence of mercy itself. From the beginning the Pharisees had rejected and opposed Jesus, and they had stood as a barrier to others who would otherwise have believed in Him. His words were God's judgment upon them and their empty religious system. Like a whiplash He repeatedly hurled at them the term *"hypocrites."* They were mere play actors or pretenders portraying a role for men to see. Even now one shudders as he hears these words of the Lord.

"Woe to you, scribes and Pharisees, hypocrites!" (Mt 23:13), because they slammed the door of the kingdom of heaven in the faces of men. They would not enter themselves —neither did they permit others to do so.

"Woe to you, scribes and Pharisees, hypocrites!" (Mt 23:15). For they traveled over land and sea to make one Gentile a convert to Judaism, but they lacked the spiritual power to redeem him from paganism. In their empty system they merely substituted for his pagan gods their own gods of ritual and ceremony. Therefore, he was twofold more a son of hell than they were. He was still a pagan but left without hope.

"Woe to you, blind guides" (Mt 23:16–22), because in their system of graduated oaths they devised means of evading them as though one was less binding than another, when all the while God did not recognize their machinations. They made a mockery of what should have been a sacred and binding thing.

"Woe to you, scribes and Pharisees, hypocrites!" (Mt 23:23). They were so meticulous in keeping the law of the tithe and all the while they ignored God's weightier laws concerning justice, mercy, and faith. They should not neglect the former, but they should keep the latter also. In their spiritual blindness they were so careful to filter out a little gnat from their cup, but

Jesus used hyperbole to make a serious point with humor. He described some of the religious leaders of His day as straining a gnat out of their cup but swallowing a camel.

they were oblivious to a camel which they gulped down—hair, hide, hoof, hump, and all!

"Woe to you, scribes and Pharisees, hypocrites!" (Mt 23:25–26), for they so scrupulously cleansed the outside of their eating utensils, but within themselves they were filled with robbery and graft.

"Woe to you, scribes and Pharisees, hypocrites!" (Mt 23:27–28). They were like whitewashed tombs. Outwardly they appeared so beautiful, but inwardly they were filled with decaying flesh and dead men's bones. For a Jew to touch a tomb made him ceremonially unclean and so unfit for worship for seven days. Therefore, as a warning to worshipers, all tombs were whitewashed with powdered lime just before the Passover. This would be

true as Jesus spoke, so that His words carried a vivid imagery. The Pharisees were like these tombs. Outwardly they appeared so righteous, but inwardly they were filled with putrid sin.

"Woe to you, scribes and Pharisees, hypocrites!" (Mt 23:29–36), because they built sepulchers for the prophets and adorned the tombs of the righteous, both of which their fathers had slain. All the while they piously said that had they lived in those days they would not have done as their fathers did, but they were the true sons of their fathers. Said Jesus, *"Fill up, then, the measure of your fathers' sins"* (v. 32). Thus He challenged them to go ahead with their plot to kill Him. This would be a fitting climax to this long line of murders, and then echoing the words of John the Baptist, Jesus said, *"Snakes! Brood of vipers! How can you escape being condemned to hell?"* (v. 33). Upon them Jesus placed all of the righteous blood that had been shed from the time of Abel throughout all of the Old Testament. A terrible indictment indeed, but one deserved nevertheless!

Then Jesus uttered another lament over Jerusalem, as representative of the entire Jewish nation. She had killed all whom God had sent to call her back to His eternal purpose. Soon she would kill the Son of God Himself. Rebellion was in her heart. Jesus still saw the storm coming and frantically had tried to save this people, but they would neither hear nor heed: *"See! Your house is left to you desolate"* (Mt 23:38). Israel had chosen to go it alone—without Messiah. Very well! Her house was left to her—without salvation.

They would not see Jesus again, as He now appeared to them, until His Second Advent when He would come again in great glory and power. Then the true Israel or all who believe on Him shall welcome Him as *"He who comes in the name of the Lord"* (Mt 23:39), but for that generation and for the outward Israel as such, Jesus fully and finally abandoned them.

7. A Closing Scene of Beauty.

The storm had passed. The critics of Jesus had slunk away. Evidently even the Twelve stood some distance apart from Jesus, for He was alone in the Court of the Women. It was a tender scene, for the Lord of the temple sat over against the treasury, watching the people cast in their gifts. Many of the wealthy cast in their gifts with no comment coming from Jesus. Then there came a poor widow to cast in two mites or lepta. She was a pauper whose gift was worth about two-fifths of a cent.

Seeing this, Jesus called the Twelve to Him. He told them that this poverty-stricken widow had given more than all of the others combined. They had given out of their overflow of wealth, but she out of her deep poverty had given all that she had, even her living itself. Truly Jesus does not count gifts; He weighs them in the scales of love! What a pity to see some rich person who claims to give the *"widow's mite!"*

With this touching scene Jesus left the temple, never to enter it again. Thus God abandoned the temple. It truly was left unto itself.

CHAPTER IX
THE GATHERING GLOOM
THE FINAL WARNINGS

Except for Jesus' words at His trial and at Calvary, His public ministry was over. All that remained now was that He should enter into the ever-deepening shadows that led to the darkest day in the history of the world, the day when Jesus died.

As would be expected Jesus spent these closing days among His friends. But even within this intimate circle, the most diabolical of sins raised its evil head. The serpent was soon to bruise the heel of the seed of the woman, but in the end He would crush its head.

This period of gathering gloom extended from Tuesday afternoon until possibly after the midnight hour on Thursday, or until early Friday morning. And it was a time largely consumed by the teaching of Jesus to His inner circle of Twelve, or to the Eleven as the case might be. The Shepherd was soon to be taken from the sheep, and everything possible was done to prepare them for it.

JESUS' DISCOURSE ON THE MOUNT OF OLIVES

The Twelve had been stunned by Jesus' words of condemnation spoken against the house of Israel, and they understood this to include the temple itself. Therefore, as they were passing from the temple area, they pointed out its beautiful buildings, paying special attention to the large stones used

The Mount of Olives as seen through an arch on the Temple Mount in Jerusalem

in its construction. One may still see some of these Herodian stones later used in rebuilding the walls about Jerusalem. But Jesus told them that the time would come when not one of these stones would be left standing upon another. As impossible as this may have seemed to the disciples, it actually became true in the utter destruction of Jerusalem by the Romans in AD 70.

Jesus and His little band left the city through the eastern gate, crossed the Kidron Valley, and began their ascent of the Mount of Olives. At a point somewhere on this mount directly across the valley from the temple, they sat down to rest. Here the disciples asked Jesus three questions: *"Tell us, when will these things happen? And what is the sign of Your coming and of the end of the age?"* (Mt 24:3). As one follows the discourse of Jesus, it is well to keep these questions in mind, for even though at times He seems to be dealing with first one and then another, in large measure Jesus answered them seriatim.

"When will these things happen?" The destruction of Jerusalem. *"What is the sign of Your coming?"* The Second Coming of Christ. *"And of the end of the age?"* The end of the age. Jesus had touched upon all of these in His discourse to the Pharisees. So it is understandable that the disciples should inquire concerning them, and they were not left without an answer.

1. The Warning against False Signs.

The disciples had asked about signs. Therefore, before answering their specific questions, Jesus warned them against being misled by false signs, and this warning was most fitting then, as it is now.

Jesus warned against false christs. These are not the *"antichrist,"* or those opposing Christ, but pseudo christs, those who claim to be the Christ. From time to time such have appeared through the ages. Josephus relates that Palestine was plagued with them just prior to and during the

The Siege and Destruction of Jerusalem by the Romans under the Command of Titus, AD 70. Artist: David Roberts, 1850.

Jewish War against the Romans in AD 66–70. They not only contributed to the causes of the war but also added greatly to the Jews' suffering during it.

Furthermore, Jesus warned against cataclysmic disturbances between nations, in the social order and in nature. It is of interest to note that even today when these things occur, there are those who herald them as signs of the approaching Second Coming of Christ. But Jesus said that *"wars and rumors of wars . . . famines and earthquakes in various places"* are but parts of the normal course of history. Christians are not to be troubled about these things, with respect to the end of the age, for *"the end is not yet"* (Mt 24:6).

"All these events are the beginning of birth pains" (Mt 24:8). The words *birth pains* were used by the Jews to refer to the sufferings of the Messiah which would preceding His appearance. However, these, said Jesus, are not a sign of the end, but of the *"beginning."* This statement, then, introduced the thought of the sufferings the followers of Christ would endure

through the ages as they endeavored to carry out the Great Commission. He enlarged upon it in the following verses as He described many of the things that would happen to them in their endeavor (cf. Mt 24:9–13; Mk 13:9–13; Lk 21:12–19). Those who endure to the end, or until death, *"shall be delivered."* This speaks of the care of God for them in their trials and the successful culmination of their purpose in Christian witnessing.

The one sure sign that Jesus gave with respect to the end of the age, involving the Second Coming of Christ, is that *"this good news of the kingdom will be proclaimed in all the world as a testimony to all nations. And then the end will come"* (Mt 24:14). But even here Jesus spoke not of time but of condition. He never set a time, but He did describe the condition, and with this Jesus proceeded to answer the disciples' three questions.

The Arch of Titus was constructed in the AD 80s. Domitian, the younger brother of Titus, built the Arch to honor Titus. On the inside wall of the Arch is depicted the Romans' destruction of Jerusalem and the temple in AD 70. Titus, commanding general for Rome, is shown in triumphal procession in his four-horse chariot. He is accompanied by Roman soldiers carrying the Menorah from the temple, the table of showbread, and the silver trumpets that called the people to worship.

2. The Destruction of Jerusalem.

In answering the first question Jesus did not speak of time, even though He might have done so, for it happened just forty years after His Crucifixion. However, again He spoke of condition. He used the word *when*

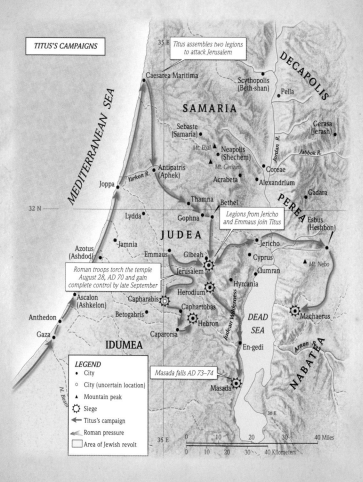

TITUS'S CAMPAIGNS

Titus assembles two legions to attack Jerusalem

DECAPOLIS

Caesarea Maritima

Scythopolis (Beth-shan)

Pella

SAMARIA

Gerasa (Jerash)

Sebaste (Samaria)

Mt. Ebal

Neapolis (Shechem)

Mt. Gerizim

Coreae

Jordan R.

Jabbok R.

Antipatris (Aphek)

Acrabeta

Alexandrium

Yarkon R.

Joppa

Gadara

PEREA

Thamna

Bethel

32 N

Lydda

Gophna

Esbus (Heshbon)

Legions from Jericho and Emmaus join Titus

JUDEA

Jericho

Cyprus

Azotus (Ashdod)

Jamnia

Emmaus

Gibeah

Mt. Nebo

Qumran

Jerusalem

Roman troops torch the temple August 28, AD 70 and gain complete control by late September

Herodium

Hyrcania

Judean Wilderness

DEAD SEA

Capharabis

Caphartobas

Ascalon (Ashkelon)

Betogabris

Hebron

Machaerus

Anthedon

Caparorsa

En-gedi

Gaza

IDUMEA

Arnon R.

NABATEA

LEGEND

- • City
- ◦ City (uncertain location)
- ▲ Mountain peak
- ⚙ Siege
- ← Titus's campaign
- ◄ Roman pressure
- ☐ Area of Jewish revolt

Masada falls AD 73–74

Masada

36 E

35 E

0   10   20   30   40 Miles

0   10   20   30   40 Kilometers

(hotan) referring primarily to condition. In it the time element is conditioned by the condition.

"When you see 'the abomination that causes desolation,' spoken of by the prophet Daniel, standing in the holy place" (let the reader understand) (Mt 24:15). Luke simply says that when they saw Jerusalem surrounded by armies, then they should know that Jerusalem's desolation was at hand. These, then, are the conditions heralding the end of the city, and Jesus referred His disciples to the prophecy of Daniel in order that they might understand His meaning. To what did Jesus refer?

The prophet Daniel speaks of certain abominations when someone shall cause the sacrifices and oblations to cease in the temple (9:27; 11:31; 12:11). Some interpreters view this as the act of Antiochus Epiphanes, a Seleucid ruler (175–164 BC), who defiled the temple by erecting an altar to Zeus on the altar of Yahweh and thereon sacrificed swine. Furthermore, he converted the priests' rooms and the temple chambers into public brothels. No doubt Jesus' words called this to the minds of His hearers.

That this was not what Jesus had in mind is seen in the fact that He referred to some future event. Josephus relates that following the destruction of the temple, Roman soldiers proclaimed Titus as emperor and offered sacrifices to their ensigns placed by the eastern gate. However, this was after the fall of the city. Jesus referred to something that immediately preceded this event.

When Jesus spoke of the *"holy place,"* it does not necessarily refer to the Holy of Holies alone, even though it is included in His statement. It could include the entire holy city and its environs. If this be true, then the specific reference would be to the siege of the city by Titus, a siege that foretold the other events connected with its fall (Lk 21:20). Pagan armies with their pagan ensigns surrounding the city would truly be an abomination of

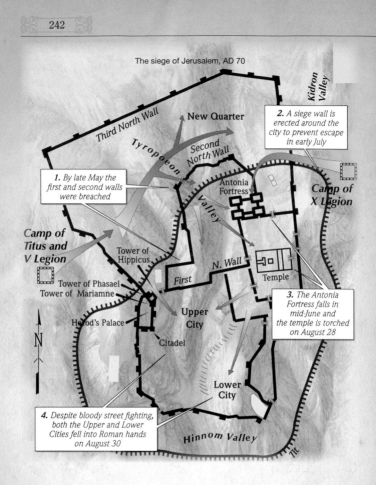

The siege of Jerusalem, AD 70

New Quarter

Third North Wall

Tyropoeon

Second North Wall

Kidron Valley

2. A siege wall is erected around the city to prevent escape in early July

1. By late May the first and second walls were breached

Antonia Fortress

Camp of X Legion

Valley

Camp of Titus and V Legion

Tower of Hippicus

Tower of Phasael
Tower of Mariamne

Herod's Palace

Citadel

First

N. Wall

Temple

Upper City

Lower City

3. The Antonia Fortress falls in mid-June and the temple is torched on August 28

4. Despite bloody street fighting, both the Upper and Lower Cities fell into Roman hands on August 30

N

Hinnom Valley

desolation, which finally resulted in the end of the sacrifices and oblations. When the disciples should see this siege begin, they would know that the destruction of the city was near.

So when they shall see these armies approaching the city, they are to flee to the mountains. Eusebius says that the Christians actually fled to Pella at the foot of the mountains about seventeen miles south of the Sea of Galilee. Those who shall be on the housetop, probably looking for the approach of the Romans, should not go down into their houses to get anything to carry away with them. They should escape the city by what the rabbis called *"the road of the roofs."* Anyone working in the field, and who had laid aside his outer cloak or had left it at home, should not return for it. Haste would be of the essence. It would be difficult for pregnant women or those nursing infants, for this would slow them down. Furthermore, they were to pray that this would not occur in winter, lest fleeing their homes they should be exposed to the cold. Or that it should not be on a Sabbath day on which Jews are forbidden to travel more than a short distance. Some rabbis said that it was permissible to ignore these regulations in order to escape danger, but many would die rather than do so.

Jesus said that the tribulation suffered during and following this Roman siege would exceed anything ever seen on the earth up to that time or

Pella, Jordan, a city just east of the Jordan River and southeast of the Sea of Galilee. It received a large part of the Jerusalem church when they fled there before the Roman destructions of the Holy City AD 66–70.

which would ever come in the future (Mk 13:19). This latter time element shows that here Jesus was not thinking of some *"tribulation"* in the last days of the age. He was speaking of the destruction of Jerusalem, and Josephus vividly describes these conditions, especially during the closing part of this siege and at the time of the fall of the city. Titus himself said that God was against the Jews on that day, and Jesus said that had not God shortened these days of suffering, *"for the elect's sake"* (Mt 24:22), the Christians themselves would have been wiped out.

As mentioned above, false messiahs would appear preceding and during this terrible time, and they led many astray, adding to their suffering. However, Jesus told His followers beforehand in order that they might not be led astray (Mt 24:25). At this point His warning extends beyond the immediate future to include all time until the end of the age. What follows may apply equally to the period through the destruction of Jerusalem, even up to and including the Second Coming of Christ (cf. Mt 24:26–28).

3. The Second Coming of Christ.

Jesus introduced His answer to this second question by specific warnings against false predictions as to His return. The warning is particularly against any claims of a secret coming of Christ. Pretenders would/will appear either in some isolated place or in some secret place within a city. Such places would make it difficult or impossible to check on their claims. Jesus warned against any such secret coming, for when the Son of man comes, He will be seen by all, as when lightning flashes it is seen from east to west (across the sky) by all simultaneously. Furthermore, He said that where the carcass is there will the vultures be gathered together. In other words, in this realistic picture He said that whenever conditions are right, the Son of Man will appear (Mt 24:28).

Then Jesus began to speak in apocalyptic language, a sort of sign language commonly used by the Jews to portray divine events (cf. Rv): *"Immediately after the tribulation of those days"* (Mt 24:29). What days? Not merely some days of tribulation near the end of the age. Jesus used the sweeping, panoramic language of prophecy to span the entire scope of time from His Ascension until His return. These are the days of tribulation that will be endured by His followers through the centuries (v. 8) as they witness to a lost world. Jesus did not say how long or how short this period would be. The matter of time was not in His thinking. He was thinking of condition.

Whenever that condition shall come, then, in apocalyptic language, He described certain phenomena in the heavens: *"Then the sign of the Son of Man will appear in the sky"* (Mt 24:30). And what will that "sign" be? It will be *"the Son of Man coming on the clouds of heaven with power and great glory"* (24:30).

At this point Jesus dealt with both the destruction of Jerusalem and His Second Coming. It is as though He were summing up these two events before passing on to answer the third question. He said that when a fig tree puts forth its leaves one knows that summer draws near. Likewise, when one saw *"these things"* (Mt 24:33, the conditions preceding the destruction of Jerusalem), he would know that *"He is near— at the door"* (24:33). The text reads *"He is near,"* but either *"He"* or *"it"* is an accurate translation. Although HCSB has "He" in the main text, it shows "it" as a valid alternative in a footnote to this verse—*"it"* referring to summer. And since Jesus said that *"this generation will certainly not pass away until all these things take place,"* it does not refer to Jesus' return. But the destruction of Jerusalem did occur within that generation, so the translation "it" is preferable.

Then Jesus spoke of His return when He said, *"Concerning that day and hour no one knows—neither the angels of heaven, nor the Son—except the Father only"* (Mt 24:36). This latter statement involves the limitations of the Incarnation voluntarily assumed by the Son. But the certainty of both the destruction of Jerusalem and of the Lord's return is assured, for Jesus had predicted them, and even though heaven and earth would pass away, His *"words will never pass away"* (Mt 24:35).

The date of the destruction of Jerusalem is a matter of history. The time of the Second Coming is hidden in the mind of God, but as the former came to pass, so will the latter do so. In the meantime, Jesus said, life will move along its natural course until without warning the Lord will return. When He does, there will be a sudden separation between those who are His and those who are not His. *"Therefore be alert, since you don't know what day your Lord is coming"* (Mt 24:42).

4. The End of the Age.

Of course, the end of the age is simultaneous with the return of the Lord. As He spoke of the one, He spoke of the other. Therefore, to drive home this truth Jesus closed this Olivet discourse with a series of parables, followed by an actual description of the scene of the judgment, which will occur at the end of the age.

Like a landowner watching for a thief in the night, who comes unexpectedly, so should the Lord's people be alert to await His coming. No servant of His should be a *"wicked slave"* (Mt 24:48) in abusing the responsibility entrusted to him. Such conduct could even mean that he was not truly the Lord's servant.

Furthermore, in the Parable of the Ten Virgins (Mt 25:1–13) Jesus taught the importance of being properly related to Him. The five wise virgins were so related—they had oil in their lamps. But the five foolish ones were not—they had no oil in their lamps, and when the Bridegroom appeared, they had no further opportunity to prepare.

The Parable of the Talents (Mt 25:14–30) teaches the importance of faithfulness in the responsibility placed by the Lord upon His servants, or slaves, in the interim between His Ascension and His return. At His return there will be a reckoning. Those who are faithful in their several capacities and responsibilities will be rewarded accordingly, but those who are unfaithful will lose not only their reward but also their further opportunity. Indeed, such unfaithfulness will even prove that they were not really servants of Christ at all. So instead of receiving everlasting reward, they will be cast from Him into everlasting punishment.

Then came the scene of the final Judgment (Mt 25:31–46). When the condition is right for the coming of the Son of man, He will sit on the throne of His glory. Before Him will be assembled all nations or ethnic groups, and as a shepherd separates the sheep from the goats, so shall the Son of man separate all men, the *"sheep"* on His right hand and the *"goats"* on His left. Some see the following scene as the Judgment of the Nations, but nations as such are judged in the context of history. Therefore, this

First-century BC pottery lamps

judgment may more likely be considered one of several pictures of the judgment of individuals.

"Then the King will say . . ." Note that the Son of man is now called a King. What shall the King say? To the *"sheep"* He shall say, *"Come, you who are blessed by My Father, inherit the kingdom prepared for you from the foundation of the world"* (Mt 25:34). The basis of this inheritance is the benevolent attitude they have shown toward the King (25:35–36), and this attitude is expressed toward Him in their treatment of those about them who are in need (vv. 37–40).

Conversely, to the *"goats"* He shall say, *"Depart from me, you who are cursed, into the eternal fire prepared for the Devil and his angels"* (Mt 25:41), and the basis of this condemnation is the malevolent attitude shown toward the King, as expressed in this same attitude toward their needy fellowmen (vv. 42–46). In other words, in each case had these two groups been with Jesus in the flesh, they would have acted toward Him as they acted toward their fellowmen.

What may be understood by this scene of judgment? The basis of judgment will not be one's works. It will be the kind of character one brings to the judgment, a character as revealed in his works. So the judgment will not determine character. It will only reveal it. The judgment will not decide whether one is saved or lost. It will reveal or declare one's saved or lost condition.

And the destination of each group will be fixed and final. The lost will enter into *"eternal punishment, but the righteous into life eternal"* (Mt 25:46). Some people prefer to deny the fact of *"everlasting punishment."* If this denial be permitted, then one must deny the fact of *"life eternal"* also. For the same word (*aionion,* eternal) describes both punishment and life. The language is quite plain. Jesus spoke of both punishment and life as *"eternal,"* and the thought of eternal punishment is all the more real when one remembers that it was expressed by Him who is infinite love and mercy.

So the Olivet discourse was ended. But before Jesus and the Twelve continued their journey toward Bethany, He told them that after two days the Passover would be observed, and the Son of man would be handed over to be crucified. Thus Jesus foretold the very day on which He would be crucified.

Probably at that moment the Sanhedrin was in session. It had been called by Caiaphas, the high priest, to plan how Jesus should be arrested quietly and be killed. However, they agreed to wait until after the Passover, lest they should find a revolt against their actions on the part of the people.

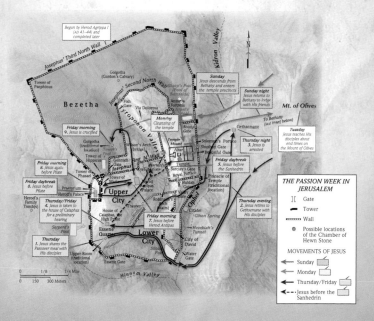

THE PASSION WEEK IN JERUSALEM

Little did they know that the time and manner of Jesus' death was not theirs to choose. Both had already been predetermined by God.

A DINNER AMONG FRIENDS

It was Tuesday evening in Bethany. The place was the home of Simon the leper, one who probably had been healed by Jesus. The occasion was a dinner in honor of Jesus. Present also were Lazarus and the Twelve. As might be expected Martha joined in serving the meal.

During the meal Mary, in characteristic fashion, came with an alabaster cruse of very precious ointment or nard. It probably was her prized possession, a gift fit for a king. In a great expression of love she broke the cruse, and anointed Jesus' head and feet with the ointment. Then she wiped His feet with her hair. It was an act of utter devotion.

Seeing this act Judas criticized her, and the other disciples joined with him in the criticism. Failing to understand this deed of love, they regarded it merely as a *"waste."* Judas asked why it was not sold and the proceeds used to relieve the poor, but John notes that he had no concern for the poor. Instead, since he kept the money for the little band, he merely wanted to get his greedy hands on the money and steal it for himself.

Jesus rebuked His disciples by reminding them that they could minister

An alabaster jar

to the poor at any time. Mary had anointed Him for His burial, and wherever the gospel should be preached, this deed of love would be known as a memorial unto her. So this precious fragrance did more than permeate the banquet hall. On the winds of time it has wafted down the centuries and throughout the world.

What a contrast is seen between Mary and Judas! Both had known the love of Jesus. Both had heard His words and had seen His wondrous works but with such diverse reactions. In all likelihood Mary and Judas were the first two who completely realized that Jesus was going to die, and with this realization each asked a question. Mary asked, "What can I do for Jesus to show that I love Him, understand, and sympathize with Him?" So she anointed Him for burial. Judas asked, "In view of the fact that Jesus is going to die anyway, what can Jesus do for me? What can I get out of this debacle for myself?" So he betrayed Jesus for thirty pieces of silver, the price of a slave, for Judas went directly from this dinner to seek out the chief priests and drive a bargain with them for his dastardly deed.

At this point one wonders again why Jesus chose Judas as one of His disciples. Some have supposed that Judas was chosen for the express purpose of his betrayal, but this would relieve Judas of all guilt and make him a mere puppet on a string held in God's hands. Such a thought not only is contrary to the Gospel record; it is in direct opposition to God's nature and His dealings with men as personalities endowed with the privilege of choice. In trying to relieve Judas of guilt they make God guilty of an unrighteous act.

In truth one is driven back to a recognition that Jesus saw a peculiar worth in Judas, which, if surrendered to Him, would make Judas of definite value to the kingdom of God. But Judas never truly gave himself to Jesus. He remained self-centered to the end.

Some even see in Judas' betrayal an effort to force Jesus' hand. It seems that on other occasions he had tried to do so but to no avail. To Judas's nationalistic mind Jesus had missed His chance to establish His kingdom on the occasion of His royal entry, so to Judas Jesus was an impractical dreamer. Perhaps if he created a situation that endangered Jesus' life, He

The traditional site of the upper room, or Hall of the Coenaculum, in Jerusalem. This was restored in the fourteenth century using the upper parts of antique column shafts and capitals. A gothic-style vaulted ceiling was added. The stone flooring may well be from the original structure.

would declare Himself. But again this attributes to the betrayer a motive not borne out by the record.

More likely Judas felt that he had forsaken everything to follow Jesus, hoping that thereby he might receive a place of prominence in the new kingdom. His dreams however were soon to be trampled in the dirt, so he sought to cash in on the failure as best he could. For his treason he received a little less than twenty-five dollars. It was a sorry bargain indeed for him, but his treachery appeared to be a windfall to the chief priests. They had not hoped for betrayal from within Jesus' little circle of intimates. It was no longer necessary to wait until after the Passover. They now had only to wait until Judas could find an opportune moment to deliver Jesus into their hands.

THE TWO MEALS

The Passover Meal

Nothing is known as to Jesus' actions on Wednesday of Passion Week. Perhaps He spent the day in seclusion as He rested and taught His disciples, but about noon on Thursday He made ready for His final visit to Jerusalem, a visit that would end in His death.

1. The Preparation for the Passover Meal.

On Thursday Peter and John were sent into the city to prepare for Jesus' last Passover meal with His disciples. They were told that there they would see a man carrying a pitcher of water. Following him they would be led to the house in which they were to make preparations for the meal.

This fact is suggestive of previous preparation on the part of Jesus. Judas must not know this location in advance. A man carrying a pitcher of water would be most conspicuous, for it was customary only for women to do this. So this man evidently was to do this as a prearranged sign. Jesus called him *"such a man."* In the papyri this very phrase was used in the sense of "Mister X." It is so used in modern Greek.

There they made ready for the meal. They went to the temple and secured a lamb slain by a priest. The lamb, in turn, was roasted, and together with certain other specified food this comprised the Passover meal.

2. The Arrival for the Passover Meal.

About 6:00 P.M. Jesus and the other disciples came to the home and entered the Upper Room. A contention ensued among the Twelve as each sought to get the chief place next to Jesus at the table. But Jesus rebuked them with a lesson concerning greatness in the kingdom, and then He proceeded to demonstrate His lesson.

On such a festive occasion it was customary for the host to provide a slave to rinse the dust from the feet of the arriving guests, but since Jesus had no such slave, He assumed that role Himself. He laid aside His outer garments, girded Himself with a towel, filled a basin with water, and began to rinse the disciples' feet. But when He came to Peter, He was met with a protest. That disciple refused to let Jesus render so menial a service for him.

One can almost see a twinkle of humor in Jesus' eyes in the play upon words that followed. Peter said, *"You will never wash my feet—ever!"* (Jn 13:8). Jesus replied, *"If I don't wash you, you have no part with Me"* (v. 8). Then Peter, in characteristic fashion, said, *"Lord, not only my feet, but also my hands and my head"* (v. 9). Give me a bath all over! And then Jesus replied, *"One who has bathed . . . doesn't need to wash anything except his feet"* (v. 10). In other words, if Peter took a bath before coming to supper, he needed only to have his feet rinsed free of dust.

Then Jesus added that not all among them were clean. Thus He spoke of Judas and his purpose of betrayal. Jesus ended this episode by applying the lesson. As He had rendered a menial service to them, if they wished to be great in the kingdom, they must do so to one another. In this act Jesus did not give to His followers an ordinance. He merely taught them a lesson in humility.

3. The Betrayer Indicated.

Jesus and the Twelve were now reclining about the table as they ate the Passover meal. In all likelihood the Lord, as the host, had already recounted the events commemorated in the meal. While they were eating, Jesus tossed a bombshell among them as He said, *"I assure you: One of you will betray Me"* (Jn 13:21). This must have been greeted by a moment of stunned silence as the disciples looked about at each other, and then one by one they began to ask, *"Surely not I, Lord?"* (Mt 26:22). The form of the question invited a negative answer. "Surely not I, Lord?" Such a thought was incredible to the Eleven. Jesus replied by saying that it was one who was dipping his hand into the dish with Him. This did not specifically point out Judas, since all of them were doing this. It merely indicated the intimacy that was to be betrayed. That Judas was not a puppet in the hands of fate is seen in Jesus' following words: *"The Son of Man will go just as it is written about Him, but woe to that man by whom the Son of Man is betrayed! It would have been better for that man if he had not been born"* (Mt 26:24).

Up to this point Judas had remained silent, but lest his silence indict him he finally asked, *"Surely not I, Rabbi?"* (26:25). His question also invited a negative answer. He had to try to bluff it out, but there is one decided difference in his question. Whereas the others addressed Jesus as "Lord," Judas merely called Him "Rabbi." To him Jesus was a rabbi and nothing more. This fact is reflected in Jesus' reply, *"You have said it yourself."* This means "yes."

Just prior to Judas' question there was a movement about the table, for Peter came to John who was reclining on Jesus' right side, the place of honor. He asked him to ascertain from Jesus the name of the traitor. The Lord said to John, not to Peter, *"He's the one I give the piece of bread to after I have dipped it"* (Jn 13:26). All were dipping their bread in a common bowl of gravy. Customarily on such occasions the host honored a guest by dipping a morsel in the gravy and giving it to him. So Jesus did this for Judas. Was this a last effort to reclaim Judas from his evil purpose? At any rate the act would carry no particular significance to Peter and the others. Otherwise Judas might well have been mobbed on the spot. But Judas knew. When he knew that Jesus was aware of his purpose, *"Satan entered him"* (Jn 13:27). Satan was already there, but this was John's way of saying that there was no longer any hindrance to the traitor's embarking on his purpose. So he prepared to leave the room.

Seeing this Jesus said, *"What you're doing, do quickly."* It was customary at the Passover to buy food to give to the poor. The disciples thought that Jesus was sending Judas on such an errand of mercy. John notes that as soon as Judas received the piece of bread, he left immediately, and then he commented that *"it was night"* (13:30). Since it was the time of the full moon, this can hardly refer to natural darkness. It was John's mystical way of noting the darkness in the soul of Judas.

JESUS' WARNING ABOUT DANGER AND DESERTION

With the departure of Judas, Jesus turned His interest to the Eleven. He spoke of the imminence of His rapidly approaching Crucifixion and of their need to love one another. Then He said that that very night all of them would be caused to stumble because of what would happen to Him. The Shepherd would be smitten, and the flock would be scattered. However, Jesus promised that after His Resurrection He would meet them in Galilee.

The idea of stumbling brought a protest from Peter. Even though all others might forsake Him in His hour of danger, he said that he would never do so. He was ready to go to prison and death for his Lord. But Jesus knew him better than he knew himself, so He said that before the cock should crow before daylight Peter would deny Him three times. Still Peter continued to affirm his loyalty, and the other disciples joined with him in it.

Jesus was aware of the danger for Him stalking the streets of Jerusalem that night. Soon under Judas's guidance the temple police would be searching for Him. In this light one may understand Jesus' words in

Luke 22:35–38. Jesus was going to die, but it would be according to God's plan and not by mob violence. So He reminded the Eleven that on a previous occasion when He had sent them forth to preach, they went without purse, wallet, or extra shoes and they had lacked nothing. *"Then He said to them, 'But now, whoever has a money-bag should take it, and also a travel bag. And whoever doesn't have a sword should sell his robe and buy one"* (Lk 22:36). In the original Greek it is clear that Jesus said that if any of them had either a purse or a wallet, he should buy a sword, but if he had neither, then let him sell his robe and buy one.

In the light of the extreme pacifism so often attributed to Jesus, these words appear strange indeed. Some interpreters endeavor to tone them down by comparing them to Jesus' words to Peter in the Garden of Gethsemane (Mt 26:52). But these are plain words and must be interpreted in their context. Light is thrown upon them by the statement that follows: *"For I tell you, what is written must be fulfilled in Me: 'And He was counted among the outlaws. Yes, what is written about Me is coming to its fulfillment"* (Lk 22:37; cf. Is 53:12). Jesus has a goal ("end") that must be fulfilled by His death on the cross (between two thieves). Nothing must prevent it. The Gethsemane experience still awaits Him, and He must not be arrested until it is finished.

So Jesus told the disciples to get a sword. They were to protect Him until He was ready to be taken. The sword was for defensive purposes only. He would not establish His kingdom through the sword, but for the present situation a sword might be necessary in order that the kingdom should be established according to God's will.

In response to Jesus' admonition, the disciples said, *"'Lord, . . . look, here are two swords.' 'Enough of that!' He told them"* (Lk 22:38). Probably they found two swords belonging to the owner of the house in which they were gathered, so the disciples took the swords in accordance with Jesus' instruction.

THE INSTITUTION OF THE MEMORIAL SUPPER

Judas had left the room to go on his evil errand. This left only Jesus and the eleven believers. Judas, along with the others, most likely had been baptized; but he was not a believer, so this memorial supper was observed only by Jesus and these baptized believers.

Grapes on a vine

As they were eating the Passover meal, Jesus took bread, blessed it, and broke it, and gave it to His disciples, saying, *"Take and eat it; this is My body"* (Mt 26:26). Then He took the cup, saying, *"Drink from it . . . for this is My blood that establishes the covenant; it is shed for many for the forgiveness of sins"* (Mt 26:27–28). Thus in the simplest of action and language He instituted the ordinance of the Lord's Supper.

Jesus concluded this beautiful moment by saying, *"I will not drink of this fruit of the vine until that day when I drink it in a new way in My Father's kingdom with you"* (Mt 26:29). But His followers are to *"eat this bread, and drink the cup . . . until He comes"* (1 Co 11:26).

Unleavened bread and the fruit of the vine

THE FAREWELL DISCOURSE

The memorial supper had been instituted, and the hour was rapidly approaching when it would find meaning in the grim reality of Jesus' death. He was now ready to give to the disciples His final teaching before the Shepherd was to be taken from the sheep, and this final discourse may be divided into two parts.

1. In the Upper Room.

The words and deeds of Jesus this night had plunged the disciples into gloom. The passion that all the while had been so real to the Savior was finally taking hold of them. So Jesus sought to comfort and encourage them, not only for the hours immediately ahead of them, but for the unfolding years ahead. Indeed, He enveloped the centuries as He spoke to His followers until the end of time.

"Your heart must not be troubled. Believe in God; believe also in Me. In My Father's house are many dwelling places; if not, I would have told you. I am going away to prepare a place for you. If I go away and prepare a place for you, I will come back and receive you to Myself, so that where I am you may be also" (Jn 14:1–3).

One might as well try to adorn an American Beauty Rose as to comment on these words, for they were a pillow for broken hearts then, as they have been through the centuries, and will be until the end of time.

But quizzical minds did inquire after them then, even as they do so now, and the answers received are eternal gems of truth. Jesus said, *"You know the way where I am going."* Thomas said that since they did not know where Jesus was going, how could they know the way? Jesus replied, *"I am the way, the truth, and the life. No one comes to the Father except through Me."* He then said that He fully revealed the Father. If they knew

Him, they knew the Father also. These words evoked a prayer from Philip: *"Lord, show us the Father, and that's enough for us."* In turn this evoked surprise from Jesus that after all this time the disciples did not yet know the intimate oneness of Father and Son: *"The one who has seen Me has seen the Father. How can you say, 'Show us the Father'?"* (vv. 4–9). This led Jesus to emphasize again this oneness. Both His words and His works were of the Father, and if they did not believe His words, at least they should see God's presence in His works.

Furthermore, if they committed themselves to Him, they would do even greater works than He had done, not greater in kind but in scope, and this was because He was going to the Father. In His absence He promised that whatsoever they should ask in His name He would do, that the Father might be glorified in the Son.

The thought of His bodily absence introduced Jesus' promise of the abiding presence of the Holy Spirit. He said, *"And I will ask the Father, and He will give you another Counselor to be with you forever. He is the Spirit of truth. The world is unable to receive Him because it doesn't see Him or know Him. But you do know Him, because He remains with you and will be in you. I will not leave you as orphans; I am coming to you"* (Jn 14:16–18).

Even though Jesus was going away, they were not to be left as orphans after all. He would come to them in the presence of the Holy Spirit, who would be their Comforter or Encourager. He would be *"another Counselor"* or *"another"* of the same kind as Jesus.

Jesus then spoke of Christian love. This is the love God has for man, to which man responds in love for God through Christ, and they would show their love for Him by keeping His commandments. If they do, then they will know the abiding love of God in Christ who will indwell them.

Jesus spoke these words during His bodily presence, but the Comforter will teach them all things and will bring to their remembrance all that Jesus had said to them throughout His sojourn with them.

Finally, Jesus left with them the legacy of His peace. It is not the temporary, shallow peace of the world, but the abiding peace of His spiritual presence. Therefore, they were to be neither troubled nor afraid. If they truly love Him, they would not grieve because He was leaving them. Instead, they would rejoice because He was returning to the Father. He told them now of His impending departure in order that when it occurred they would believe.

Hereafter He would not talk much with them, because He would soon be taken from them by the power of evil. He was ready for it in order that the world might know fully God's redeeming purpose.

"Get up; let's leave this place" (Jn 14:31), and with these words Jesus led His little band of sheep from the safety of the Upper Room to go to the tryst awaiting Him in Gethsemane.

2. On the Way to Gethsemane.

Jesus often used the peripatetic method of teaching. That is, He taught as He walked along. So on the way to Gethsemane, as they walked along Jerusalem's dark streets, He continued to teach.

He had already spoken of His departure and of the coming of the Holy Spirit, and in His power they were to witness concerning the gospel in the unfolding future. This they would do as in the Spirit they abode in Him.

Jesus likened Himself to *"the true vine, and My Father is the vineyard keeper"* (Jn 15:1). The followers of Jesus are the branches on the Vine, and the Father expects them to bear fruit. This they will do as they abide in Jesus, for apart from Him they will be fruitless. Failure to do so will result in lost usefulness. The result will be that they will be pruned from the Vine and their useless works will be burned. This does not refer to a lost redemption but to a lost opportunity. In fact, they had been chosen for the express purpose of bearing much fruit to the glory of God, and in their efforts at fruit bearing they have the assurance that God will give them the object of their prayers, as long as they come to God by the merits and in the authority of Jesus' name.

As they seek to witness, they must expect to endure the enmity of the world. It hated Jesus; it will hate them. It persecuted Jesus; it will persecute them. Nevertheless, they will not be alone in their work, for the Comforter will be with them. He will testify of Jesus, and in His power and presence they shall bear witness also.

Then Jesus reiterated the necessity of His departure. It was in order that the Holy Spirit might come. Of course He had been present all the while, but in a special way He will now work in and through the followers of Jesus.

He will reprove or convict the world of sin, righteousness, and judgment (Jn 16:8). *"Of sin,"* because the world believes not on Jesus—and this unbelief is the greatest of sins. *"Of righteousness,"* because Jesus goes to the Father, and the world shall see Him no more—but with Jesus' righteousness as the standard, the world will be made to realize its lack of righteousness before God. *"Of judgment,"* because Satan is judged permanently—and those who cling to him are judged accordingly.

There were many things Jesus would have spoken to the Eleven, but they were unprepared to receive them. However, the Holy Spirit would continue to teach them. He would guide them into all truth. He will not speak of Himself but of Jesus. He will not glorify Himself but Jesus. He will receive the things of Jesus and will show them to the disciples.

Then with a final promise of answered prayer, Jesus said, *"Look: An hour is coming, and has come, when each of you will be scattered to his own home, and you will leave Me alone. Yet I am not alone, because the Father is with Me. I have told you these things so that in Me you may have peace. You will have suffering in this world. Be courageous! I have conquered the world"* (Jn 16:32–33).

THE PRAYER OF INTERCESSION

Jesus had been walking as He taught, so possibly by this time they were somewhere in the vicinity of the temple area. If so, this adds meaning to that which ensued, for Jesus began to pray. This has been called His high priestly prayer. He will soon become the Sacrifice, but now the prayer of the High Priest rises as sweet incense to gladden the heart of God.

First, Jesus prayed for Himself. *"Father, the hour has come. Glorify Your Son so that the Son may glorify You"* (Jn 17:1). He came to give eternal life to all who would believe on Him. *"This is eternal life: that they may know You, the only true God, and the One You have sent—Jesus Christ"* (Jn 17:3). He had fully done the Father's will, a will anticipating the cross. Now the Son prays that the Father will glorify Him *"with that glory I had with You before the world existed"* (v. 5).

Second, Jesus prayed for the Eleven, and for all those who at that time had believed on Him.

"I pray for them" (Jn 17:9). He would soon leave them alone in the world, so He prayed that the Father would keep them. Because they are not of the world, the world will hate them. He did not pray that the Father would take them out of the world but that He would guard them from the evil one. He asked that they should be sanctified (set apart for God's service) through God's Word, which is truth. Jesus was sending them into the

world to declare God's truth, even as God had sent Him into the world to reveal it. And for their sakes He dedicated Himself to the cross.

Third, Jesus prayed for all who in the future should believe in Him. He prayed that they should know unity in spirit, even as He and the Father were one. Furthermore, He prayed that all who believe in Him should be with Him in glory. He wants them to behold His glory the Father has given to Him, *"because you loved Me before the world's foundation"* (Jn 17:24).

Then Jesus closed this prayer with words of wondrous beauty: *"Righteous Father! The world has not known You. However, I have known You, and these have known that You sent Me. I made Your name known to them and will make it known, so that the love with which You have loved Me may be in them, and that I may be in them"* (Jn 17:25–26).

What a beautiful way to close His public ministry! Having done so, Jesus went through the eastern gate of Jerusalem to rendezvous with destiny—a destiny that would give His greatest revelation of the love of God.

THE AGONY IN GETHSEMANE

It was now possibly past midnight when Jesus and the Eleven arrived at Gethsemane. This was a garden just across the Kidron brook from Jerusalem. Tourists today may visit such a garden in which stands the Church of All Nations. Gnarled olive trees may still be seen there, and one may view the Rock of Agony, reported to be the very rock on which Jesus prayed. Whether this is the actual spot or not, it must have been one nearby.

The word *Gethsemane* means "olive press," so evidently this was an olive orchard. It could have belonged to some friend of Jesus. He had often retired within its shaded retreats to spend time in prayer.

When Jesus arrived at Gethsemane, He left eight of the disciples near the entrance, probably as an outer guard against His being interrupted before He was ready to be arrested. Did this group have one of the two swords?

Then going farther into the garden, He left Peter, James, and John. Their near presence not only would strengthen Jesus but would also afford Him further protection. Peter carried one of the two swords. Luke says that Jesus told them to *"pray that you may not enter into temptation"* or trial (Lk 22:40). Both Matthew and Mark note that He told them to remain in that spot and *"watch"* or be on the alert.

Then with great sorrow of soul Jesus went still further into the shadows. There with only God to see, He knelt, fell on His face, and prayed. With a physician's touch Luke says that His *"sweat became like drops of blood falling to the ground."* He broke out into a bloody sweat that became clotted blood.

Three times Jesus prayed, and there is a progression in His prayers. The first prayer was, *"My Father! If it is possible, let this cup pass from Me.*

Inside the garden of Gethsemane (Mk 14:32–42), the olive trees and foliage provide a beautiful and tranquil scene.

Yet not as I will, but as You will" (Mt 26:39). He prayed for the cup to pass away if it be possible.

The second and third prayers were, *"My Father, if this cannot pass unless I drink it, Your will be done"* (Mt 26:42). The original language reveals that, realizing that the cup cannot pass away, *"unless I drink it,"* He was resigned to drinking it although He had not yet done so.

Was this struggle in prayer between Jesus and Satan? Or between Jesus and the Father? Or was it a struggle within Himself, within His own soul? Some hold that in Gethsemane Satan again tempted Jesus to avoid the cross. True, he did not want Jesus to die on the cross, but the struggle at this point does not seem to have been between Jesus and Satan. Nor can one say that it was a struggle between Jesus and the Father. There is no evidence of conflict between their wills. Indeed, in each prayer Jesus prayed that God's will should be done. Therefore, it would seem that the struggle was one within the soul of Jesus Himself.

This struggle is depicted in what the *"cup"* involved. Does it mean that Jesus feared physical death? The entire record of the Gospels is to the contrary. Jesus must become sin for a lost world. His sensitive and sinless soul drew back from the prospect of becoming the very essence of sin itself. If there were any other way! Since there was not, He willingly surrendered Himself to the Father's will. He took the *"cup"* to drink its last bitter dregs.

After each of the first two prayers, Jesus had come to the three disciples to find them asleep. Physical exhaustion had taken its toll. The first time He found them asleep, He awakened them and cautioned them to be on the alert; but the second time He did not bother them. The spirit was willing, but the flesh was weak.

However, the third time, with the victory fully won, He said to them, *"Are you still sleeping and resting?"* (Mt 26:45). He no longer needed their protection, for *"the time is near. The Son of Man is being betrayed into the hands of sinners. Get up; let's go! See—My betrayer is near"* (vv. 45–46).

The hour truly had come. And the Son of Man was ready.

CHAPTER X
THE CRUCIFIXION OF JESUS
THE TRIAL OF JESUS

The actual crucifixion of Jesus consumed a period of about six hours. It began about nine o'clock on Friday morning, and Jesus died shortly after three o'clock in the afternoon of that day. But the larger picture involves the time from His arrest until His death and burial, and the arrest took place sometime after midnight and long before dawn on Friday.

THE BETRAYAL OF JESUS

Even as Jesus said, *"Get up; let's go,"* Judas appeared, accompanied by the temple police and a cohort of Roman soldiers. Since leaving the Upper Room, Judas had been quite busy. In all probability he went first to the home of Caiaphas where he received a detachment of temple police. It took time for the high priest to secure the cohort of Roman soldiers from the Tower of Antonia. Perhaps these were sent along in case of a riot among the friends of Jesus.

Judas likely led this armed band to the home where he had left Jesus, but when they arrived, He and the Eleven had departed. Remembering Jesus' custom of praying in Gethsemane, Judas must have surmised that He had gone there again, so he led his group to the garden. They got by the outer guard of disciples who, like the inner guard, may have been asleep.

When they came to Jesus, He asked whom they were seeking. They said, *"Jesus the Nazarene"* (Jn 18:5). He replied, *"I am He."* Upon hearing this, the guard, in fearful awe, moved back so quickly that they fell to the ground. Regaining their composure, they again, in answer to a second question from Jesus, said that they sought Him.

Judas had agreed to point out Jesus to them by kissing Him, and even though Jesus had identified Himself to them, Judas stepped up to Him and said, *"Greetings, Rabbi!"* (Mt 26:49; to him Jesus was still only a rabbi) and with that he kissed Him. Actually, he *"kissed him much."* Since Judas called Jesus *"Rabbi,"* he probably kissed Him on the hand, the customary greeting of a pupil to his rabbi. With that, the officers seized Jesus.

By this time the disciples were wide awake. They asked Jesus if they should attack with the sword. Since they had been asleep, they were unaware that Jesus was now ready to be taken. Without waiting for an answer from Jesus, Peter, who may still have been somewhat dazed from

Model of the Tower of Antonia, which served a number of purposes including where the Roman soldiers were billeted

The old city of Jerusalem

sleep, pulled out his sword and swung away. He was trying to cut off some-body's head, for when he swung, Malchus, the high priest's slave, dodged expertly toward the direction from which the blow came, so that instead of being beheaded, he lost only his right ear. Jesus quickly healed the ear, and then He rebuked Peter. He took him in hand as He said, *"Put your sword back in place because all who take up a sword will perish by a sword"* (Mt 26:52).

Why did Peter react as he did? And why did Jesus rebuke him? When Peter saw Jesus being taken, and not knowing that He was now ready for it to take place, he did exactly what he understood that Jesus had told him to do. He was protecting Him from His enemies. But Jesus had now accom-plished His purpose in coming to Gethsemane. He no longer needed this protection, so He told Peter to put up his sword lest he get himself killed.

Note Jesus' further word: *"Or do you think that I cannot call on My Father, and He will provide Me at once with more than twelve legions of angels? How, then, would the Scriptures be fulfilled that say it must hap-pen this way?"* (Mt 26:53–54). More than twelve legions of angels! Over seventy-two thousand! One legion for each disciple, including Judas. He no longer needed guarding. Had He spoken just one word to the Father, the very forces of heaven would have rescued Him, and against such an assemblage what could a few temple police and Roman soldiers have done? No, Jesus was ready—His hour had come. The Scriptures must be fulfilled in Him. No man took His life from Him—He laid it down of Himself.

So with a word of rebuke for His captors, He permitted them to bind Him and lead Him away, and despite the disciples' avowals of loyalty, they all forsook Jesus and fled. They could with a sword dare the power of the armed band, but they lacked the moral courage to stand helpless in the face of evil.

Mark notes that a young man fled naked, as some officer grabbed after him (14:51–52), but he only got hold of a loose linen cloth which the lad had thrown about his body. Was this John Mark himself? If so, he had probably been awakened from sleep when the band came to his mother's home. With a boy's curiosity, perhaps he hurriedly put this linen cloth about his body and followed them to Gethsemane. At least, it is an interest-ing theory.

As the armed band led Jesus away, He said to them, *"This is your hour—and the dominion of darkness"* (Lk 22:53). Jesus had taken the *"cup,"* and for all practical purposes had become sin. Until this time God had kept evil on a leash. He permitted it to go so far in its wicked purpose, but no farther. Now it seems that He unleashed evil to let it do its worst. It is as though God were saying, "Do your worst. You want to destroy God. Now you have your chance. But when you have expended all of your tyrannical power, I will still triumph over you!" It is thus that one can understand the utter abandon of evil in the hours following. In this light both the cross and the empty tomb take on their ultimate significance.

THE TRIAL ITSELF

The trial of Jesus comprised two phases, the Jewish and the Roman, and each of these was composed of three stages.

1. The Jewish Trial.

(1) The Preliminary Examination.

Jesus was taken first before Annas, the father-in-law of Caiaphas. It was before dawn on Friday. Even though Annas had been deposed as high priest by the Romans, he continued to wield great power with both the Jews and the Romans. So any charge brought against Jesus having his support would bear weight with both groups.

Furthermore, the sudden turn of events brought on by Judas' treachery had probably caught the Sanhedrin unprepared. Therefore, it was considered wise by them to let Annas hold a preliminary examination in order to try to learn some definite charge to bring against Jesus.

When Jesus appeared before him, Annas asked Him about His disciples and His teachings. Jesus reminded him that He had always spoken openly in the synagogues and the temple itself, so let those who had heard Him answer Annas's question. One of the temple police struck Jesus with a rod for thus answering the high priest. *"If I have spoken wrongly,"* Jesus answered him, *"give evidence about the wrong; but if rightly, why do you hit Me?"* (Jn 18:23).

It was evident that Annas had failed to evoke a charge from Jesus. Therefore, he sent Him on to Caiaphas.

(2) The Predawn Trial before the Sanhedrin.

This stage of the trial was held in the home of Caiaphas. When word reached him that Jesus had been arrested, he hastily summoned the Sanhedrin, excepting Joseph of Arimathea and Nicodemus, to his home. It would appear that they had prepared two men to bear witness against Jesus, but events were moving so rapidly that they had not yet arrived. Therefore, the Sanhedrin sought to get other witnesses to bring some testimony against Jesus that would justify the death sentence. Apparently they had difficulty finding such, and even those who came forward gave conflicting testimony.

By this time the coached witnesses arrived, but even their testimony did not agree. One reported Jesus as having said, *"I can demolish God's sanctuary and rebuild it in three days"* (Mt 26:61). The other's account was that He had said, *"I will demolish this sanctuary made by human hands, and in three days I will build another not made by hands"* (Mk 14:58). Evidently the chief priests had remembered but misunderstood Jesus' words at the first cleansing of the temple. However, the witnesses did not do so well in following their coaching.

So failing here, the high priest took charge. As though to imply that these witnesses had produced damaging evidence, he asked if Jesus could answer the charge. But He remained silent. Then Caiaphas became desperate: *"By the living God I place You under oath: tell us if You are the Messiah, the Son of God!"* (Mt 26:63). Had Jesus remained silent, He would have been denying His identity as Messiah and Son of God. So under oath He admitted that He was, saying, *"You have said it"* or "Yes."

This would have been enough evidence for Caiaphas. But he received more than he expected, for Jesus continued, *"But I tell you, in the future you will see 'the Son of Man seated at the right hand' of the Power, and*

The Church of St. Peter in Gallicantu on the north slope of the Hinnom Valley. According to tradition this is the place where Peter denied Jesus.

'coming on the clouds of heaven'" (Mt 26:64). The day will come when He will be the Judge and Caiaphas will be the judged.

Caiaphas had heard enough. So charging Jesus with blasphemy, he asked as to what further evidence they needed. Then he began to tear his garments. When they heard blasphemy, the Jews were supposed to tear their garments and never wear them again. In all likelihood the remainder of the Sanhedrin followed their high priest's example, and when Caiaphas asked for their verdict, they all cried, *"He deserves death!"* (Mt 26:66).

Then pandemonium broke loose. They began to spit in Jesus' face and to beat Him on the neck. The temple police joined in the debacle. After blindfolding Jesus, they beat Him with rods and mocked Him, saying, *"Prophesy to us, Messiah! Who hit You?"* (Mt 26:68). It was a sickening spectacle. A court of justice had become a kangaroo court of injustice. What should have been a dignified occasion had become mob violence. It was the hour of the tyranny of darkness, as these men vented their hatred upon the Holy One of God.

While all this was transpiring within Caiaphas' house, a tragic event was taking place in the court outside. Peter, after a momentary panic, had followed afar off to see the outcome of Jesus' arrest. Three times he was asked by those around him if he were not one of Jesus' disciples. He first pretended not to understand the question. Later he took an oath that he did not know Jesus. Finally someone noted that he was a Galilean, because his peculiar dialect proved it. Apparently Peter then decided if language had anything to do with it, he would show them some language. His fisherman's vocabulary came to the surface as he began to curse and swear, saying, *"I do not know the man!"* (Mt 26:74). Then from somewhere, probably outside the city, he heard a rooster crow. With this he recalled Jesus' words about his three denials.

Evidently Jesus heard it also, for He turned and looked at Peter, who was also looking at Him. That look broke Peter's heart, and weeping bitterly, he slipped away into the darkness.

(3) The Post-Dawn Trial before the Sanhedrin.

This stage of Jesus' trial was a mere formality, for the Sanhedrin had already decreed that He deserved to die. But Jewish law forbade that trials should be held at night, so to ratify the action already taken under cover of darkness, and to preserve the semblance of legality, after dawn the Sanhedrin assembled in its regular chambers and formally pronounced Jesus to be liable to death. It was after dawn, indeed, but it was the dawn of the blackest day in the history of the world!

A post mortem to the Jewish trial of Jesus was the remorse and suicide of Judas. When he saw that Jesus was condemned to death, he was *"full of remorse"* (Mt 27:3). The word rendered *"full of remorse"* is not the word for true repentance, meaning a change of mind, heart, and attitude. It carries the sense of "regret" but does not result in change within the person. Paul says that it may lead to true repentance (2 Co 7:8–10) but not necessarily so. Judas's regret did not do so. He regretted that he got caught in his deed. He suffered remorse, but he did not truly repent. Like some rapist who suffers remorse after he has satisfied his lust but will commit his foul deed again, so Judas suffered remorse. However, it involved no change of heart, mind, or attitude.

In his fit of remorse he sought to ease his conscience by returning the thirty pieces of silver, but the chief priests would have none of it. They had used Judas in their nefarious deed and now were through with him. So he flung the blood money at their feet and went out and hanged himself. He is one of five suicides mentioned in the Bible, the only one in the New Testament. Where he did this is not known. Tradition places it in the Valley of Hinnom. Such a place is still pointed out to tourists. This would have been a fitting place for so foul an end, for it was Jesus' symbol of hell, the eternal destiny of Judas as he went *"to his own place"* (Ac 1:25).

The chief priests never appeared more hypocritical than at this point. They had probably taken this blood money from the sacred treasury or Corban. They had no compunction of conscience in using God's sacred money to carry out their evil purpose to destroy an innocent man, even the Son of God. Yet when it was thrown back at their feet, they said, *"It's not lawful to put it into the temple treasury, since it is blood money"* (Mt 27:6), a price which they themselves had paid. So after taking counsel, they used it to purchase a potter's field in which to bury, not Jews, but foreigners! (v. 7; cf. Ac 1:18–19). They did not even name it "Judas's Memorial Cemetery!" Judas selfishly reached for the stars, but he got nothing. Yea, less than nothing; for he lost even that which he had, including his immortal soul.

2. The Roman Trial.

(1) The First Time before Pilate.

Under Roman rule the Sanhedrin was permitted to try cases involving civil and religious matters, but the Romans reserved to themselves the right to try criminal cases involving capital punishment. So even in this light, the Jewish trial was a farce. The most that it could accomplish was to determine some capital charge against Jesus to present to the Roman governor Pilate.

Since it was early on Friday morning when the chief priests brought Jesus to Pilate, the place was probably the Herodian palace. Lest they be defiled for the Passover, the chief priests refused to enter the dwelling of

Excavations of Herod's Palace on the west side of Old Jerusalem adjacent to the Phasael Tower, one of the three towers constructed to guard the palace. This is one of three possible sites for the Praetorium, the site of the Roman phases of Jesus' trials.

a Gentile. Therefore, when they arrived, Pilate came outside to meet with them.

The interplay of scorn between Pilate and the Jewish rulers is quite evident in the proceedings. In response to the governor's question as to the charge against Jesus, they said that had He not been an evildoer they would not have brought Him to Pilate. However, of necessity they stated a charge: *"We found this man subverting our nation, opposing payment of taxes to Caesar, and saying that He Himself is the Messiah, a King"* (Lk 23:2). They themselves had accused Jesus of blasphemy, but they knew that Pilate would consider only a charge involving political implications. However, even the charge which they named was a false one.

Pilate sensed that the whole thing involved only religious matters, so he told them to judge Jesus according to their own laws. Even though the Roman had not yet examined Jesus, the Jews reminded him that they had no authority to handle capital cases. To them Jesus was condemned prior to a legal trial.

So Pilate had Jesus on his hands. Therefore, he took Him inside the palace to examine Him. Here, then, is one of the most dramatic moments in history—Jesus, the Son of God, before a pagan Roman governor. Pilate thought that Jesus was on trial before him, when all the while he was on trial before Jesus. Take interest in the regal bearing of Jesus throughout this entire series of trials. It is evident that He, not His judges, was directing the proceedings. He would die, but it must be as a King.

The governor never asked Jesus about the charge of forbidding the payment of Roman taxes. This is significant, since this was a particularly tender spot for the Roman Empire. It shows that Pilate realized the falseness of the charge and that the matter was religious in nature. However, the chief priests had charged that Jesus made Himself a king, so the governor asked if He were the King of the Jews. Jesus replied that according to Pilate's own words He was; but He emphasized the fact that His kingdom was one of truth and not of politics. However, the fact remained that both the Sanhedrin and Pilate had called Jesus a King.

With a contemptuous question as to *"what is truth?"* Pilate led Jesus outside again. He told the Jews that he found Him guilty of no crime. The chief priests and elders, Sadducees and Pharisees, repeated their charge, which met only the silence of Jesus. Evidently expecting a denial from Him, Pilate asked if He had anything to say about the charge. *"But He didn't answer him on even one charge"* (Mt 27:14). Once He had led them to charge Him with kingship, Jesus had nothing more to say. This silence caused the governor to marvel greatly.

Apparently the Jews sensed that Pilate was about to release Jesus. Therefore, they began to say more urgently, *"He stirs up the people, teaching throughout all Judea, from Galilee . . . to here"* (Lk 23:5). When Pilate heard the word *Galilee*, he saw a way out of his predicament, for Galilee was under the jurisdiction of Herod Antipas who was in Jerusalem at that moment. Even though the two men were not on good terms, Pilate sent Jesus to Herod for judgment. He cared little for showing the puppet tetrarch any courtesy. He merely wanted to get Jesus off his hands.

(2) The Appearance before Herod Antipas.

Herod Antipas was quite pleased when Jesus was brought before him. He had long wished to see Jesus, hoping that He would perform a miracle in his presence; but even though he questioned Him at length, amid the repeated charges of the Jewish rulers, Jesus did not so much as speak one word to him. Knowing Herod's true nature, He ignored him altogether.

Herod soon became bored with the entire proceedings. Therefore, he and his soldiers began to treat Jesus with contempt. They regarded Him as nothing, a zero. So they mocked Him, their supreme mockery being to array Him in robes of regal splendor. A king indeed! Therefore, they dressed Him as one, and then they sent Him back to Pilate. The Roman governor still had Jesus on his hands.

(3) The Second Time before Pilate.

When Jesus again stood before Pilate, the governor called a counsel with the Jewish rulers. He told them that neither he nor Herod had found Jesus guilty of their charges, but to placate them he proposed to whip Him and then to release Him. Whip an innocent man? But such was the conniving of an evil mind and a weak character. Of course the Jews would have none of this.

In desperation Pilate sought some other way to escape his uneasy predicament. Suddenly he remembered a custom of the Romans. On festive occasions, in order to placate the Jews, they would release some prisoner of their choosing. At that moment Pilate was holding a notable prisoner named Barabbas. He was guilty of insurrection, robbery, and murder, and, together with others, probably was scheduled to be crucified that very day. He may have been one of the false messiahs whose mission had failed, and like so many others of his kind, he had become the leader of a robber band that pillaged and murdered. Pilate thought that the Jewish people surely would not want him turned loose on them again.

Therefore, he proposed to release either Jesus or Barabbas. The Jews could have their choice. It may well be that the people were about to select Jesus for release, but at that point the proceedings were interrupted. For at that moment Pilate received a message from his wife. She urged him to have nothing to do with this righteous man. In a dream she had suffered many things because of Him, and since the Romans placed much importance on dreams, this disturbed Pilate all the more.

The Jewish rulers had used this interruption to advantage. Moving among the people, they urged them to choose Barabbas. Thus when Pilate asked them to make their choice, they chose Barabbas for release. In consternation Pilate, perhaps hoping that their choice might even extend to Jesus, asked, *"What should I do then with Jesus, who is called Messiah?"* (Mt 27:22). Unanimously they cried, *"Crucify Him!"*

What was the choice that they made? It involved more than a man, for they proposed to release one who had claimed to be their kind of messiah and to crucify the Messiah of God. It is interesting to note that Origen, the early Christian scholar (AD 185–254), claims to have seen a Gospel of Matthew calling Barabbas "Jesus Barabbas," and some manuscripts in existence today so read. There is tremendous suggestion in this thought.

The word *Jesus* means "Jehovah is salvation." *Barabbas* means "son of father." So here was "Jesus, the son of his father" and "Jesus, the Son of His Father." The former offered himself as a political messiah; the latter offered Himself as a spiritual Messiah. The one proposed to give political redemption; the Other proposed to give redemption from sin. The one brought revolution; the Other brought regeneration. Jesus Barabbas offered to save the Jews by the shedding of their blood. Jesus Christ would save them by the shedding of His own blood. But the Jews chose Jesus Barabbas and rejected Jesus Christ. Truly, they chose, and rejected, more than they knew.

Still Pilate made one last effort to release Jesus—he beat Him unmercifully. This was done by tying Him to a post, having first bared His back. The whip was made of leather thongs. In the end of each thong was placed a piece of bone or metal. With each lick these pieces tore out bits of flesh, leaving the back of the victim a bloody, lacerated mass. In such a condition Jesus would appear to be everything else but regal. So, partly in derision of the Jews and perhaps also hoping to appeal to their sympathy for so pitiful a spectacle, Pilate brought Jesus before them, saying, *"Here is the man!"*

But Jesus was to know no sympathy that day. Instead, the mob cried, *"Crucify Him."* Still protesting the innocence of Jesus, Pilate tried to escape a decision by a weak yet taunting suggestion that the Jews should crucify Jesus. *"See to it yourselves,"* he said. But they could not put anyone to death, let alone crucify them. And they would not let Pilate escape. By their law Jesus should die because He had made Himself the Son of God. Hearing this, the superstitious Roman feared all the more. Again taking Jesus inside the palace, he questioned Him once more, but no answer came from Him. Pilate reminded Jesus that he had the power either to release or to crucify Him. Then Jesus spoke the second time to the governor. He reminded him that the only power which he had over Him was not from Rome but from heaven. Pilate's abuse of that power was a sin, to be sure. However, since he was a pagan who was ignorant of the revelation of God, those who knew that revelation and yet had handed Jesus over to Pilate for crucifixion must bear the greater sin.

When the governor sought once again to release Jesus, the Jews reminded him that if he did so he was no friend of Caesar. Here was a veiled threat to bring this whole

The Jewish leadership got Pilate's attention when they told him if he released Jesus, he would be no friend of Caesar. At that time Tiberius Augustus was Caesar (AD 14–37).

matter to Caesar's attention, along with Pilate's other misdeeds. That did it! Because as a procurator he was directly accountable not to the Roman senate but to Caesar.

So Pilate gave up the struggle. He caused his judgment seat to be brought forth for the purpose of sitting thereon as he pronounced upon Jesus the sentence of death by crucifixion. Before he did so, however, in scornful defiance of the Jews, he pointed to Jesus saying, *"Here is your King!" The chief priests completely denounced the kingship of Jesus, even of God Himself, as they said, "We have no king but Caesar"* (Jn 19:15).

When, therefore, he saw that the case was hopeless, Pilate performed a customary ritual to declare his innocence in the whole debacle. Calling for a basin of water, he washed his hands before the multitude, saying, *"I am innocent of this man's blood. See to it yourselves"* (Mt 27:24).

But Pilate could not escape his guilt so easily. In his cowardly surrender to mob violence, he made a travesty out of Roman justice. He continued on his evil way, until in AD 36, just six years after he had sought so tenaciously but weakly to escape the judgment of Caesar, he was recalled to Rome and banished to Gaul. Just outside Lucerene, Switzerland, stands Mount Pilatus. Tradition says that when storms rage on that mountain, Pilate's ghost in the rain seeks to wash the guilt from his hands, saying, "It won't come off! It won't come off!" Nor will it ever do so.

What about the Jews who stood before him on that terrible day in Jerusalem? All the people answered, *"His blood be on us and on our children!"* (Mt 27:25).

This is all the more terrible when one remembers the teaching of the Mosaic Law in this regard. Pilate knew nothing of it; but the Jewish people knew. In Deuteronomy 21 the law took account of the problem of innocence in cases of unsolved murder. If someone was found slain in the field by an unknown slayer, the distance should be measured from the body to the surrounding cities. The one nearest to the body was regarded responsible. So to be cleansed of guilt the elders of the city were to follow a prescribed rite. A heifer was to be slain in an uncultivated valley. This was to be done in the presence of the priests, the sons of Levi. Then the elders were to wash their hands over the slain heifer, all the while saying, *"Our hands did not shed this blood; our eyes did not see it. Lord, forgive your people Israel You redeemed, and do not hold the shedding of innocent blood against them. Then they will be absolved of responsibility for bloodshed"* (vv. 7–8).

No absolution was sought on this day. Instead, the crowd embraced responsibility for the crime that was about to take place.

Pilate released Barabbas, but he caused Jesus to be scourged and crucified. The soldiers made quite a sport of the whole affair. So Jesus was a king, was He? A king should have regal robes! Therefore, they put about Jesus a scarlet cloak belonging to one of the soldiers. He should have a crown! So they plaited one out of thorns and thrust it on His head, the thorns gouging into His brow. He should have a scepter! A reed of grass growing nearby was plucked and placed in His hand. Then in procession the soldiers passed by, kneeling before Him, hailing Him as King of the Jews, spitting on Him, and beating Him on the head.

When they had tired of the cruel sport, they led Jesus away to be crucified. The ordeal to which He had been subjected took its toll, for on the way He fell under the weight of His cross that He was required to carry. A passerby, Simon of Cyrene, probably a Jew from North Africa who had come to Jerusalem for the Passover, was made to carry the cross for Jesus. Two malefactors, perhaps companions in crime with Barabbas as their leader, were also taken to be crucified. So they came to Golgotha, a hill shaped like a skull. (The Latin name is *Calvary*.)

No one knows for certain the location of this place. Tradition places it at the site of the Church of the Holy Sepulchre. In modern times Gordon's Calvary has been mentioned as a possibility. This is a small knoll outside the city wall, which to this day has the appearance of a skull. It is now the site of an Arab cemetery. A guide told the writer that this was once the place where the Jews executed by stoning. The Romans continued to use it, only they employed the method of crucifixion. One thing is known. Calvary was outside the city wall (Heb 13:12). Archaeologists are not agreed as to whether the Church of the Holy Sepulchre stands outside the wall of that day, but most certainly Gordon's Calvary does.

THE DEATH OF JESUS

1. Some Significant Matters.

A benevolent society of women in Jerusalem always provided a drink of drugged wine for crucifixion victims in order to dull the pain, but when it was offered to Jesus, He tasted it and then refused it. He would endure the cross in full possession of His mental powers. Upon this refusal the soldiers proceeded with the crucifixion, an ordeal so terrible that Roman law forbade that it should be used in executing a Roman citizen.

One end of the upright part of the cross was placed in a hole in the ground. The crosspiece was placed flat on the ground. After stripping the victim of his clothes, he was made to lie flat on the ground with his arms outstretched along the crosspiece. In order to render him helpless, his arms and legs were jerked out of joint. Then, after his hands had been nailed to the crosspiece, his body was drawn up into a position, perhaps two feet above the ground, where the crosspiece was fastened to the upright part. Finally, his feet were crossed, and a spike driven through them into the wood. Then a board, on which was written the victim's

Gordon's Calvary, one of two possible sites where Jesus was crucified

crime, was nailed above his head. In the case of Jesus it read, *"JESUS THE NAZARENE THE KING OF THE JEWS."* Thus Jesus, stark naked, was nailed to a cross between two thieves. Truly, He *"was counted among the rebels"* (Is 53:12).

The crucifixion detail was composed of four soldiers under the command of a centurion. Customarily the four soldiers divided among themselves the clothes of their victims. Usually such clothing consisted of five garments: head gear, sandals, girdle, an outer garment, and an inner garment. Each of the soldiers took one of the first four items, but Jesus' inner garment was seamless or in one piece. Therefore, rather than tear it, the soldiers gambled for it. Little did they know that they were fulfilling Psalm 22:18.

In the meantime the chief priests returned to Herod's palace to protest the wording written on the superscription above Jesus' head. They insisted that it should not read, *"THE KING OF THE JEWS,"* but that He said, *"I AM KING OF THE JEWS."* However, Pilate stood his ground. Therefore,

Courtyard of Church of the Holy Sepulchre in Jerusalem. One of the two possible sites of Jesus' crucifixion

the official Roman crime for which Jesus died was that He was King of the Jews.

John notes that this "title" was written in Hebrew (Aramaic), Latin, and Greek. Obviously Pilate's purpose in using this trilingual title was that the crime of Jesus might be known to all. Aramaic was the language spoken in Palestine at that time. Latin was the official language of the Empire, and Greek was a somewhat universal language that would be understood by all who did not read the other two.

However, knowing John's mystical nature, one can but wonder if he did not mention these languages with another purpose in mind. Was it not to point out the universal guilt for Jesus' death? Hebrew, Latin, and Greek suggest the three great streams of life in the Roman world. At least these languages suggest that the three great streams converged to nail Jesus to the cross. Hebrew was the language of religion; Latin was the language of government; Greek was the language of pagan culture. Religion rejected Jesus; government crucified Him; pagan culture ignored Him. Surely there was/is guilt enough for all.

What of the ordeal of the crucifixion itself? During this time Jesus spoke seven times, and in these "seven words from the cross" one may under-stand partly that which transpired as *"in Christ, God was reconciling the world to Himself"* (2 Co 5:19).

2. The Seven Words from the Cross.

(1) *"Father, forgive them, because they do not know what they are doing"* (Lk 23:34).

This was a prayer prayed by Jesus, probably while He was being fastened to the cross. Over and over He prayed it. It was a prayer that God would forgive all whose sin helped nail Him to the cross.

In a distinct way, however, it was a prayer for those who had an actual part in the crucifixion itself. The basis upon which He asked this forgiveness was that they did not "know" what they were doing. Paul says that had the rulers of this world known, they would not have crucified the Lord of glory (2 Co 2:8).

When Jesus prayed, He used a word for "know" which means to perceive through experiential knowledge until it becomes a conviction of the soul or soul knowledge. In their sin-mastered state they did not know in their souls what they were doing. They had asked for a sign from heaven as to Jesus' deity. That sign would be His bodily Resurrection. Thereafter they would have a basis upon which to acquire soul knowledge. If then they repented, they should be forgiven. Otherwise, there would be no forgiveness.

The people passing by on the nearby road railed against Jesus, calling upon Him to come down from the cross. Even the chief priests, scribes, and elders, having returned from their fruitless mission to Pilate, joined in. They said literally, *"He is the King of Israel! Let Him come down now from the cross, and we will believe in Him"* (Mt 27:42). They even dared God to save Him. *"He has put His trust in God; let God rescue Him now— if He wants Him! For He said, 'I am God's Son'"* (v. 43). The two thieves dying on either side of Jesus joined in with His tormentors.

This raises the question as to who or what nailed Jesus to the cross. Certainly it was in the will and purpose of God, but this is not to say that He actually did it. One might say that Satan did it. He had tried repeatedly to kill Jesus, but in no sense did he want Him to die on a cross. From the outset he tried to steer Jesus away from it. Even now through the mockers in the crowd Satan was challenging Him to leave the cross, for he knew that it was in such a death that God would utterly defeat him. In this light one can only say that evil running rampant nailed Jesus to the cross. It had even gotten out of Satan's control. God had unbridled evil to let it do its worst, and even then He would triumph over it and destroy its power.

Could Jesus have come down from the cross? He could have, but He would not, for He was on the cross to die for the sins of the world. If He saved Himself physically, He could not save man spiritually. So, in fact, He was held to the cross, not by spikes, but by divine love expressing itself in God's saving will and purpose.

(2) "Today you will be with Me in paradise" (Lk 23:43).

The howling mob continued, but to Jesus through its din came the voices of the two thieves. At first they both reproached Him, parroting the words of the Jewish rulers. Suddenly there was a change, for in one sense of the word both men began to pray to Jesus. They were asking that He do something for them.

One thief yelled insults at Him. He demanded that since Jesus claimed to be the Christ, He should save both Himself and them. There was no note of repentance and confession. He said nothing about sin, only about his present peril. There was no change in his heart. He only wanted off that cross. Jesus heard him with His ears but not with His heart. There was no basis whatever for a divine response, so this thief entered hell with a so-called prayer on his lips.

The other thief prayed quite differently. He rebuked his companion in crime, admitted their sin, but confessed the sinlessness of Jesus. Then he prayed, *"Jesus, remember me when You come into Your kingdom!"* (Lk 23:42). The light had broken through to his soul. He knew that Jesus was the Christ of God. In that knowledge he forgot all about his present predicament. His one thought was for his soul. On the cross both he and

Jesus would surely die, yet his only desire was to be remembered by Jesus in His kingdom.

However, he received more than he asked for. Jesus said, *"Today you will be with Me in paradise."* He prayed for remembrance; he received fellowship. He thought of a far distant kingdom; Jesus said, *"Today."* Before the sun set on that day, Jesus and the redeemed sinner walked arm in arm through the gates of glory.

(3) *"Woman, here is your son! . . . Here is your mother"* (Jn 19:26–27).

There was a little island of love in that ocean of hate, for three women and a man had drawn near to the cross. One woman was Jesus' mother, and the man was John the beloved disciple. When Jesus saw them, He spoke to them words of comfort and courage.

Mary had learned to lean on Jesus, her eldest son. Now He was dying. The sword truly was piercing through her soul. The future must have been bleak indeed. To whom could she turn, for her other children did not believe in Jesus as the Messiah!

John also was bent down with grief, for the One whom he loved with a passion was now hanging on a cruel cross. What could life possibly hold for him?

Then they both heard Jesus' blessed words. To Mary they meant that she could now turn to the one person on earth who, besides herself, loved and understood Jesus the best. To John it meant the comfort and encouragement of a committed responsibility. Jesus had faith in him so that to him He entrusted His dearest and best. As Jesus was his substitute on the cross, so John would be Jesus' substitute in caring for His mother.

From that hour he took Mary to live in his own home. One tradition says that she lived with John in Jerusalem for a few years and then died there. Another holds that she died at an advanced age in Ephesus, where she had continued to live with the beloved disciple. In either case they most surely were a comfort and strength to each other, and they had fellowship together in their living Lord.

(4) *"My God, My God, why have You forsaken Me?"* (Mt 27:46).

These are the opening words of the twenty-second psalm, a psalm which describes the crucifixion in vivid detail. It must have been much in Jesus' mind and heart throughout His life, but this was not a mere recital of a verse of Scripture. It came up from the very depths of Jesus' soul. Matthew gives this verse from the original Hebrew, but Mark gives it in Aramaic, the native tongue of Jesus. Either is correct, but more likely Mark gives it exactly as Jesus uttered it. In His deep grief and suffering, the Lord, who doubtless spoke Greek, went back to the language of His childhood to give utterance to this cry.

With this saying one enters into the very Holy of Holies of Calvary. A strange darkness had hovered over the land since the noon hour, as though the sun covered its face before such a scene. It was now about three o'clock in the afternoon. It was indeed the hour of darkness both natural and spiritual.

It is impossible for mere man to plumb the depths of the meaning of this word of Jesus, but note that He no longer called God *"Father."* In some indefinable way the Father had forsaken the Son, so that now He can only say, *"My God."* Even this was a cry of faith, although there is the difference in relationship.

Was it not that Jesus now had drunk the last dregs of the bitter "cup"? He had become sin. A holy God cannot look with favor upon sin. In that moment the Son of God wrestled with sin in its deepest depths. The Son of man, now become sin, endured the sufferings of hell as all of the vial of God's abiding wrath was poured out upon sin. It was for only a moment, but it was the infinite God suffering infinitely for the infinite guilt of finite man. In a very real sense Jesus had been left by God in the lurch, which is itself a good translation of this cry.

(5) *"I'm thirsty!"* (Jn 19:28).

At the outset of the crucifixion, Jesus had refused drugged wine, but now He asked for something to drink. While the struggle with sin raged, He gave no thought to His own physical needs. Now that the battle was over, and the victory won, He called for some liquid.

This was a natural thing for Him to say, for thirst was one of the greatest sufferings accompanying death on the cross. Through bleeding Jesus lost body fluid. The suffering and nerve-racking experience caused Him to perspire profusely. Every ray of the hot sun became a leach sucking water from every pore of His naked body, so that His lips were parched and cracked. His mouth was dry, and His tongue thickened. Fever ravished His body, and His inflamed vocal cords became raspy.

There were two reasons Jesus uttered this one word *(dipsō)*. John says that Jesus knew all things were now finished, that is, the purpose of His being on the cross had been achieved, but he added also *"that the Scripture might be fulfilled"* (cf. Pss 22:14 15; 69:21). Except for the acts of dying and being raised again, every prophetic Scripture concerning His redemptive work other than those connected with Jesus' thirst had been fulfilled. So when He said, *"I'm thirsty,"* the picture up to that point was complete. Jesus did not utter this as a merely mechanical recital of Scripture, but coming, as it did, out of His physical agony, it did fulfill Scripture.

However, there was another reason for this word. Jesus was about to utter the word of victory or completion. He wished it to be not the rasping utterance of one who was completely spent. It must be clearly enunciated in order that it might be heard and understood.

There was also a touch of pity in this gruesome scene. A soldier took a sponge and dipped it in the vinegar provided for the crucifixion detail. Then placing it on a reed, he pressed it to the lips of the Savior.

(6) *"It is finished!"* (Jn 19:30).

This was Jesus' word of completion. It means that "it is finished and stands finished." It was a word of full and final completion. Nevermore will Jesus die on a cross. Nevermore will He suffer for the sin of the world. He had made the once-for-all sacrifice. All that was necessary for the Son to do for man's redemption had been accomplished.

The Greek papyri add greatly to the meaning of the word *tetelestai*. It belongs to a family of words used in the legal and commercial life of Jesus' day. One word of this family was used to express the idea of completing a legal deed by dating and signing it. In a very real sense, before the foundation of the world, God had drawn up a deed of redemption for all men who would receive it, but the deed had never been dated or signed. So just before Jesus died He inserted the date of His death, and He signed it in His indelible blood.

The word uttered by Jesus was used in the sense of making full and final payment of a note. Again, in eternity the Son had made out a promissory note of redemption. In this light one may understand the manner of salvation for those who died before Calvary. They were saved on credit, the credit of the Son of God, looking toward that day when He would pay the note. Therefore, all the Old Testament righteous, like Abraham, had looked forward in joy to Messiah's day.

Now on the cross the promissory note had been paid. So Jesus wrote across it TETELESTAI! Nevermore can payment again be demanded! All who lived before that hour, and since that hour, may in faith receive the redemption God in Christ provided as He died on the cross.

Even more to the point is a papyrus usage of this verb where a father sent his son on a mission, saying, *"Until you accomplish this for me."* It is inferred that upon the successful completion of the mission the son reported, *"It is finished."*

In the above examples, therefore, Jesus' sixth word from the cross takes on added meaning. To the Father He said, "Mission accomplished!" To the host of Old Testament saints who were in heaven "on credit," He said, "The note has been paid and receipted. The deed to redemption has been dated and signed." As this word TETELESTAI gave assurance to those who in faith looked forward to Calvary, even so it continues to give assurance to all after the event who look back to it believing in the Savior.

(7) *"Father, into Your hands I entrust My Spirit"* (Lk 23:46).

Having uttered this word Jesus died. Mark and Luke say that He *"expired"* or *"breathed His last."* John says that He *"yielded up His spirit,"* but Matthew says that He *"gave up His spirit."* In other words, when His mission was accomplished, He permitted His spirit to return to the Father. King all the way!

What did Jesus mean when He said, *"Father, into Your hands I entrust My spirit"*? You will notice that once again He addressed God as Father. There never was a time when He and the Father were not one, but, now that the struggle is over, the representative Prodigal of prodigals has been clasped to the Father's bosom. The Son committed or placed His spirit alongside the Father.

The papyri add meaning to this statement also, for this word *commit* was used in the sense of filing a report or of inserting something in the register. The Son, therefore, filed the report of His completed mission. The receipted note and completed deed He inserted in the register of heaven.

Another such use of this word was to commit a thing to another to be safeguarded and used for its intended purpose. A derivative of this word is used of a "deposit," as in a bank. The Son deposited His redemptive work in the bank of God's grace, to be kept safe and used for the redemption of all who shall believe in Him as Savior.

What these various words meant to those who first heard them from the cross enhances their meaning through the ages. They are the substance of the gospel itself, and they are committed by the Father to all who receive the Son in faith, that through the Holy Spirit they may be the power of God unto salvation to everyone who believes in Him who became everything that men are, apart from sin, that they may become everything that He is.

THE PHENOMENA ACCOMPANYING JESUS' DEATH

When Jesus died, strange things happened in and near Jerusalem. Nature itself responded to the death of its Creator. The earth quaked, and the rocks were split. The temple itself must have reeled, for the veil of the temple, which separated the Holy of Holies from the Court of the Priests, was torn in two from top to bottom. This signified that through the redemptive work of Christ every man might come to God with boldness.

Josephus tells of a quaking of the temple before its destruction, and the Jewish Talmud even says that such a phenomenon happened forty years before its destruction. This would mean AD 30, the very year that Jesus died!

Furthermore, tombs about Jerusalem were opened as the earth heaved, and many of the saints who had died came forth to appear to many in Jerusalem. Apparently they were raised after Jesus' resurrection (Mt 27:53), since He was the *"firstfruits"* from the dead (1 Co 15:23).

Quite naturally the earthquake frightened the people. Probably someone came running with the news about the temple veil. The centurion who

The temple veil is a curtain that separated the most holy place from the holy place (2 Ch 3:14). Only the high priest was allowed to pass through the veil and then only on the Day of Atonement (Lv16:2). At Jesus' death the temple veil was ripped from top to bottom, illustrating that in Christ God had abolished the barrier separating humanity from the presence of God (Mt 27:51; Mk 15:38; cp. Lk 23:45). Hebrews 10:20 uses the tabernacle veil, not as the image of a barrier, but of access. Access to God is gained through the flesh of the historical Jesus (cp. Jn 10:7).

commanded the crucifixion detail, together with the soldiers, said, *"This man really was God's Son"* (Mt 27:54). It is to be hoped that they came to know Him as the Son of God.

The multitude who had raged about the cross returned to the city, smiting their breasts in great grief. Well they might, for they had participated in the crime of the ages. But far out on the edge of the crowd stood a little band of women, faithful to the end, and their faith would soon be rewarded with assurance.

THE BURIAL OF JESUS

The Jewish rulers were meticulous to the end. Since it was the *"prepa-ration"* (Jn 19:31) or Friday, they requested that the three bodies should not remain on their crosses over the Sabbath. When they wished to hasten death, the soldiers did so by breaking the legs of their crucified victims. If left to die naturally on a cross, they might even linger for days. Therefore, the soldiers broke the legs of the two thieves, but when they came to Jesus, they found that He was already dead. So they did not break His legs, but one of the soldiers ran a spear into His side. These also were fulfillments of Scripture—that none of His bones should be broken and that they should look on Him whom they had pierced (Jn 19:36–37).

However, an even more significant thing happened. When Jesus' side was pierced, there came out blood and water. In dealing with the physical cause of Jesus' death, a medical doctor says that the spear pierced His left side near the heart. He concluded that since blood and water came out together, this shows that the inner walls of Jesus' heart had ruptured. Thus

Garden Tomb

An interior view of a representation of the garden tomb where Jesus was buried and was raised from death

He actually died, not from the throes of the Crucifixion itself but from a broken heart.

Nevertheless, when it was found that Jesus was dead, Joseph of Arimathea requested of Pilate that he be permitted to bury His body. Had not he, or some other person, claimed the body, it would have been thrown into the Valley of Hinnom. But having received permission, Joseph and Nicodemus prepared Jesus' body for burial and placed it in Joseph's new tomb in which no body had been buried.

Where was this tomb located? Tradition says that it was on the site of the Church of the Holy Sepulchre. The same problems exist here as are found in the attempt to locate Calvary. Perhaps the location will never be known. Maybe God does not intend that it should. One thing is certain. It was located in a garden near Calvary. Adjacent to Gordon's Calvary one may visit Gordon's Tomb. It is today located in a beautiful garden.

Joseph of Arimathea was a married man, and he may have had children. If such a person were preparing a tomb, would he not prepare for others than himself? The tomb in the Church of Holy Sepulchre provides for only one body, but Gordon's Tomb has places for two bodies on one side and two on the other. Furthermore, one side is unfinished, as though the *"new tomb"* (Jn 19:41) had been put to use hurriedly and unexpectedly. Just outside this tomb has been excavated a small chapel of the Byzantine period. Evidently at that time the place was considered as a Christian shrine. To be sure, this is not conclusive evidence that this was considered to be the tomb in which Jesus' body was placed, but it is interesting nevertheless.

After the tomb was closed by rolling a stone across the entrance (Gordon's Tomb has a groove for such a stone), some of the faithful women lingered before it. Theirs was a love that would not let go.

However, there were other feelings concerning this tomb, for the chief priests and Pharisees went to Pilate with a request. They claimed to have remembered suddenly that Jesus had said that after three days He would rise from the dead. Had it ever been out of their minds? However, they asked that the tomb be sealed with the Roman seal and that a Roman guard be placed in front of it. They feared that the disciples might steal the body. Then, according to them, the last *"error"* would be worse than the first.

Pilate granted their request: *"You have a guard of soldiers . . . Go and make it as secure as you know how"* (Mt 27:65). Literally, "Make it sure for yourselves, as you know how." Therefore, they made the sepulchre secure, sealing the stone, with the guard watching them do it. The guard was then left to protect this seal of Roman authority and power. Poor soldiers! Was ever a detail assigned to so hopeless a mission!

The Jewish rulers were careful to protect their place and power, but in so doing they furnished one of the greatest proofs of Jesus' resurrection from the dead.

CHAPTER XI
THE RESURRECTION AND
ASCENSION OF JESUS CHRIST

The day when Jesus Christ died is the blackest day in the history of
the world, but the brightest day is when He arose from the dead. As someone has said, these days are but one day apart. According to the ancient
Jewish method of reckoning time, any part of a day was considered as an
entire day. Jesus was buried late on Friday—first day. He remained in the
tomb throughout Saturday—second day. He arose from the dead early on
Sunday—third day. When Jesus spoke of being in the heart of the earth
"three days and three nights" He was speaking within the context of the
thought of His day. The grand truth is that even though He was *"killed,"* He
was *"raised again the third day."*

THE DAY THAT CHRIST AROSE

Late on the Sabbath day Mary Magdalene and another Mary visited the
tomb of Jesus. It was more than a Sabbath day's journey from Bethany to
the tomb. The Sabbath ended at 6:00 P.M. Therefore, after this hour these
two women and Salome went to buy spices to use in a further anointing of
Jesus' body after the hasty burial on Friday. Then before dawn on Sunday
these two Marys left Bethany to go to the tomb bent on their errand of
love.

In the meantime, even before daylight, there was a great earthquake, as two angels from heaven came down and rolled away the stone. Their brilliant appearance, along with the earth tremor, frightened the soldiers almost to death. Therefore, they fled from the scene in terror.

As the women made their way to the tomb, they wondered who would roll away the stone for them. In their fondest dreams they did not anticipate the scene awaiting them, for when they arrived, they found the tomb opened. Even while they wondered about this, they saw the angels and became frightened. But one of the angels allayed their fears as he spoke to them: *"Don't be afraid, because I know you are looking for Jesus who was crucified. He is not here! For He has been resurrected, just as He said. Come and see the place where He lay"* (Mt 28:5–6). He had been lying in the tomb, but now the tomb was empty. The angel reminded them that Jesus had repeatedly told them that this would be so, and then they

Beams of light illumine the Church of the Holy Sepulchre in Jerusalem, believed by many, to be the site where Jesus was buried

A recent tomb discovered in Israel which dates back to the first century. Jesus would have been buried in a similar tomb with the stone rolled over the entry.

remembered His words. They went into the tomb and found that Jesus' body was not there.

This naturally raises the question as to why the angels rolled away the stone. Was it to let Jesus out? No mention is made as to the exact moment that He came forth, but the entire tone of the Gospel record is to the effect that Jesus came forth, unassisted, except by the power of God. It would seem, therefore, that the tomb was empty even before the stone was removed. Therefore, the purpose of rolling away the stone was not to let Jesus out but to let the women in. They received proof that the body was not there.

Having shown the women the empty tomb, the angel told them to go quickly and tell the other disciples, and that He would meet them in

Galilee. With this the angels departed. Their mission concerning the risen Lord was finished. Thereafter it was up to the disciples to tell the glorious news to all the world.

Accepting this commission the women ran to tell the apostles. Apparently, they found only Peter and John. At first their report seemed to the two apostles as nothing more than the talk of hysterical women, and they did not believe it. Nevertheless, they would investigate the matter, so they ran to the tomb. John, being the younger, outran Peter and came to the tomb first. However, he hesitated at the entrance, only peeping in and glancing about. But Peter, when he arrived all out of breath, rushed in and looked around. The tomb was empty, all right, but he saw nothing more in the spectacle. Insofar as he was concerned, it could have been a grave robbery or something else. Then John, perhaps emboldened by Peter's example, went into the tomb, and with a discerning eye he saw more. He saw the linen clothes in which Jesus' body had been wound. Evidently they were lying in the form of a body but with the body removed. Then he noticed the napkin which had been on Jesus' head. It was not lying with the linen cloth but was carefully rolled up in a separate place in an orderly fashion. To John this meant that the empty tomb was not due to grave robbers. It indicated to him that Jesus truly had been raised from the dead. Peter went away still wondering, but John went away believing in the bodily Resurrection of Jesus.

THE REPORT OF THE GUARDS

While these events were transpiring, another more sinister one was taking place. Some of the guard detail that had been posted at the tomb, having overcome their panic, had gone to report the supernatural event to the chief priests, but instead of visiting the tomb to check on their story, they called a meeting of the Sanhedrin. The discussion that developed must have been an odd one. Quite naturally the Sadducees would want to deny that a resurrection had taken place. It would seem, however, that the Pharisees would have welcomed the guard's report. Here was proof positive that they were right and the Sadducees were wrong. However, they were partners in crime, and their blind hatred of Jesus united them on the very thing dividing them. Both groups had their *"sign from heaven,"* but they refused to believe it.

Therefore, they came up with what to them was a brilliant idea. They had warned Pilate of the possibility of a grave robbery, so now they bribed the soldiers to say that while they slept, the disciples had stolen the body of Jesus. If the soldiers were asleep, how did they know?

Acting on warnings from Jewish leaders, Pontius Pilate sought to secure the body of Jesus. Until 1961, some scholars doubted that Pilate was a historical figure. In that year a team of Italian archaeologists led by Dr. Antonio Frova discovered this limestone slab at Caesarea Maritima. It contains a building dedication to the Roman emperor, Tiberius Caesar. The dedication is made by Pontius, Prefect of Judea.

Where did the Sanhedrin get the *"large money"* for the bribe? Most likely it came from the sacred treasury. Probably they had taken the money from it to pay Judas for his act of treachery. Now they did the same to buy a denial of the Resurrection, and if Pilate heard of the failure of his soldiers, they could always use the Corban to seal his lips. They knew from experience that he was not above receiving a bribe, and they were not above giving it.

The soldiers did their job well, for years later, when Matthew wrote his Gospel, the concocted story was still being spread abroad. Nor did it stop with that generation, for more than a century later Justin Martyr mentions that this report was still being spread among the Jews by *"chosen men"* who had been sent throughout the Roman Empire to propagate it.

This event suggests that through the centuries various theories have been proposed to account for the empty tomb other than that claimed by the disciples—that Jesus was raised from death. Some have suggested that Joseph of Arimathea removed the body to another place, but why would he change his attitude so suddenly? Even had he done so, what about the guard? Another theory says that the women got lost and went to the wrong tomb. Did Peter and John also lose their way? One proposal is that the disciples made up the story to prove the deity of Jesus. However, in the first place, none of them expected Jesus to rise from the dead. In the second place, it would have been psychologically impossible for them to have endured untold suffering in preaching the Gospel, had they known that it was based on a fraud. One theory is that Jesus did not really die. He merely fainted, later revived, and came from the tomb. But the soldiers, who were experts in killing, said that He was dead. Had this theory been true, how could Jesus have gotten out of the grave clothes, or even the tomb itself? Furthermore, it is inconceivable that such a risen Savior, broken and emaciated, could have commanded the faith of His followers. Then there is the theory that the entire story is based upon hysteria brought on by grief. Indeed, Peter and John did think, at first, that the women were hysterical, but a visit to the tomb confirmed their story. Were all to whom Jesus appeared victims of such an emotional disturbance? Even more than five hundred at once? On the face of it these theories are preposterous.

Perhaps the most widely held position today, which would discount the Resurrection account, is that the Resurrection does not mean that Jesus' body arose from the grave. It means that His spirit lives on. However, the word *resurrection* means that something or someone who was once dead is alive again. No one claims that Jesus' spirit died. Such a theory robs Jesus of His uniqueness, for all men's spirits live on, and if this be the meaning of Jesus' Resurrection, then why believe in Him? Why not believe in Buddha, Gandhi, or some other great teacher? Jesus has influenced history and the human race as no other person has done. If one denies His unique deity, as proved by His Resurrection, then there is no reasonable explanation for this.

However, when men have exhausted their theories, they still must explain the empty tomb. All of the Gospels, which are credible historical documents, say that Jesus' body was placed in the tomb on Friday. It was found empty on Sunday, and all of the wisdom of men has never improved on the explanation of that which was given by the angel: *"He is not here! For He has been resurrected, just as He said. Come and see the place where He lay"* (Mt 28:6).

THE APPEARANCES OF JESUS

For forty days after His Resurrection, Jesus remained bodily on the earth. During that time He made ten appearances to various of His followers, ranging all the way from one person to more than five hundred at one time. The first five occurred on Resurrection Sunday. The others were scattered over the remaining period of His sojourn on earth.

1. The Appearance to Mary Magdalene.

When Peter and John ran to the tomb, they were followed by Mary Magdalene. After these men had left, she stood outside the tomb weeping. Hers were not tears of joy but of sorrow, for, not yet believing that Jesus was risen, she thought that someone had removed His body to a place unknown to her. Finally, she turned to leave the tomb. Before her stood Jesus, but, perhaps because of tear-blinded eyes, she did not recognize Him. He asked her why she was crying. Thinking that He must be the gardener, she said, *"Sir, if you've removed Him, tell me where you've put Him, and I will take Him away"* (Jn 20:15). Then Jesus spoke her name. Mary! Recognizing His voice, she said, *"Rabboni"* or "My Teacher." Evidently she fell at His feet, and clung to Him, for He said, *"Don't cling to me."* He said this because He had not yet ascended to His Father. This suggests that no longer should she know Him merely by sight, sound, and touch. Their fellowship was to be a spiritual one. His final state of glory had not yet begun. It would do so after His Ascension. Thereafter she would know a more intimate relationship through the Holy Spirit.

Instead of clinging to His person, she was to go and tell His *"brothers"* that He would soon ascend to His Father and their Father, to His God and their God. This is suggestive of that more intimate fellowship in the Heavenly Father through the Spirit.

So Mary ran to tell them that she had seen the risen Lord. It was His first appearance. Of interest at this point is that after the Resurrection of Jesus, no enemy of His ever visited the tomb. They were afraid that they might find it to be empty. After Mary Magdalene left the tomb, having seen

Jesus, no friend of His is recorded as having returned to it, for they knew that it was empty.

2. The Appearance of Jesus to Other Women.

At some time early on Sunday morning, Jesus appeared to a group of women. Matthew records this as coming immediately after the women had discovered the tomb to be empty, but in harmonizing the four Gospel accounts, this probably came after the appearance to Mary Magdalene. At any rate Jesus met them and greeted them with *"Good morning"* on this new day when the Son of righteousness had risen with healing in His wings. With this greeting, Jesus told them to bear the news to His disciples that He would keep His promise to meet them in Galilee.

3. The Appearance on the Road to Emmaus.

Sometime on Sunday afternoon two disciples, Cleopas and perhaps his wife, were walking along the road to Emmaus, a village located about seven miles from Jerusalem. They had been in the city during the last few terrible days, but they had left before the news of the Resurrection had been confirmed. Theirs was a gloomy walk, as they tossed words back and forth about the recent tragedy.

Jesus also was traveling that road, but when He drew near to them, for some reason they failed to recognize Him. As He walked along with them, He inquired as to their conversation. They expressed surprise that He seemed to be unaware of the events of recent days. When He asked what they meant, they recounted the death of Jesus, and one sees the depth of despair in their hearts as they said that they had hoped He should redeem Israel. But now He had been dead three days. True, word had come about the angels and the empty tomb. Some of the disciples had even investi-

Emmaus (Imwas). According to the Sinai manuscript, Emmaus is thought to be the site of the house of Cleopas. Ruins of a Byzantine church stand on the site of the house.

gated the report and had found the tomb to be empty, but to their knowledge no one had seen Jesus alive.

They had informed Jesus of recent events. Now He proceeded to teach them about the significance of these events. He gave to them an exposition of the messianic Scriptures which taught that these very things would happen to the Christ. How fortunate they were to hear these things from Christ Himself!

Presently they were in the village, at the door of their home. Jesus acted as though He would go by it, but upon their invitation He entered the home with them. As they sat down to eat, Jesus took a loaf of bread, blessed it, and gave some to them. Suddenly they recognized Him in the breaking of the bread, but just as suddenly He vanished from their sight. Then they noted how their hearts had burned within them as He had opened to them the meaning of the Scriptures.

4. The Appearance to Peter.

These two disciples of Emmaus hastened back to Jerusalem to tell the other believers the glad news, but upon arrival they found that they already knew about the risen Lord. It was now Sunday evening, and the group had assembled behind closed doors to share experiences. Therefore, when these two from Emmaus arrived, they were greeted with the news that Jesus had appeared to Simon Peter.

Peter had known that the tomb was empty, but apparently he did not believe that Jesus had risen until He appeared to him. The despair which had gripped this little group was now turned into exceeding joy, and they must have hung on every word of the disciples of Emmaus as they related in detail their experience with Jesus that day.

5. The Appearance to the Assembled Disciples.

Their greatest experience of the day was yet to come. As the group eagerly drank in every word of this report, suddenly Jesus Himself stood in their midst. Evidently the door was locked because of the disciples' fear of the Jews, but unlike the arrival of the disciples from Emmaus, who must have gained entrance by knocking on the door and giving proof as to their identity, Jesus was suddenly in their presence without having entered through an open door.

Thinking that they were seeing a spirit, naturally the group was terrified. But Jesus allayed their fears by giving to them the customary Jewish greeting: *"Peace to you!"* (Jn 20:19). To prove to them that He was more than a spirit He showed them His hands, feet, and side. He challenged them to handle Him that they might know that His was a resurrection of the body. It was too good to be true! But it was true, and as further evidence of it, Jesus ate some broiled fish they gave to Him upon His request.

In this picture certain things may be learned as to the nature of Jesus' resurrection body. It was not subject to time, space, or density. He could appear and disappear suddenly. He entered the room without opening the door. Yet He could be seen with the natural eye. He could speak and be heard. He was conscious of His surroundings. He had a body of flesh and bones and was subject to the touch of others. He could eat food. And, most interesting of all, His body still bore the marks of the nails that had held Him to the cross.

Whether these things should be pressed as to the resurrection bodies of all believers, they are suggestive nevertheless. Paul said that these bodies will be of such nature as to be suited to the conditions existing in the post-resurrection manner of life (1 Co 15:38–41).

The disciples were overjoyed. They must have listened intently as Jesus repeated His legacy of peace: *"Peace to you"* (Jn 20:21). It was at this time that He gave to them the first of three commissions. As the Father had sent Him into the world, even so was He sending them into the world. His language reveals that He is still sent, but they are to go for Him. Then He breathed upon them saying, *"Receive the Holy Spirit. If you forgive the sins of any, they are forgiven them; if you retain the sins of any, they are retained"* (Jn 20:22–23). He gave them a foretaste of Pentecost as He repeated the charge concerning their use of *"the keys of the kingdom"* which He had given twice before. Then He left them.

One of the apostles, Thomas, was absent from this happy event. It is not told where he was. He simply was not there, and what a blessing he missed! When later he heard of Jesus' appearance, he said, *"If I don't see the mark of the nails in His hands, put my finger into the mark of the nails, and put my hand into His side, I will never believe!"* (Jn 20:25). For such a stupendous thing he demanded proof, but he was no more a doubter than the others, for he only demanded the proof which they had already received.

6. The Appearance to the Eleven, including Thomas.

The next Sunday night the disciples were together again, and this time Thomas was with them. Once again the door was shut. As He had done on the previous Sunday, Jesus suddenly appeared among them. Following the Jewish greeting of peace, immediately He spoke to Thomas: *"Put your finger here and observe My hands. Reach out your hand and put it into My side. Don't be an unbeliever but a believer"* (Jn 20:27). It was as though Jesus had heard Thomas's condition of faith, for He challenged him with almost the exact words Thomas had used.

This was too much for Thomas. Confronted with the evidence of the bodily Resurrection, he forgot his demand. Instead of making the physical examination, he confessed, *"My Lord and my God!"* (Jn 20:28). He believed through sight, not touch, but he had missed the higher blessedness which would have been his had he believed without seeing.

Nevertheless, one cannot discount the faith of Thomas. Unfortunately, he has become a byword in modern language that refers to him as "Doubting Thomas," but even time cannot erase the fact that this heroic man, who once was ready to die with Jesus, made the greatest confession of the deity of Jesus that is recorded in the Gospels. No other faith reached the height of his faith as he confessed, *"My Lord and my God."*

7. The Appearance by the Sea of Galilee.

Jesus had said that He would meet His disciples in Galilee, so after the appearance on the second Sunday night, they evidently returned to Galilee to await the appointed time. As they waited, one evening Peter announced that he was going fishing. This was a natural thing for him to do, since

Sunrise on the Sea of Galilee at Tiberias. Here the Risen Christ prepared breakfast for seven of His disciples.

fishing had once been his trade. There were six other disciples, including John, with him, and all seven spent the night in an effort to catch some fish. They caught none.

At daybreak Jesus stood on the beach. However, because the disciples were some distance from shore, with possibly a morning fog hovering about, they did not recognize Jesus. He called to ask if they had any meat, and when they answered in the negative, He told them to cast their net on the right side of the ship. When they did, they caught so many fish that they were unable to draw them in.

Remembering a similar occasion John told Peter that the one on the shore was the Lord. Peter was stripped for work, but hastily donning a coat, he jumped into the water and swam ashore. The others brought in the boat, dragging the filled net behind them.

When they got to shore, they found that Jesus had already built a fire, had cooked a fish, and had bread with which to eat the fish. So in the early morning the seven disciples ate breakfast together. It is not stated that Jesus ate with them, but the assumption is that He did.

After they had eaten, Jesus spoke to Simon Peter: *"Simon, son of John, do you love Me more than these?"* (Jn 21:15). *"These"* could refer either to the boat, net and fish, or to the other six disciples. In all likelihood it is the latter. Peter had boasted that his devotion to Jesus exceeded that of all others, but his subsequent denials proved how utterly wrong he had been. Now Jesus gently reminds him of that fact. He asked him if he now feels that his love is greater than that of the others.

Peter ignored the *"more than these"* as he replied, *"Yes, Lord . . . You know that I love You."* Jesus said, *"Feed My lambs."* A second time Jesus asked, *"Simon, son of John, do you love Me?"* Not *"more than these,"* but do you love Me? Again Peter gave the same reply. Jesus said, *"Shepherd My sheep."* A third time Jesus asked, *"Simon, son of John, do you love Me?"* Peter was grieved because Jesus asked him the third time if he loved Him, but he replied, *"Lord, You know everything! You know that I love You."*

Why did Jesus' third question grieve Peter? It could have been because His questions matched in number the denials of Peter, but the original language reveals a deeper reason for his grief. In this interplay of questions and answers, two different words are used for *"love."* The one expresses a superior love. It is akin to the word John used when he said, *"God is love"* (1 Jn 4:8). The other word for *"love"* expresses the love as of a friend. In the first two questions Jesus used the verb for this superior love, but Peter answered with the verb meaning love as of a friend. In His third question Jesus changed to the verb Peter had been using. When he failed to rise to the level of love for which Jesus asked, then Jesus came down to Peter's level. He did not ask if he loved Him with this God-kind-of-love but did he even love Him as a friend. Peter, then, was grieved, not because of the three questions but because of his failure. It certainly taught him a lesson in humility.

Having taught this lesson, Jesus then told Peter that the time would come when, in his old age, he would be taken by another where he did not want to go. John, writing long after Peter's death, interpreted this to mean the manner of death which Peter would die. Tradition says that he was crucified head downward at his own request. His Lord had been crucified upright, and since he had denied Him, Peter said that he did not deserve to die in the same manner as did Jesus. However, this is only a tradition.

Peter had been humbled, but it did not lessen his curiosity. Therefore, looking at John, he asked Jesus what would happen to him. In effect, Jesus told him that this should not be his concern. If He willed that John should live even until His return, *"What is that to you? . . . follow Me"* (Jn 21:22).

8. The Appearance to More Than Five Hundred.

This probably was the appearance mentioned by Paul (1 Co 15:6). At the time he wrote, many of these people still were alive. In a sense Paul was saying that if anyone wanted proof as to the bodily resurrection of Jesus, eyewitnesses were still available to avow the truth.

This was the appearance to which Jesus referred even before His death, and of which the angel reminded the women following the Resurrection. It occurred on a specified mountain in Galilee. Possibly as the Eleven, and others who had seen Jesus alive in Jerusalem, journeyed to the appointed place, they had been joined by other disciples from Galilee, so that when Jesus appeared to them *"they worshiped, but some doubted"* (Mt 28:17). This latter group would be those who saw Jesus for the first time after His Resurrection. It was simply too good to be true!

Then Jesus spoke to them: *"All authority has been given to Me in heaven and on earth. Go, therefore, and make disciples of all nations,*

The mountain where Jesus gave the Great Commission has been traditionally thought to be Mount Tabor in Lower Galilee.

baptizing them in the name of the Father and of the Son and of the Holy Spirit, teaching them to observe everything I have commanded you. And remember, I am with you always, to the end of the age" (Mt 28:18–20).

The word *authority* means "out of being." So out of His being as the crucified, resurrected, and living Lord, Jesus gave this Great Commission. It was given not to the apostles only but to all who believe on Him. The commission was not to *"go."* This word is a participle meaning "as you are going." He assumed that they would go to declare the blessed news. The only imperative form in these verses is *"make disciples."* This is Jesus' command, and by a further series of participles, He told them what to do. As they discipled all nations, they were to follow this by baptizing and teaching them. *"To observe"* means to preserve and pass on to others His commandments, and in the doing of it they were assured of His presence until the consummation of the age.

9. The Appearance to James.

This little gem is preserved only by Paul (1 Co 15:7), but it speaks volumes. James was a half brother of Jesus. Along with his other brothers and sisters, he did not believe that Jesus was the Messiah. There is evidence in the Gospels that Jesus' mission was an embarrassment to the half brothers and sisters and that this may even have caused a strained relationship to exist between Mary and these children. These things all enter into the reason for Jesus' special appearance to James.

That James thereafter did believe in Jesus is quite evident. Afterward he became a leader of the Church in Jerusalem. Furthermore, he wrote one of the books of the New Testament, and his testimony about this appearance must have led his other brothers and sisters to share his faith in Jesus, for another brother, Jude, also wrote one of the New Testament epistles. But neither James nor Jude in their epistles mention their family relationship to Jesus. They call themselves a *"servant"* or *"bond slave"* of Jesus Christ. Through faith in Him they had found that higher relationship of which He had spoken.

10. The Last Appearance in Jerusalem.

At the end of forty days following the Passover, Jesus appeared to His disciples who had returned to Jerusalem. This probably occurred in the Upper Room where Jesus had instituted the Lord's Supper. In this appearance He evidently spent quite some time with them, for He opened their minds concerning the Old Testament Scriptures as they related to the redemptive work of Christ, including both His death and His Resurrection. Now this gospel of redemption is to be preached unto all nations, beginning from Jerusalem. The Eleven had seen these things, and, therefore, were to share their knowledge and experience with others.

Jesus met with His disciples in Jerusalem and then led them up the Mount of Olives to Bethany where He ascended to the Father. Pictured is the path that led the two miles from Jerusalem to Bethany on the southeast side of the Mount of Olives.

Then Jesus promised to send the Holy Spirit upon them, even as the Father had promised. In turn, they were to wait in Jerusalem *"until you are empowered from on high"* (Lk 24:49). The Father will send the Holy Spirit to them at Pentecost, but they must surrender to His power in order that He may do His work through them. The intervening ten days until the Day of Pentecost must have been days of earnest self-examination on the part of this little group and other fellow believers, because when the Holy Spirit did come in mighty power, they were instruments of God surrendered to His will.

THE ASCENSION OF JESUS

Once again Jesus and the Eleven left the Upper Room to walk through the streets of Jerusalem. Apparently they went unnoticed by the people of the city, who long since had put the unpleasantness of forty days ago behind them. The little group went past the temple area, leaving the city by the eastern gate, but this time they went on by the Garden of Gethsemane. They continued on up the Mount of Olives, probably following the route Jesus had taken into the city on His royal entry.

In spite of all that had happened, the disciples were still looking for an earthly kingdom, because, as they walked along, they asked Jesus if He would at this time restore the kingdom to Israel. He told them that they should not be concerned to know about this. This was a matter the Heavenly Father had appointed in His own authority. In the meantime, they had another responsibility, that of being used to bring the kingdom into the hearts of men. He repeated the promise about the Holy Spirit's coming upon them in power: *"And you will be My witnesses in Jerusalem, in all Judea and Samaria, and to the ends of the earth"* (Ac 1:8).

By this time they had arrived at a place just across from Bethany. There Jesus lifted His hands and pronounced a final benediction upon His

In the Church of the Holy Ascension, claimed by some to be the place from which Jesus ascended into heaven is an indentation in stone that some believe to be Jesus' footprint.

disciples. Even as He was blessing them, He began to ascend into heaven. With eager and longing eyes they followed Him until a cloud obscured their vision, and they could see Him no longer. But their eyes continued to focus on the spot where they had last seen Him.

As they stood with fixed gaze into the heavens, two angels (were they the ones at the empty tomb?) appeared, standing beside them. They said, *"Men of Galilee, why do you stand looking up into heaven? This Jesus, who has been taken from you into heaven, will come in the same way that you have seen Him going into heaven"* (Ac 1:11). Implied in these words is the truth that their responsibility was not merely to stand gazing into the heavens where the Lord had gone and from where He will return. They were to be busy about the task of spreading the glad tidings of salvation to all men, and through the age they and their successors in the faith are to continue to do so until they see the Lord in the air, coming in the clouds with the angelic hosts, in great power and glory, at the consummation of the age. *"Amen! Come, Lord Jesus!"* (Rv 22:20).

THE TRIUMPHAL ENTRY

Even as the disciples gazed into the heavens, other eyes were looking over the ramparts of glory to welcome the Conqueror home. Heaven's streets range with shouts of joy as the hosts of heaven viewed His triumphal entry.

Paul describes it when he says, *"When he ascended up on high, he led captivity captive, and gave gifts unto men"* (Eph 4:8). In ancient times a returning conqueror rode through the streets of his capital city amid the shouts of acclaim from the populace. As evidence of the completeness of his victory, behind his chariot in chains walked notable prisoners, maybe even a defeated king, and the conqueror tossed gifts to his rejoicing people.

Through the streets of heaven rode the triumphant Jesus. In chains behind His chariot trudged sin and death. The procession proceeded up to the throne of God, before whom the Son placed the evidence of His redemptive work as an abiding intercession for the souls of men. Then He sat down at the right hand of God, where He sits through the ages, expecting, until His enemies shall become the footstool of His feet.

What about the gifts given by the conquering Christ?—*"and gave gifts to men."* He gave them not to the heavenly hosts, but *"to men."* Men who were yet on earth waiting to hear the gospel of redemption, of justification, sanctification, and glorification—complete salvation, both here and hereafter. What were these gifts?— *And He personally gave some to be apostles, some prophets, some evangelists, some pastors and teachers, for the training of the saints in the work of ministry, to build up the body of Christ, until we all reach unity in the faith and in the knowledge of God's*

The blocked Eastern Gate on the Old City Wall of Jerusalem, Israel is traditionally known as the gate through which Jesus Christ will return when He returns to earth.

Son, growing into a mature man with a stature measured by Christ's fullness. Then we will no longer be little children, tossed by the waves and blown around by every wind of teaching, by human cunning with cleverness in the techniques of deceit. But speaking the truth in love, let us grow in every way into Him who is the head—Christ." (Eph 4:11–15).

Therefore, *Make your own attitude that of Christ Jesus, who, existing in the form of God, did not consider equality with God as something to be used for His own advantage, instead He emptied Himself by assuming the form of a slave, taking on the likeness of men. And when He had come as a man in His external form, He humbled Himself by becoming obedient to the point of death—even to death on a cross. For this reason God highly exalted Him and gave Him the name that is above every name, so that at the name of Jesus every knee will bow—of those who are in heaven and on earth and under the earth—and every tongue should confess that Jesus Christ is Lord, to the glory of God the Father." (Php 2:5–11).

"What should I do then with Jesus, who is called Messiah?"

— *Pontius Pilate, Procurator of the
Roman Province of Judea, AD 26-36*